WARDAY
AND THE JOURNEY ONWARD

**Warday was merely a flicker of hell; what remains
are the consequences.**

Nothing makes the case against the continuing arms
race so compellingly and with such immediacy as
WARDAY. Marrying the clinical details of non-fiction
with the passionate humanity of a novel, WARDAY is a
heart-wrenching work of total authenticity and
conviction. Nothing in it is beyond the realms of
possibility, technologically or politically, and this is
what gives it its awesome power and terrifying reality.
It is filled with many voices and many stories, stunning
in its intensity, overwhelming in its truth.

Lifelong friends from boyhood, WHITLEY STRIEBER
and JAMES W. KUNETKA wrote WARDAY out of the
conviction that unless we do something soon, we will
face a nuclear war before the end of the century. In this
novel they have successfully blended the skills of the
science writer (James Kunetka is the author of *Los
Alamos* and *Oppenheimer*) and the novelist
(Whitley Strieber is best known for *The Wolfen*
and *The Hunger*).

The result is utterly convincing.

Also by Whitley Strieber

THE WOLFEN
THE HUNGER
BLACK MAGIC
NIGHT CHURCH

Also by James W. Kunetka

CITY OF FIRE: LOS ALAMOS AND THE ATOMIC AGE
OPPENHEIMER: THE YEARS OF RISK

WHITLEY STRIEBER
AND
JAMES W. KUNETKA

WARDAY
AND THE JOURNEY ONWARD

CORONET BOOKS
Hodder & Stoughton

Copyright © 1984 by Wilson & Neff, Inc. and James W. Kunetka

First published in Great Britain 1984 by Hodder and Stoughton Ltd.

British Library C.I.P.

Strieber, Whitley
  Warday and the journey onward.
  I. Title.   II. Kunetka, James W.
  813'.54[F]   PS3569.T6955

  ISBN 0-340-35849-1

Printed and bound in Great Britain for Hodder and Stoughton Paperbacks, a division of Hodder and Stoughton Ltd, Mill Road, Dunton Green, Sevenoaks, Kent (Editorial Office: 47 Bedford Square, London, WC1 3DP) by Richard Clay (The Chaucer Press) Ltd, Bungay, Suffolk. Photoset by Rowland Phototypesetting Ltd, Bury St Edmunds, Suffolk.

This book is respectfully dedicated to
October 27, 1988,
the last full day of the old world

Contents

INTRODUCTION

PART ONE: THE WEST

PART.TWO: CALIFORNIA DANGERS

PART THREE: ACROSS AMERICA

PART FOUR: NEW YORK

PART FIVE: RETURNING HOME

INTRODUCTION

However and wherever we are
We must live as if one never dies.

– Nazim Hikmet,
'On Living'

Whitley: A Survivor's Tale

The survivor's tale is the essential document of our time. All of us have them; even babies have them. To be born now is no guarantee that you will not be touched by Warday. Indeed, birth makes it certain.

So we are all survivors, and those of us who actually lived through that day carry our histories with us, our stories of how we did it, of what particular luck or strength or cleverness saw us through.

We are not the people we were on that sharp October day in 1988. I see the change in my wife and son, certainly in my collaborator, Jim Kunetka. And in all whom I know. Sitting here with my pad and paper, I find that writing about it evokes obscure and powerful feelings. Am I bitter, or angry, or simply sad? So much of what I saw as basic to life is gone; what I counted valuable, worthless.

I have my own particular artefacts of that time, mostly small things and mostly relating to the security of my former life. I have been marked by the economic disaster as much as, or more than, by the radiation. In the final analysis, for so many of us, the closed bank and the worthless money are truer expressions of Warday than is some distant mushroom cloud. My last stock statement from Shearson/American Express, for example, is probably my most treasured talisman of the past. It reminds me of the fragility of complex things. Somehow, age has given it beauty. I can imagine that such a thing, covered with symbols and symbolic numbers, associated with a mythical time of plenty, could one day become an object of worship.

I open the document, smooth it out. My feelings about it are so strong that they are almost silly. I have sat staring for hours at the anachronistic names: Raytheon, General Foods, American Motors, Dow Chemical. I got eighteen gold dollars in the distribution of '90. How ironic that nine hundred paper dollars will now buy a house. In 1987 you could spend more on a suit.

More even than to this paper, though, I cling to the memories of my family. These five years later I still find myself waiting for the phone to ring, expecting my younger brother, Richard, to be on the other end of the line. Richard, the determined, tiny rival, the childhood enemy who became as an adult my best friend, who understood me and whom I understood. Whom I loved. We talked every afternoon, no matter where we were in the world. So now, each day at four, I remember. That is my monument to him.

New York was my home in the eighties, and I was there on Warday. We remained there through the dangerous twilight that followed. In fact, the only reason I am alive now is that we stayed as long as we did.

I saw New York in her gaudy evening, and I saw her dead, and so – a little bit – I comprehend. My difficulty is with my childhood home, San Antonio. How a whole place, all of its people, all the details of its life, could just disappear is beyond my understanding.

Nobody would have put San Antonio on a list of prime targets – nobody except the Russians.

They thought not of the quiet streets or of the fun we had, but of the repair and refitting facilities at Kelly Air Force Base and of the burn centre at Brooke General Hospital, and of the massive concentration of spare parts and equipment in the area. But they did not think of kids running through sprinklers, or of the River Walk or the genteel silence of the McNay Art Institute, or of the enormous, vital, striving Chicano population.

My family had a history in San Antonio. I was deeply connected to the place; in so many ways, my identity flowed from it. Though I lived in New York, I kept a membership in the San

Antonio Writers' Guild. When I was there I used to walk by the river for hours, and then eat Mexican food at Casa Rio. At age ten, I would sit in my father's office in the Alamo National Bank Building and look out over the flat, smiling land and dream boy's dreams, of having wings, or of riding shotgun on the stagecoach to Dallas.

How can it be that the place where I was formed is gone? The Alamo National Bank Building was a tremendous skyscraper, or so I remember it. Did it fall over at the end, crashing into Commerce Street, or did it simply disintegrate?

My brother had just opened his own law office there, on the eighteenth floor. Did he feel anything? Say anything? I visualise him on the phone, hearing a noise, glancing up, then gone. Or was it horrible and slow? Death by fire in an elevator? Or by suffocation in some sub-basement parking garage?

And my mother. Looking back to the placid life we knew, it seems so impossible that her fate was to be killed in a war. She was seventy-one years old, and for her the end was almost certainly instantaneous. She lived in an apartment house two storeys high, of rather light construction. She was either there or at a neighbour's house at the moment of death. Whichever was the case, there wouldn't have been the least protection.

So many bombs exploding simultaneously over such a relatively small area caused the temperature to exceed that of the surface of the sun. People have told me that they heard the explosion in Oklahoma City and Monterrey, Mexico.

We are the first generation to see places instantly vaporised. Hiroshima and Nagasaki were destroyed, but not so completely as this. In a vaporised place, not even rubble remains.

I understand so very well the thing that impels refugees to cluster at the borders of the San Antonio Red Zone. I myself have thought of going back. And yet the blackened land must be terrible to see, and the smell of it, the stench of millions of tons of rotting ash, almost beyond enduring.

I have thought of memorials. Many times I have copied out the forty-seven names of the members of my family who died in San Antonio. And I have wondered – are they all really dead? Ours was a prosperous clan. Maybe some of them were travelling. One aunt and uncle, for example, often went to Europe in the autumn. Are they there now, perhaps engaged in a new life? They had investments in Germany; they could have got a refugee visa if they had applied for it early enough. But the rest – I have a feeling about them that is common to those who lost people close to them on Warday. They disappeared so suddenly and so completely that they don't seem dead so much as lost. My relationships with them continue as if they will sometime soon come back and take up the thread.

We've all read and heard about the details of blast effect. But there is one detail that is usually overlooked: the heart does not understand this sort of death, neither the suddenness nor the scale. Blast effect has trapped me in a maze of expectancy from which I cannot seem to escape.

I know a little bit more about blast effect. I was riding a Number 5 bus down Fifth Avenue when the New York Pattern detonated. Of course, I have thought many times about the consequences of the miss. I have wondered what subtle imbalance of technology caused it. And I have thought: a nuclear miss doesn't mean much. The city died of it anyway.

The bomb that would have exploded about eight thousand feet directly over my head detonated instead on the eastern edge of Queens.

As I sit here, my yellow pad in front of me, I find that my mind shifts focus from the broad to the tiny: the shin splints I had that day from too much jogging; the breakfast cereal I had eaten.

October 28, 1988.

I was trying to remember to call my sister in Houston, to congratulate her on becoming forty-four years of age.

But Pandora's Box was sprung, and nobody was going to be making any phone calls for a while.

October 28, 1988: a clear blue afternoon, just pushing towards five o'clock. While I read the *New York Post* and sucked a Velamint, the world cracked asunder. I was sitting in the bus, just behind the rear exit door. I remember that it was one of the GM buses, with the darkly tinted windows. All of a sudden it was lit up inside with a chalky brilliance, a strange and unpleasantly hot light that penetrated everything.

Sudden darkness followed – due to our eyes of course being stunned by the intensity of the flash. The driver shouted, 'Jesus Christ!' and stopped the bus. I just sat there. We all did. We couldn't see a thing. I heard a horn honking.

Then the blast hit. There was no warning, just a sudden cataract of sound and wind. The bus rocked violently. There were deep thuds and shattering noises as pieces of roofing and glass came down. The noise rose and rose until I thought it would never stop. People were trying to get out of the bus. I crouched down on the floor. My heart was pounding; I was gasping. I had my eyes shut tight. At that moment I was thinking in terms of a terrorist attack or maybe of the Con Ed plant in the East Thirties blowing up. The thought of a nuclear bomb didn't occur to me until the noise subsided and my eyesight got back to normal. Then I looked out.

The chaos was so great that my mind simply went blank. I was vision only. The images swept all thought away. Windows were broken, cars were up on the sidewalk, and people were running, staggering, lying in the street. A dark yellow haze of dust cast everything in eerie light.

My first clear thought was of my family. My son was in the third grade at Grace Church School and taking an after-school gymnastics class. As far as I knew, my wife was at home. I thought I'd better call her and tell her that there had been some kind of an explosion but I was all right and not to worry. By this time the driver had gotten the doors open. He was trying to restart the bus and not getting anywhere at all. Of course, we didn't know a single thing about electromagnetic pulse back then. He had no idea that the bus's electronic ignition had been destroyed.

Because the bus was broken down, the driver gave us all transfers, and we filed off. A few people went to the Twentieth Street bus stop to wait for another bus. The wind was gone, its roar replaced by the sound of glass still raining down from above, the screams of the injured and the terrified, and a complex mix of car horns, sirens, the hissing of a broken fireplug, and the blue-streak cursing of a hot dog vendor whose cart had exploded.

Suddenly all I could think about was my boy. I started off down Fifth Avenue at a trot. It wasn't long before I was turning east on Fourteenth. I knew by then that things were terribly wrong. People were lying everywhere, in every condition. Lots of them were bloody from flying glass, many more livid with flash burns. I did not know it, but I was bleeding too, the blood running down my neck and soaking my shirt like sweat. I'd had a slice taken out of my scalp that I wouldn't feel until much later.

I saw gangs of kids coming out of the Fourteenth Street stores with everything you could name in their hands: radios, records, clothes, candy bars. They were laughing and shrieking. I saw one of them get blown almost in half by a storekeeper with a shotgun.

My mind was still far from clear. I just couldn't seem to grasp what had happened. There was no reason to think that there had been a nuclear attack, though I kept considering and then rejecting that thought. US–Soviet tensions weren't high. There'd been no sign of impending conflict, none at all. In fact, the news was full of the reestablishment of détente.

It was the sky over Queens and Brooklyn that enforced the notion of a nuclear bomb. Through the dusty air I could see ash-black clouds shot through with long red flames. These clouds were immense. They stretched up and up until they were lost in their own expanding billows. There was no impression of a mushroom cloud, but I knew that was what it was, a mushroom cloud seen so close that it didn't look like a mushroom. The coldest, most awful dread I have ever known came upon me then.

I knew it for certain: a nuclear device had been exploded at the eastern edge of the city. I thought, My God, the lives. Later it was estimated that a million people had died in the instant of the explosion. Hundreds of thousands more were dying right now.

I was walking on a grate above the Fourteenth Street subway station when a blast of dank, dirty air from below practically blew me off my feet. It was accompanied by the most horrible screaming I have ever heard, then the nasty bellow of water. Though nobody knew it then, the tidal wave caused by the bombs that had detonated at sea had arrived and was filling the subway system. Those screams still come to me in the night.

A man came up out of the station, wet from head to foot, his right arm dangling. '*Agua*,' he kept saying, '*agua!*' Then he made a bleating noise and staggered off into the swaying crowds. My mind said: Grace Church School, Grace Church School, Grace Church School. I ran.

My greatest fear was fire.

I found the school closed and locked. There were lots of broken windows, but the lower floors were barred. I shouted and the Latin teacher opened the front door for me. Inside, the kids were sitting quietly in the great hall with their teachers. 'What's going on?' Mr Lewis asked me. 'I think we've been hit by an atomic bomb,' I replied. He nodded. 'We all think that.'

I went to my boy. He jumped up and flew into my arms, and then started screaming because he saw all the blood on my back. The school nurse came over to tend the wound. She said I needed at least five stitches. But what could we do? I ended up with a brushing of Betadine and a bandage.

The phones weren't working, so I couldn't call Anne. It was then that I made the decision that saved my life.

I didn't know it at the time, but like all people caught outside during the initial stages of the disaster, I had received a radiation dose. If I had gone out even another fifteen minutes at the height of the fallout period, I would have quickly dosed red and then lethaled. What kept me from doing so was my belief that my wife's instinct would also be to come to the school and I was more likely to find her by waiting than by searching.

Not ten minutes later she appeared. She was wearing my felt hat and carrying an umbrella. I will never forget how it felt to kiss her at that moment, to feel her in my arms. And then Andrew said, 'Let's have a family hug.' We held each other, and I told them both what I thought had happened.

Anne is a practical person. She had no idea what had happened – in fact, her theory was that a volcano had erupted – but she suspected that in any case we might get hungry, so she'd brought a box of freeze-dried food we had put aside years ago for a camping trip and never used. She'd also brought a little news of home: the power was out, the radio and TV were dead, the phones weren't working, and there was hardly any water pressure. Every window in the apartment was broken. The dishwasher was stopped on rinse and the clothes washer on spin. She reminded me that I had the video recorder set to tape a movie on HBO at five o'clock, and the power failure was going to mean that I would miss it.

Other parents were now arriving at the school. The Head moved the children into the gym, which had no windows, and we decided to make that a shelter for all the families who wanted to stay. Anne and I went to the changing room and took long showers. Some of the parents who did not take this precaution died in days. Others were unaffected. For the most part it depended on how long they had been outside, and whether or not they had been shielded from the initial burst of gamma rays from the blast.

We had the church right there, of course, attached to the school. Grace is probably New York City's most beautiful church, and it served us well in the next few days. It could be reached from the school without going outside. While the city died we prayed there. At that time I wondered if humanity would prevail. Despite what was happening, I found myself trusting the goodness in us more than hating the violence. I still feel that way.

Of that night there remains with me the memory of a particular noise: footsteps on pavement. It was persistent thunder, and mixed with the cries of the hurt and desolate, it defined those hours.

By 6.00 p.m. the sky was black, the air very still [the sun a lifeless maroon shadow on the western horizon]. Many parents were at the school, but not many families were complete. Some of the kids were still waiting. Some had left. They didn't come back. Every so often another mother or father would appear out of the gloom, and we would count a victory.

By now it had occurred to us that there must be dangerous radiation, so we were trying to keep trips outside to a minimum, and had hung blankets over the windows.

Throughout the night, the rattle of walking continued as people crossed Manhattan, heading for the tunnels and bridges, trying to get out of the city on foot. Once we saw a fire truck – obviously too old to have an electronic ignition and so not immobilised by the electromagnetic pulse – making its way down Fourth Avenue, trying to negotiate a path among the reefs of stalled cars. It was soon lost in the gloom. The eastern sky glowed like the inside of a furnace, a deep, fearsome orange. Towards midnight it began to rain pieces of burning tar. They looked like meteors coming down into the streets and on to roofs. I thought then that this was the beginning of the end – the firestorm was crossing the river.

By this time the little group at Grace had become a community of sorts. We organised ourselves as best we could, trying to find our way to survival. There was no information, only the crowds and the confusion and the burning streaks of tar. Two of our group went to the roof to put out any fires that might start there. They held plastic dropcloths from the art room over their heads as protection from cinders and radiation. The fallout worried us even more than the fire. We knew little about it. Was there still too much radiation in the air, or should we join the exodus west instead of trying to fight the fire? We just couldn't recall. On balance, most of us decided to remain at the school a little longer. At least we were reasonably safe there for the time being. We also had light from church candles, food from the school's larder, and water from the tower, which we hoped wasn't contaminated by radiation.

Our first case of radiation sickness started at about eleven that night. Meg Parks began sneezing. She had walked down First Avenue all the way from Eighty-ninth Street, where she had her office. She was a psychiatrist, and her two girls were in the school. By 2.00 a.m., Meg had fever and was breaking out in a rash. She was vomiting and suffering from severe diarrhoea. We tried to get water into her, and the school nurse gave her Kaopectate. But it was all quite useless. Her husband, Peter, still had not appeared, and by morning we decided to take her over to St Vincent's Hospital. Bob Tucker and Fred Wallace volunteered to be stretcher bearers. We suspected that the streets might be dangerous, so three more of us went along: Jerry Fielder, Tom Roote, and myself. As Tom had a .38, we considered ourselves relatively safe.

We were less concerned about radiation now. A brisk west wind had come up about midnight, blowing not only the fire-storm away from Manhattan, but the fallout as well. As we went down the street, though, I wondered; our feet crunched on a thick dusting of ash. We kept on – it was unthinkable that we should just let Meg die because we were afraid to go out.

We carried her in a hammock made from a blanket. She lay quite still. She was coherent and she joked that swinging her in a hammock had to be the hardest labour any of us had done in years. She was having frequent convulsions, and she looked very weak.

To the east the sky was now filled by a massive grey-white cloud. Closer, there were tall columns of smoke.

On our way across Thirteenth Street we counted many dead. Forty, I think, all shot or beaten or, in one particularly horrible case, burnt. There were fires smouldering here and there, but nothing devastating. We didn't know it, but at this time hundreds of thousands of people were dying on Long Island as the firestorm swept eastward.

We were a block away from St Vincent's when we understood our mistake. The crowds were so thick we couldn't move a step forward. There was the disgusting tang of vomit on the air, and many people were lying in the street, sick to death and helpless. There were burned people everywhere, many of them also suffering from radiation sickness. We could hardly stand to see it. We fell silent, we turned away.

It was like the aftermath of a great battle. The hospital itself must have been a scene of unspeakable horror.

We took Meg back to the church, where she expired at four o'clock that afternoon, after a very hard five hours. The father of her daughters never showed up. I do not know what happened to the two Parks girls.

As soon as we were back at Grace we all took long showers. Anne and Andrew and I decided that we would remain inside this building, away from the windows, for as long as we could. We did not know then that the hot cloud from Washington was on its way up the seaboard, spreading extinction. If we had tried to leave then, we would have been caught in it with the millions whose footsteps still had not stopped.

The teachers organised activities. The children threw themselves into work on a folk song festival. Along with myself and Tucker and a couple of others, the rector of the church and the Head formed a survival committee. We inventoried the food and discovered that we could do about a thousand calories a day per person for two more weeks. We wouldn't starve, but as far as quality was concerned, we were going to have protein problems. There were cans of beans and soup, but the only meat was the six freeze-dried hamburgers Anne had brought. There was no longer any gas pressure, but we worked out a method of using the stove anyway. We found that we could heat food by building a fire from paper and pieces of chairs on top of the burners and hanging the pots up in the exhaust flue.

Our first meal consisted of spaghetti with marinara sauce from cans, and pork and beans. It was washed down with fruit juice. Not much, but I suspect that it was better than many got in New York on that day. We ate in the gym, off paper dishes saved from last year's May Fair and intended for use at the Christmas party.

All during that day, neighbourhood people had been congregating in the church. Our food situation improved rapidly. Everybody brought canned goods, so the increasing numbers were no drain on those resources. We began to worry instead about water, and drew up strict regulations about those long showers we had been taking. No baths unless you made an 'approved excursion'.

We were determined to live through this, somehow, even though most of us felt that the rest of the world had been destroyed.

Falling water pressure rapidly became a more and more serious problem. Already high-rise apartment buildings were uninhabitable above the sixth floor because of a lack of electrically pumped water. Low-rises were suffering too, as was Grace Church School. Broken mains in the bombed boroughs were draining the system dry. Soon our rooftop tank would be all we had left.

More even than the lack of water and power, though, people were scared because of the lack of news. Those who had ventured as far east as the river confirmed that there was a holocaust going on in Brooklyn and Queens. They had been able to feel the heat on their faces even on this side of the river, and the wind being pulled into the fire was stiff enough to make it hard to stand up. People reported that the conflagration made a great, hissing roar. They described it variously as sounding like a railroad train, a hurricane, or the voice of an angry crowd.

The electromagnetic pulse generated by the huge bombs the Soviets had detonated in near space was the answer to the mystery of why even portable radios wouldn't work, and why people with recent-model cars couldn't get them started. The vast majority of electronic devices – computers, televisions, radios, microwave stations, radar, avionic devices on aeroplanes, electronic car ignitions – had been shorted out by Soviet bombs detonated in outer space. The explosions had been invisible and had had no effect except to blanket the country with a brief, massive burst of electromagnetic energy. Certain military equipment had been shielded, and even some computers owned by big banks and corporations.

They shielded such devices, during the mid-eighties, to resist a 50,000-volt pulse. So the Soviets simply generated a larger one. Recent estimates are that it exceeded 150,000 volts. Thus they overcame billions of dollars worth of shielding with bombs worth at most a few million. An efficient means of destruction.

Because of the electromagnetic pulse, we had no access to news.

I will never forget the moment when somebody outside started yelling about the *Times*. The next thing I knew, there was a man coming in with a paper. It was the famous sixteen-page extra, which was the last news we were to see for a long time. I still don't know how the *Times* managed to get that paper out. Someone told me it was produced in New Jersey before local electric power was lost.

I remember the headline: NUCLEAR ATTACK BY AT LEAST THREE MISSILES DEVASTATES CITY. And the lead: 'Nuclear weapons detonated over Queens and Brooklyn on October 28 at approximately 4.45 p.m., causing catastrophic devastation and leaving both boroughs in flaming ruins. An estimated two million people lost their lives.'

It was there also that we read of Washington. We were stunned, confused. Washington no longer existed. There was no President, no Vice-President, no Congress, nobody. We had no government. 'Washington, DC, the seat of government of the United States of America since 1800, has been destroyed by a surprise nuclear attack. Reports from the area indicate catastrophic destruction on a scale previously unknown in human affairs. The city was swept away in a sea of fire. Not a building remains standing, not a monument intact. Observers are unable even to approach within ten miles of the city. Baltimore, Maryland, is also burning, as are the majority of smaller communities surrounding the District of Columbia.' It went on, but I find that my memory does not serve me to quote the rest.

The paper recommended that people stay indoors, reported the flooding of the subway system, and announced that the police department had opened Madison Square Garden, the Armoury, and the Convention Center as protected public shelters.

I would say that the appearance of that newspaper was one of the few good things that happened in those terrible days. It served first notice that humanity still existed, that we had been hurt but we were not going to give in just yet. I know that people lost their lives doing the reporting that went into it, not to mention transporting and delivering it. Not only *Times* people were involved in the edition, but also news crews from the television networks and the staff of the *Daily News*, which was without power to run its own presses.

Still, reading in black and white that Washington was gone made me frantic.

Until that moment I hadn't thought beyond the immediate situation: how to live through the next few hours, and would I come down with radiation sickness? Every passing moment of queasiness or faint chill was terrifying. We had set up a hospital in the parents' lounge, which was also an interior room, and there we attended the sick and dying as best we could. The school's science teacher, Mrs Dannay, had managed to rig up a thing called a Kearney Fallout Meter, and was engaged in dividing the school into safe and unsafe areas.

The KFM was made in a Folger's coffee can and consisted of two leaves of aluminium foil hung side by side on strings inside the can. It was covered by the clear plastic top from a Tupperware container in which the fourth grade had been hatching frogs' eggs. The bottom of the can held crushed gypsum, used as a drying agent because humidity can affect the ability of the foil strips to respond to the presence of radiation. Mrs Dannay had dug the gypsum out of the wall in the lab. It was just ordinary wallboard.

She could tell by the way the leaves of foil spread apart or came together how much gamma radiation was present in a given area. It wasn't accurate enough to measure hot spots on people, but it did help us to confirm that our water was not highly contaminated and that our top two floors and the area of the church closest to the main doors were as well as all areas on the main floor of the school near doors and windows, and the whole central foyer.

That Kearney Fallout Meter probably saved the lives of most of the people in our school. It also enabled Mrs Dannay to develop a rough estimate of ambient radiation outside. She told us that trips out were safe only for fifteen or twenty minutes, and that no individual should make more than one trip.

It was on the third day that I began to have symptoms. My head had become infected despite copious applications of Betadine and plenty of soap and water. Of course, I had been exposed to radiation and that had lowered my resistance to disease. (Lowered resistance caused by the combination of radiation and starvation is undoubtedly the reason that the Cincinnati Flu took so many lives the year before last.) In any case, I began to get symptoms of radiation poisoning and infection. My head hurt terribly.

When I started vomiting, Anne and Andrew took me off to a corner of the hall and tended me there. They did not want to put me in the parents' lounge, which had become a virtual dying room. Just about everybody who went in there died within a few hours. Of course, people had no notion of how to protect themselves from radiation, and many of them had got very severe doses. I hoped that my dose wasn't too terrible, but I also suspected that, combined with the head wound and the rough conditions, it might weaken me enough to threaten my life.

We prayed a good deal. Over the past few years we had gone from being agnostics to becoming Christians again. We had been parishioners at Grace for about six months. I am a Roman Catholic by birth, and have had a stormy relationship with my Church. During the early eighties I went through a period of what could be described as confused neutrality. By Warday, I was temporarily uninterested in religion, though I felt comfortable with my son in an Episcopal school. Since the Reunion of '90, I have been a Catholic worshipping in the Episcopal rite.

It was the prospect of death that brought me back once and for all to the Church. I am not a strong man, spiritually. I returned because I was facing pain and destruction and I was scared. Since Warday my faith has become so essential to me that I can hardly imagine being without it. When I thought I was dying, I began to pray to the Blessed Virgin, to whom I used to turn in times of childhood crisis. I was not afraid to die, but I felt awful that I must leave Anne and Andrew at such a time.

The sickness grew in me until it was an invincible horror, a devastating, agonising thing that wracked me with convulsion after convulsion and left me so weak I could not even move my hands, let alone talk. Our rector came and gave me the last rites. With my wife and son at my side, I waited for death.

By this time Dr Leo Stein had arrived. Leo's son Jeremy and my boy were best friends, and Leo and I had gotten to know each other pretty well. He had been working since Warday. The moment he heard the explosion, he had simply packed up what he had on hand in his office and hiked to the nearest hospital, which was Bellevue. The hospital had reeled under the strain, but Bellevue was a powerful institution and had managed to organise itself well enough to provide at least routine care to every serious case that presented itself. This was before triage, and doctors were still treating people on a most-serious-first basis. Best-prospect-first classification was still six months away. When Leo had been relieved after seventy hours of work, he had put on a whole-body radiation suit from the hospital's stores, acquired a gun from its armoury, and come down here on foot, bringing what medicines he could.

He treated me with ampicillin for my infection, then dressed the head wound. To replace electrolytes lost in vomiting and diarrhoea, he prescribed the now-familiar salt, baking soda, and potassium solution that is routinely used in such cases. We managed only the salt and baking powder. I recovered without the potassium. Nine days after Warday I was on my feet again. I weighed a hundred and thirty-one pounds. In nine days I had lost forty-six pounds.

Since then, my lifedose level has been diagnosed as terminal, so I am on the triage, waiting for the inevitable outbreak of cancer. It could start tomorrow, or next year, or in five years. It might never start, but the odds in favour of that are very small.

By the time I recovered, the radiation level in the streets was not detectable on our Kearney Fallout Meter. Our food supplies were dwindling, and water was strictly rationed. About a third of the families had left the school.

On November 6, 1988, Anne and Andrew and I started out on our own journey home. It was to be a long and bitter trip, ending in sorrow.

Home is where one's family lives. For Anne and Andrew and me, this was San Antonio. Not until ten hard days of travelling later, when we were on a bus in Arkansas, did we learn that it had suffered the same fate as Washington and was no more.

Jim: What's It Like Out There?

I was forty-four years old on Warday. By prewar standards I had lived somewhat more than half of my life.

I was forty-nine when I left with Whitley on an adventure through postwar America. I was very conscious that the five years that had just passed had been the equivalent of at least twenty prewar years. I kept wondering how many more I would use up on the journey.

And I wonder now how many are left.

War is about death and change, but it is also about numbers, about counting. Because there was a war, our numbers have changed. If it did nothing else, the war and its after effects have aged us. But how do we measure an epidemic of shortened lives?

Whitley and I have been friends a long time. We went to grade school together. Our prewar literary careers certainly didn't parallel, but they happened in tandem. I was writing *Oppenheimer* while he was doing *The Wolfen*, for example. I doubt that those books are even known now.

(It makes me feel terribly uneasy to think of J. Robert Oppenheimer. He has appeared from time to time in my dreams. He stands there, silent. When I realise who it is, I wake up with a shout.)

But beyond friendship or an interest in writing, there was a shared vision. Two men in their forties, white-haired, thick of voice, slowed, but wanting to find what is happening in ordinary, everyday America. Poor communications have made a secret of experience we all need and deserve to share.

When Whitley and I first considered the notion behind this book, my impulse was protective: I wanted to stay right here at home and cling to what life I have left. But then I began to wonder: What is the country actually *like* now? Everything certainly seems different. If there has been fundamental change, is it productive? Or is cultural psychosis threatening us?

At first, I must admit, even my curiosity was not enough to move me. Even in tranquil times, one tends to hold on to anything definite and stable, and my job with the Dallas *Herald News* was a good one. Whitley and I talked about the book needing to be written, but I'm not sure I buy that. I don't think there is such a thing as a book that needs to be written.

But the question of the state of the country – the way it feels for ordinary people to live in its various regions – wouldn't go away. Since the wire services were reconstructed in '90, we have all been getting a certain amount of outside news. But facts can't reveal the things that are really important: how it feels and tastes and smells in America, what work is like and what hopes are general. The only way to find such things out is to walk the streets and talk to the people.

Travel is not easy, and in many places it's far from safe.

I live in a nice house and, with two others, I own a fairly good car. I cherish my safety passionately. On Warday both my wife and my mother disappeared, my mother in the maelstrom of San Antonio, my wife in Austin. Mother I know is dead. But my wife – there is always the chance she remains alive, caught in the great shuffling departures that have marked the famine and the flu. I wrote only my mother's name in the Governor's Book of the Dead.

I ate dandelion leaves during the famine. I know what it is to have the flu and get told to leave the hospital or face arrest. I know what it is to lose relatives, home, possessions, friends.

And I know how I feel when I watch the sunset over the roofs of the neighbourhood and hear the snick of the scythe as my neighbour cuts his lawn.

But the things I did not know seemed to me more important. What, for example, was life like in the least affected parts of the country, such as California? How was the federal government functioning now, with its new capital in Los Angeles and a whole new breed of bureaucrats? Have they documented the history of the war, and what are they saying about it now?

More importantly, what do ordinary people know about the war, and what have they learned from it? Will we ever rebuild the old 'United States', or is that as much a part of history as the USSR?

So curiosity became interest and I found myself drawn into working on the book. We both knew it couldn't be done from Dallas, that we would have to do our research by travelling, talking with people, getting in touch with the landscape, gathering the vitally important personal stories and sensations even more than the official facts.

There would be risks, of course. We could get hurt or even killed. We could run out of money. Whitley would be away from his family for an indefinite time. Travel is not easy. We would have to do a lot of walking. We might, in fact, end up for a while in one of the civilian detention centres the Army uses to control migration. We would have to use every contact we had and all the salesmanship we could muster to go where we wanted and meet the right people.

I also wanted to gather government reports, documentary evidence. Not to place blame, but to see and perhaps understand.

Transportation was the most immediate obstacle. Air travel is quick, but there isn't much chance of doing it on a regular basis without government approval or foreign papers, unless you are willing to wait months for a reservation. Also, you don't meet ordinary people on planes. We would go TBF – train, bus, and foot. Just like everybody else.

Travel passes aren't commonly needed except, as we found out, in California. Washington State and Oregon also have stringent immigration restrictions. War Zones were off limits, of course, but my government contacts could help us there.

Whitley is in somewhat more jeopardy than I. He is triaged because of his high lifedose. His chances of getting cancer in the next five years are seventy per cent. His ten-year survival probability is zero. This comes from his living through Warday and the week after in New York.

I have lost so much: wife, mother, friends, expectations. All of my references are to the here and now, and I found I wanted to expand and enrich them. The trip would do that.

Besides, I remember something my grandfather used to say whenever someone would offer him a scotch and water: 'Why not, I can't dance.'

As much as any, that was a good reason for doing this.

Dallas to Aztlan to California, then back across the continent to New York, then home through the old South. A call to Amtrak confirmed that the rail service is not only running but somewhat expanded since prewar times. Amtrak's diesels did not suffer from the effects of EMP because they have no delicate electronic parts like aeroplanes.

We made phone calls and sent letters. The telephone system is quixotic. Some large areas are still completely without service. Others were never affected at all. To find out if a place has service it is easiest just to call. Austin is as easy to reach as ever. A call to Los Angeles was interrupted by an operator asking us to state our business – our first taste of California's raging paranoia about outsiders.

When you call San Antonio, a recorded voice says, 'We're sorry, but the number you have called does not exist in the 512 area code. Please consult your directory and try again.'

Each regional telephone company has dealt with its destroyed areas in different ways. Call Cheyenne and you'll get an announcement that the number has been disconnected. New York clicks on the third ring, and returns silence.

As we called here and there, we found that our reputations opened some doors and closed others. But I'm a decent enough reporter, and I felt confident that I could overcome even the resistance of the military authorities and the federal government to letting their documents out.

I'm organised. Whitley is a narrative writer, a storyteller. I have a more technical bent, and a reporter's knowledge of whom to approach for documents. I made a list of people we should talk to in government agencies, and drew up an assessment of the ease or difficulty we could expect with each one. Then I mapped out our journey, assessed transportation problems, estimated expenses, and evaluated expected roadblocks of both the human and highway kinds, identified radzones on our path, and marked out areas of the country where there might be bandits or aggressive survivalist bands.

Both Whitley and I wished that we could have organised all our data on our lost computers. He was rich before the war; he had an Apple. I had an old Osborne. They are missed accomplices, the best tools either of us ever had.

Families and friends had mixed reactions to the trip. Whitley's wife, Anne, and his son, Andrew, hated it, but in the end they accepted it. One of my friends called it 'difficult'. I suppose he was trying for understatement. My editor at the paper was excited. Given no city or state censorship problems, he would print our reports in serial fashion, assuming we were able to mail them back to him. And he'd pay. Not much, but it would help.

After our final planning session together, I left Whitley to a day alone with his family. I spent it packing, thinking about places and people.

Sometime after dark there was a knock at my door. Nobody was there; instead, on the doormat was a bottle of bourbon – very valuable – and a small unsigned note reading *Good luck*. We are more furtive now, we Americans. I never found out who cared so much about me that they would give me something as precious as that.

The next morning, waiting outside Whitley's house, I thought how hard it must be for him to leave a real, functioning family. But we've all left people before, and we've all experienced hard moments.

Our journey began in morning and sun. By some miracle, an old aunt of mine managed to catch up with us at the British Relief HQ in Dallas and give me her St Christopher medal, which she'd carried for more than seventy years.

I did not tell her that the Church removed Christopher from the calendar of saints years ago. And I wore the medal all the way.

PART ONE

THE WEST

That is no country for old men. The young
In one another's arms, birds in the trees
– Those dying generations – at their song,
Fish, flesh, or fowl, commend all summer long
Whatever is begotten, born, and dies.

– W. B. Yeats,
'Byzantium'

The Journey Begins

It is a bright August morning, the air dense and full of the smell of the wisteria that grows around our back door. I have been up since five-thirty, watching the sky go from gold to white. Jim will soon arrive, and I am beginning to count my minutes. There has been wind from the west, dusty wind, but I don't mind; west of Dallas lie the South Plains, and, unlike the Corn Belt, their dust is low-content.

Anne has given me a breakfast of eggs and a glass of goat's milk. Our eggs are small and brown, from our own bantam hens. Good town birds. The goat's milk is from the Perrys, across the street. Their son Robert keeps three goats. On the table there are hard, tart grapes from our arbour.

Anne sits across from me, her chin in her hands. Though she is only forty-six, her hair is white and as soft as down. There is about her face a nervous look that is new. It comes, perhaps, from the difficulty she has believing that our life will remain as tolerable as it has recently become. But there is also hardness in that look, a kind of determination that has developed over the years. You can see it in her eyes, a sort of flintiness. We have been married for twenty-three years and we know that our remaining time together is quite limited, and so she sees my journey as a family tragedy. But she understands my motives. I was a writer for many years, and I did not voluntarily give that up. Anne will not stop me from doing something of real value with my skill.

'I'm going to miss you,' I say. She smiles, tight-lipped. 'I'll write,' I add. Her hand comes up, touches my face. 'I'll be back as soon as I can.'

Loving and being loved is the great thing, I think. My love for Anne is as much a part of me as my eyes or my voice. For the first time in perhaps ten years, I will not tonight sleep in the same bed as she. After all we have been through to get to this peaceful corner of the world, it seems almost a travesty to leave her bed, no matter what the reason.

Andrew comes in, his eyes alight, his hands and T-shirt smeared with grease. He is really an artist with machines, my son, and he has kept our ancient Dodge in superb order since we bought it in '90. It is a '75 model with a beautiful old-fashioned electric ignition of the type that survived EMP. More modern cars, with their electronic ignitions and microchip-controlled carburation systems, were rendered inoperable. Jim says that there was an AP wire story to the effect that fourteen million electronic ignitions were destroyed on Warday. Since Warday, an average of a million replacements have been made each year. At this rate, close to half of the disabled cars will have been ruined by weathering long before they get new ignitions.

Our precious Dodge cost us twelve gold dollars, a sum it took me two years to raise. But it runs, and the highways aren't crowded, and sometimes in the dead of the night one or the other of us has the trapped dream, and then we like to get in it and drive westward, towards cleaner land, along the dark, empty Interstate.

I am leaving the car behind. It is too expensive and difficult to journey by private vehicle.

'You've got a dozen hardboiled eggs in your backpack,' Anne says. 'It's all I could get out of the banties.'

'It's a lot.'

'I made some bread.' She hands me a loaf, and my heart almost breaks. Flour is hard to get these days, and she must have hoarded this carefully. It's quite a surprise.

'What a nice gift. I had no idea.'

'Just remember that there's more where that came from.'

All her life, Anne's been insecure about her ability to keep me. But it is I who should worry. I feel she is a better wife than I am a husband. We kiss and she is fervent. Her fingers are linked at the back of my neck. 'I love you so,' I whisper into the soft white hair.

We stop at last.

I take the bread and put it in my backpack.

Andrew has washed his hands and sat down at the table. He is a tall, rangy thirteen-year-old. His memories of prewar America are fading, and I regret that. On Warday he was six weeks away from his ninth birthday. He remembers New York chiefly as a place where you could get a chocolate-chip cookie or a Danish at Cake Masters whenever you wanted it. I know that this is an awfully small memory of that glorious place, but so far I have been unable to discuss with him the true nature of our loss. That city was part of my soul. Despite its size, its loss seems a deeply personal thing. I did not lose the towers but the view of them from the roof of my building, not the museums but my own personal experience of the great works there, the paintings that were looted from Manhattan museums or rotted there, and the ones that burned in Brooklyn.

I felt comfortable working in New York. I wrote all my prewar novels there. My films were set there.

How anachronistic those books seem now, those light entertainments that were my life's work in the last days of the old world.

I was rich in New York, and there also I knew the shuddering poverty of starting out. I find, though, that my memories return to it less and less often now. As I grow older, my mind jumps back further, to the San Antonio of the 1950s and 1960s, in the fine days of my boyhood.

Andrew is looking at me. Our eyes meet. For a moment he is grave, his face full of unexpected tension. 'Good luck, Dad,' he says. We have talked at length about my journey, and he approves. He also knows the risks. 'I'll take care of Mom,' he says. 'I can do it.' I believe that. At the age of ten, this young man kept his head about him when he was starving. He organised midnight forages to abandoned warehouses, learned at the library how to recognise edible plants, and never spoke a word of complaint through all those terrible months. At twelve he helped on a disinfecting crew during the flu, then faced that disease himself, and lay in this very house between life and death. 'What happens, happens,' he said then. 'I know that God'll keep me.' He has seen the dead stacked in heaps, being dealt with by bulldozers and lime; he has lost friends many times, and seen this neighbourhood all but emptied, then refilled again by people more like us than the original residents who had been here before the war. Our newer neighbours are leather-hard.

I reached my maturity in a world of electronic ease. Andrew remembers my Apple and our RCA TV, but he is saving for a radio and eagerly awaiting the day we get listed for a Japanese computer. He has it all picked out: an Epson 221 with artificial intelligence. But he has little concept of the electronic village. When he wants to reach a friend, he is more likely to write a letter than to try to telephone. It isn't that Andrew is totally deprived of the advantages of electronics now, but that they were unknown to him during his most impressionable years. Until this year he has experienced telephones as balky, unreliable things. Before the war, we placed what now seems a fantastic level of reliance on the most fragile electronic webbing.

I think of the Japanese. Even their immense productive capacity has not been enough to rewire the United States.

There is a sound of footsteps outside, and Jim Kunetka comes in the back door. He is blade-thin, smiling, looking rather haggard. When I ask if he slept last night, he only smiles more. Anne gives him oatmeal and grapes, and he eats eagerly. He has been my friend since we were children. Lately he has been working as a journalist, while I have gone into microfarming and indoor garden design. I can build you a hydroponic garden sufficient to supply a family of four with vegetables year-round, and locate it indoors so you don't have to worry about fallout or residual buildup. Before the war I was a middle-range novelist. We were happy and fat then. My horror stories were successful, because happy people crave the luxury of artificial fear. I wouldn't write one now – the very idea is loathsome. (Although, I must admit, I've begun to get a trickle of royalties from Europe and Japan. It is strange to see the computer printouts from my British agent, like ghostly documents from a world that is gone.)

'Our appointment is at eight-thirty,' Jim says in his most brisk manner.

I swallow the last of my milk and get up. Anne and Andrew and I hold each other for a moment, our faces touching, our arms around one another's shoulders. We have always hugged like this, the three of us. For me it is a symbol of our endurance as a family and as civilised people, and of the truth of our love.

We say goodbye in the hug. Anne's expression remains firm and calm. It's not that we ignore our tears. I remember a time when people were embarrassed by such displays of emotion, but no more. We need our luxuries, and tears are cheap, but this is not the moment for them.

Jim and I leave. The hourly Dallas Transit bus will stop out on Forest Lane in ten minutes. We refuse Andrew's offer of a ride to the bus stop. I'd rather he and Anne stayed together, and, in truth, I don't think I can bear to prolong this parting.

The sun is already hot. We pass through the neighbourhood and turn on to Plano Road. Abandoned condominiums line both sides of the street. Chateau Versailles, Woodridge, Oak Park II – names from the past. There is no longer a housing shortage in this country, not with a thirty per cent population decline in five years.

Our little nuclear war was not about ultimate and final ends at all. The issue was not Armageddon, it was consequences. Seven million people died on Warday. My family and I were twelve miles from Ground Zero of one bomb, and we survived.

We are used to death, though. All of us know how easy it is to die. Not an American lives who has not lost somebody – friend, family member, lover. More than sixty million people have died in the years since Warday, of malnutrition or diseases brought on or made worse by weakness. Some have died from radiation poisoning. Others have given their lives to cancer and the new disease, NSD.

Jim tells me that the British Relief estimates that there are still a quarter of a million war-related deaths every month. If I die of cancer, I will be counted among them one of these days. Warday was a flicker of hell. The rest has been consequences.

Only the first ragged salvos of missiles were actually fired. Immediately upon their detonation, both sides experienced the collapse of their elaborate command, control, and communications nets, and the war went out like a carelessly struck match.

I don't think anybody ever seriously considered that a limited nuclear war would be as brief as it actually was. God knows what would have happened to us if there had been another exchange, or if the two sides had been able to carry out even the smallest part of their plans for each other. Consequences only have meaning when you are living in them.

In New York I learned how it felt to get caught in a 'trivial'

nuclear war. Here in Dallas I have learned every agonising detail
of the consequences – the long, unforeseen drama of the aftermath.

No planner ever dreamed that it would be as small as it was.
No doubt some prewar strategists would have felt confident
about a nuclear exchange like the one we had. I can see the memo
now: 'As minor a megadeath level as six is sustainable, and
planning must include the possibility of even greater losses
within the parameters of acceptability.'

As many died on Warday in this country alone as in all of
Hitler's gas chambers. And afterwards – all I can say is that the
death of friends no longer surprises.

On this fine Dallas morning Jim walks along beside me,
silently. He was like this years and years ago, on patrol in
Vietnam, his eyes seeming to look inward, his face in almost
meditative repose. I remember the day we got on that Pan Am jet
to come home. The moment the plane was in the air he changed
back to his old self, voluble, full of laughter, his wit at turns fierce
and gentle. Now the silence is customary. Jim has killed to stay
alive, and he has seen hard things. Because he got the flu early,
he was able to come and go as he pleased during most of the
epidemic. To this day he is short of breath from the scarring on
his lungs, but he survived. A week after his recovery he took his
camera and notepad and travelled through the Midwest on
behalf of the Dallas *News Herald*. It was the height of the
epidemic. He walked the streets of Cincinnati during the Ten
Days, and saw what a modern American city in the grip of an
uncontrollable plague was like. He took the classic photograph of
the stacks of dead burning in Eden Park. Never once has he
spoken about his experiences there, and nobody asks him to. His
pictures and published accounts are sufficient testimony.

People greet us at the bus stop. Winnie Parker embraces me, so
does John Gordon. I can understand why modern custom has
replaced the handshake. To hold others is to maintain something. A handshake confirms distance, and we don't need that
any more.

The bus comes at 8.12, right on time. We get in, jamming to
the back as best we can. Because of the cost of parts, it can be
very expensive to run a car, but the bus fare is two cents here in
Dallas.

The bus soon reaches the Central Expressway and turns in

towards the downtown area. The only time it leaves the express-way is to stop at the Meadows Building, where the Centers for Disease Control has its regional office. I suppose that it is the largest non-military agency of what remains of the United States Government. Maybe the Agriculture Department is larger, but I doubt it. CDC is heavily supported by the British. US tax collection procedures are still too minimal to guarantee the kind of budgetary consistency a massive operation like CDC requires. What the English do is simple: they pay CDC's salaries out of their general exchequer, then bill the US Federal Reserve Bank in Atlanta, which transfers gold down at Fort Knox from the American pile to the British pile.

Half the passengers on the bus get off at CDC. The rest of us continue on into downtown. A group of girls in Rat Patrol uniforms sing a familiar song, made popular by the rock group Sunshine.

> 'Earliest morning, hour of sweetness
> Surely begotten just to remind us
> That night is completed
> And we can begin now, a brand new day.'

I must confess that I don't like Sunshine's relentless good cheer any more than I liked the facile anger of The Bad back before the war. I was a Bach fan back then, and I am a Bach fan now. But the Rat Patrol girls are fresh-faced and full of the winsome joy of their song. To a man my age, the young are so beautiful to see.

'Hey, Whitley, we're here.'

'Sorry.' I follow Jim out of the bus. We are at the Adolphus Hotel, which is the Southwestern headquarters of the British Relief. And some say, also, the true seat of government of the Southwestern United States.

The Adolphus is in superb repair, unlike many Dallas structures, which have suffered mainly from this country's continuing glass shortage. There are no cracks in the façade of this beautifully restored old hotel. I can remember, dimly, coming here with my father, driving up from San Antonio in his black Cadillac, when he was doing business with a prewar billionaire named H. L. Hunt. Dad and his partners were trying to interest

Hunt in drilling for oil in Lavaca County in South Texas, but I don't think they ever succeeded.

The Adolphus of today is much more elegant. We pass through big doors elaborate with polished brass, and confront at once a receptionist behind a wide desk. To her right is a Phillips computer, its screen glowing. To her left is a communications console. She is wearing the summer uniform of the British Emergency Medical Relief Organisation, a white peaked cap with blue trim, white shirt with blue-and-gold epaulettes, white skirt, and white shoes. Altogether, she radiates health and a kind of deep, interior confidence I remember well. It was common-place in the prewar United States. Behind her, two blue-uniformed bobbies stand at parade rest in front of the elevators.

'May I help you, please?' she says quickly.

'James Kunetka and Whitley Strieber to see Mr Shandy.' Jim's voice is smooth, his manner calm and affable. He comes here often, looking for news. I cannot help but be uneasy in this foreign-controlled enclave. Like most Americans, my trust in massive central governments is nil. I am uneasy around these British civil servants with their paramilitary pretensions, though I know that their contributions to our welfare have been enormous.

The receptionist types our names into the computer. In a moment the communications console beeps. She picks up the receiver, listens, puts it down. 'You can go right up.' She presses a buzzer and one of the bobbies steps forward. By the time he reaches us, she has filled out two green tags. We are expected to put them in our shirt pockets so that, folded out, they can be seen at all times.

We are accompanied to the sixteenth floor by the other bobby. There, a third policeman shows us to Room 1620, which is marked simply CONTAGIOUS DISEASES. There is a faint smell of sausages and coffee in the hallway.

Another secretary shows us into a cramped outer office, which is dominated by a communications console and computer identical to the ones downstairs. The next moment Jim is introducing me to the inhabitant of the more commodious inner office, a man of medium height with a badly sunburned bald head and a sort of blustering joviality about him. He is in a summer uniform with large wet spots under the arms. He gets right down to business. 'I can give you an hour,' he says.

Jim takes off his backpack and pulls out his recorder. 'The idea is that you simply talk. We won't ask many questions. Just tell about your job. Your life here. Whatever you want.'

Shandy regards us. 'I'd anticipated questions.'

'Do you feel you need them?' Jim asks.

'Well, I suppose not. It's just – more convenient, you know.' His eyes meet mine. His gaze is blue and direct. 'Before we start, I want to know a little bit about your plans.'

Jim smiles. 'We're still going to Aztlan, Mr Shandy.'

Shandy's lips tighten. 'We don't recommend it.'

The Hispanic Free State that has come into being around El Paso is notorious in this part of Texas. People are terrified of Aztlan. Our visit there will be the first great challenge of our journey.

'Aztlan is extremely dangerous,' Shandy says. 'We'd really prefer that you stay in Texas.'

'Who is "we"?' I ask.

'The UK contingent,' he snaps. Then he picks up the little Sanyo recorder. 'You have a disc in this thing?'

'All set. Just start talking.'

Shandy settles back. After a moment, he begins.

Interview: Charles Shandy, UK Relief Official

My work as a public health officer has taken me to many parts of the United States, but I have spent most of my time in Texas, being attached to the United Kingdom Emergency Medical Relief Organisation, Southwest Region (HQ) in Dallas, as Director of Contagious Disease Control. I have been here in an official capacity for three years. Prior to the war, my experience in America was limited to a three-week vacation in San Francisco. We exchanged our house with a couple living there, the Mannings. I remember it as being a beautiful city and formed a very favourable impression of the American people from my experiences in California. When the King and the Prime Minister described the situation in America on the telly in the winter of 1988, I was among those who volunteered for the relief effort. One cannot fail to remember the American response during and after World War II, or the close ties between the two countries. I was then assistant managing director of the Albert Doring Company. We specialised in the transport of live vaccines to tropical areas, so I knew a good deal about contagion. At least, that was what I thought at the time.

During our prewar vacation, my wife and I travelled up and

down the West Coast on a train called the *Starlight*, and really had a great deal of fun. California was beautiful, and the Queen's having been there the previous spring – that was the summer of '83 – meant that the people were more than usually kindly disposed towards us English.

I have been once to San Francisco since the war, and found it quite a tattered and crowded version of its old self. But certainly recognisable. I went to call on the Mannings, but nobody in the road knew what had become of them. The family occupying their house would not talk to me.

My primary job is to identify outbreaks of treatable contagious disease and allocate appropriate Relief resources to them so that the problem will be minimised. It is not generally understood, but our main function is to supplement existing American services. The ordinary citizen views the country as being without any internal authority, but this is not the case. There is still a strong federal presence. Certainly in health care. All surviving physicians have, for example, been recorded in a new central registry maintained by the Centers for Disease Control. Hospitals can, as of last year, report their supply needs to the Centres also, and get fairly rapid allocation of medicines and equipment. The loss of records and trained bureaucratic personnel that occurred when Washington was destroyed was certainly damaging to health care, but it has not proved fatal.

I work very closely with the Centers for Disease Control. My experience with the CDC has been very good. The Centers have grown tremendously since the war. There has been great advance in identifying the numerous mutant disease factors that have appeared among the American population. The progress with pseudomonas plague, which has become a significant cause of death in the Southwest since the war, has been spectacular. The death rate from this illness has been reduced to forty-five per cent, primarily as a result of the development of nonantibiotic prophylaxis, which was done at CDC. We have helped in educating the population to identify and report plague cases so that isolation and treatment can be effected.

In the past year we have not had the continuous round of problems that were encountered at first. Certainly nothing on the scale of the Cincinnati Flu in '90. Worldwide deaths from that disease are estimated at approximately two hundred and thirty million, twenty-one million of them in the United States and two million in Europe. But the US population is better fed and stronger now, so we expect the next pandemic to be less damaging here than was the last. We anticipate another expression of this hybrid flu, and are relying heavily on CDC results in the development of a treatment regime.

Actually, one of our major projects at present is to teach CDC pneumonia prophylaxis, the construction of steam hats, the various means of assisting the breathing-impaired, control of circulation with hot and cold spots, and such things. CDC has really worked miracles with the very simplest materials and procedures. The objective of their work is to develop effective medical treatment for serious disease, treatment that can be applied at home by family members and by the victims themselves. On another front, we are underwriting the medical faculties at the new University of Texas Medical School here in Dallas, and providing British doctor-professors so that local medical personnel can concentrate on hospital work.

Despite all this effort, we are not out of the woods. Frankly, however, the drop in US as well as world population is also going to mean a long-term reduction in pandemic disease, if only because the remaining population groups are obviously going to be farther apart and have fewer contacts with one another. Despite this, it must be recalled that, worldwide, health systems remain frail. Supply lines are long and subject to extraordinary stresses. Fuel may be unavailable to move a shipment of drugs from the UK to America, for example. On the other hand, the lack of communications – a situation that is really improving fast, by the way – may simply mean that a disease outbreak goes unnoticed by us until it reaches an area where we have a permanent station.

This was the case with the cholera epidemic that created such suffering in South Texas last summer. We consider this to be a deeply damaged area, with the extensive residual radiation contamination from San Antonio, the uninhabitable zones, and the presence of an ill, malnourished, and restless Mexican population to the south. There was an unnoticed migration from Mexico into Texas all summer – more than three hundred thousand individuals were involved, virtually all of them starving. Many of these people moved right through the San Antonio Red Zone and began arriving in Dallas and Waco not only dying of starvation and radiation sickness, but carrying cholera.

Neither of the first two problems is contagious, fortunately, but the cholera did spread to the local population. There were eight thousand deaths among registered inhabitants of the state, according to the Statistical Services Office.

Our treatment regime consisted of oral electrolyte replacement and treatment of exposed populations with tetracycline. The outbreak was quelled, but the real solution lies not in prophylaxis but in the restoration of sanitary facilities to prewar condition.

To communicate the extent of health problems in Texas, it is only necessary to talk about birth rates. The Southwest shares with the Northeast the dubious distinction of having a death rate four times in excess of its birth rate. And the number of mutations per 100,000 live births is 1,018, the highest in North America. In the Southwest we have placed birth mutations on the epidemic list and have put priority on obtaining working sonogram and amniocentesis equipment, so that parents can have some warning that their child may not be normal. In addition, the Relief has established criteria for abortion and mandatory destruction of nonassistable live births, to relieve parents of this difficult responsibility.

We encourage relocation of individuals out of the Yellow Zones south and east of San Antonio, and routinely triage those who refuse to move. The population of these counties has dropped roughly ninety-one per cent since the war.

Since the beginning of my tour I have dealt with Cincinnati Flu, cholera, the first Nonspecific Sclerosing Disease panic in Dallas, a massive outbreak of brucellosis in Amarillo, apparently caused by the ingestion of contaminated milk smuggled up from Gonzales County, and numerous other smaller crises. I cannot say that my job is less than exceedingly challenging.

When my four-year tour of duty here is up, I expect to be posted back to England for six months of R-and-R and then down to the Argentine, where we have an extensive operation contending with malnutrition and its associated diseases.

You have asked me to be as personal as possible. What is the life of a Relief officer actually like? Do I meet with any hostility on the job? Of course, a certain amount. And I have emotional difficulties of my own. I must often make decisions that shorten and even take life. When I must isolate populations to prevent the spread of disease, and sometimes even withdraw medical assistance to allocate it to areas where help will still matter, I all but sweat blood.

On the other hand, I have been able to help enormous numbers of people. We have a large number of burn cases in Dallas, many of them scarred to the point of crippling: refugees from the South Texas firestorm, some of them profoundly crippled. I was a part of the committee that decided to allocate sufficient social resources to these people to prevent their dying of starvation or neglect and also to house them in public facilities. We do make decisions in favour of life whenever we can.

I live in an apartment at the Adolphus Hotel, along with the rest of the British here. Our government purchased the hotel because its large number of small suites are ideal for housing single public officials. Only our Commissioner has his family with him. Until the Southwest Area is reclassified as safe, the rest of us may not bring our families in. So I have two lonely rooms with a long view to the south. The hotel service has been maintained quite well, so I am comfortable. Most of our foodstuffs and all of our liquor is imported. The food is all tinned, unfortunately, because we cannot risk building lifetime dosage to dangerous levels if we are to remain in our jobs for any length of time. So we cannot eat local food or drink local water. Dallas's water supplies are from lakes, so there is a definite radiation problem, persisting even now. In the summer, long-half-life particles blow up from the south, and in the winter they come down from the north.

There is one saving grace here, though, and that is the people themselves. These are terribly determined people here. In fact, we have encountered few Americans who have not responded to the catastrophe in some positive manner. For example, Dallas normally works a six-day week now, and goes from eight to six. I have met some of the bravest and most wonderful people I have ever known here. I will never forget their calm courage in the face of death, nor their willingness to expose themselves to danger for the sake of others.

During the flu, for example, our main problem was keeping victims isolated from people who wanted to help them and were willing to endanger themselves to do so. At present we are turning away three-quarters of the applicants for paramedical training, because the teaching staff must concentrate on doctors. People in the paramedic job are exposed to contagious disease and radiation as a matter of routine. Another example of the high morale involves farmers. When we must condemn produce – which happens less and less often now, I'm glad to say – you would expect anger on the part of the farmers. We have come to anticipate complete cooperation. When crops are suspect, the farmers themselves are the first to tell us. 'I got in a thunderstorm on the way in, looked like it had blown up from the south,' they might say, and assist us in checking the shipment for hot particles. They can be trusted to give the food to the disposal teams for burial if necessary. And these are all people who have known starvation in the most personal terms.

I recall that we sent out an emergency call for cleanup teams after the hot thunderstorm in April of 1989. There were hot spots all over Dallas. And by '89 it was all long-half-life stuff. This radiation was not going to dissipate. We got more volunteers than we had gear for them to wear. People who were already triaged volunteered to work without protective clothing, which was in short supply. I think that the city was probably saved as a viable human community by the men and women who gave what remained of their lives during that cleanup.

Fortunately, most of the local thunderstorms are generated over Oklahoma and North Texas, so a hot storm coming up from the south is rare. There is the problem of radiation being carried down from the Dakotas, but this is not too severe. Most of that flow is southeastward, and affects the Midwest.

[NOTE: At this point Mr Shandy's breakfast arrived. This is the morning menu of a British Relief officer: one fried egg, one sausage, two kipper fillets, one bowl of oatmeal with cream, one small pot of tea, and one tablet of vitamin C.

Mr Shandy ate his breakfast and made two telephone calls, one to the Relief's human resources pool requesting a Spanish-speaking interpreter to accompany him on a field trip, and another to the Centers for Disease Control to enquire whether or not they were ready to try some newly designed kits intended for testing whole blood for contamination by what he referred to as 'exotics'. He did not offer to expand on the content of these phone calls. After his breakfast he asked us what we most wanted to know from him. We requested that he tell us of his experiences in and around San Antonio.]

I was a part of the South Texas Emergency Relief Project in May of '89. There were many people living between Houston and San Antonio who had been out of touch with the outside world for seven months. As it did throughout the country, the electromagnetic pulse destroyed most of the televisions and radios, along with computers, radar stations, medical equipment, and car ignitions. Add the bombing of San Antonio to the general chaos, and one can see that the conditions would be truly terrifying.

Initial reaction in rural communities was to go towards the cities. We must recall that in less than a second a silent and invisible EMP burst had plunged people from the twentieth century to the Middle Ages. So they knew absolutely nothing of what was happening beyond the borders of their own towns. People who could have direct-dialled Tokyo one second could not telephone the county sheriff the next. The disorientation was extreme. So they went towards the source of communications, which was the cities. But in South Texas this was a terrible error, because San Antonio was in flames. In fact, the city survivors were streaming into the countryside – not many from San Antonio, but hordes from Austin because of the fire and Houston because of fallout. Many Houstonians, in their confusion, went towards San Antonio, not away from it. Apparently the traffic jams to the east and north of the city were so bad that escape westward was the only alternative. The sheer massiveness of the attack on San Antonio created damage and injuries previously unexpected. There were large numbers of people with hearing loss due to blast pressure even miles from Ground Zero. Others suffered not only burns but toxic reactions to synthetic-fibre clothing that had melted into their skin. San Antonio was struck with low airbursts, creating a massive dust cloud. The large number of huge weapons detonating simultaneously at first blew immense quantities of dust into the air, then created updraughts that drew it upward where it mingled with particles created in the fission phase of the explosions.

Conditions in such places as Lavaca, Gonzales, and DeWitt counties were appalling. The populations had quadrupled in the first days after the war. Gasoline and food ran out very quickly. Radiation sickness was virtually epidemic and was followed shortly by all the diseases we have come to associate with large groups of undernourished, debilitated people.

Although we arrived in Dallas three months after Warday, it was not until three more months had passed that we were organised enough to arrange an overflight of San Antonio and South Texas. We were in an SC-7 Skyvan loaded with extra fuel tanks in the rear of the passenger compartment so that we could accomplish a round trip to and from Dallas if ground conditions were too unstable to permit us to land. You must recall that we had been broadcasting into this area on all available bands for some months, and getting no response. Military recon flights indicated an extensive population. So we did not know what to expect. The Commissioner wished to determine whether or not to extend British Military Rule to the area. This has not been done in many parts of the United States, but it is generally considered for areas where the population is in a state of confusion or upheaval, and the local authorities are not able to cope.

We flew as far south as Seguin, which is thirty miles from San Antonio. To avoid ground radiation we did not go below three thousand feet, but rather observed through binoculars. Seguin proved to be largely burnt.

At that time I got a look at the condition of San Antonio. I remember being astonished that this little city had been so terribly devastated on Warday. People had hardly even heard of it in Britain. One would have expected Los Angeles or even Houston before San Antonio. Of course, it has since come out that a good part of the planned Soviet attack didn't go off, so in a sense San Antonio was simply unlucky. The Soviets had given it first-strike priority because of the extensive US Air Force repair and refitting facilities there, and the huge complex of military hospitals, the atomic supplies dump at Medina Base, and the presence of a mechanised army that could have been used to preserve order across the whole of the Southwest as well as seal the Mexican border.

Perhaps, also, they knew that American intelligence did not expect this particular attack, and considered that there was value in surprise.

It is no wonder that the American military prohibits photography in such places. The effect on national and indeed worldwide morale would be very negative. From a distance there is nothing to see but the black landscape and the gleaming fused earth around the Ground Zero points. The land is mostly flat, with some rolling hills to the north. Although I never went to San

Antonio before the war and had never met anyone from there, my first experience of that blasted corpse was, quite frankly, shattering. I sat at the window of that plane unable to move, unable to speak.

The cabin was silent. After a time we simply flew away.

We soon found ourselves over the town of Yoakum, Texas, which showed on our charts as a population area of approximately eight thousand people.

There were two tent communities to the south of the town. The fields roundabout were planted with corn and various vegetables, but looked to be in poor condition due to post-blast weather effects. There were numerous horses about, many of them hitched to cars and pickup trucks from which the engines had been removed to lighten them.

Our appearance caused a great deal of excitement in the town. People rushed out of houses and buildings waving sheets or articles of clothing or just their arms. We were able to land on State Highway 77 on the outskirts of town. There was a local airfield, but the runway was too cracked to justify the risk of using it, and the road seemed solid.

The first to meet us were a man and a woman on horseback. They had rifles in holsters on their saddles, and as they came to a stop they drew them. I'll never forget the first question, from that lean, bewhiskered man with the hollow eyes: 'Y'all from Russia?'

They thought they had lost the war. This was, we were to find, generally the assumption in isolated populations. I explained that we were British. We were at once escorted into town. We had various emergency medicines, and our orderlies soon set up an aid station with the equipment we had brought. Our station was placed in the showroom of a local Ford dealership, the Wendell Motor Company. This offered us a large floor space and limited access via two doors. At the same time, the people waiting outside could see for themselves that we were working as quickly as we could. Ampicillin, keflex, and tetracycline were our main supplies, along with morphia and heroin for pain sufferers. We also carried cyanide and copies of the euthanasia rules. Cultural resistance to this programme is very strong, especially in rural America. But people usually come to understand that truly unspeakable suffering ought to be relieved by death if the victim has no scruples of conscience, or is indeed begging for it.

On that first day in Yoakum, our three doctors and six medical orderlies treated 211 of the thousands who presented themselves. The actual local population was approximately fifteen thousand at that time. In my estimation, there were no able-bodied individuals. It was fortunate that we brought the four soldiers, because violent disagreements kept breaking out among the patients, especially as to whose dying children were to have the first chance at the antibiotics.

On that day we performed sixteen paediatric euthanasias, for the most part on children suffering both pain and brain damage from radiation or other poisoning.

We found numerous cases of mental breakdown. Paranoia, schizophrenia, catatonic withdrawal were all present in the population. Our psychological pharmacopoeia consisted of a little Thorazine and Valium. We dispensed what Thorazine we could to the schizophrenics. We recommended that the mentally ill who were unable to function be euthanised, with the consent of their families. Nobody volunteered their psychotic relatives at first, but the prospect of being free from the burden of their presence caused people, as is usually the case, to come to us in the night to get the cyanide capsules.

We also faced numerous cases of partially stabilised radiation sickness. These individuals were usually covered with sores from secondary infections and were in great agony. Upon being told of the hopelessness of their situation, most of them willingly accepted the death alternative.

Because of their oaths or religious objections, many British doctors have refused to dispense euthanasia treatment, so this aspect of the programme was left to me. I spent my days living out tragedies with the victims, and my nights in dreams of indescribable horror, where I heard them calling me from the grave, and imagined that I had accidentally buried them alive. But it wasn't true, I was not the shadow of death. To these people, with their burns and their sickness and their tormented bodies, I was mercy.

Among the problems with which we could not cope were the various parasitic diseases. They are not much of a problem in Britain, and we simply failed to anticipate their presence here. Hookworm, tapeworm, ascaris, and giardiasis were the most serious of these. These diseases were in adults unattractive and debilitating, but in children they were devastating. The acuteness of the problem can be realised when one reflects that these people, forced to live on a below-starvation-level diet, one almost absent of proteins, were being consumed from within by their own worm loads. We instructed on the use of saline enemas, developed by the CDC as a means of temporarily reducing infestation, especially in the cases of hookworm and tapeworm. But the only real relief, namely proper medication and a good, clean source of food and water, simply was not available at this time.

Our contamination specialist surveyed the area in some detail, and found it seriously affected by radiation. Most of the population was radiation-poisoned to some degree at least. There was also malnutrition. Only a few children were free of rickets. Pellagra, the old curse of the South, had reasserted itself.

We realised, during that first day, that we were in the presence of a whole world, small though it was, that was dying before our eyes. There were only two babies under the age of six months. One had been blinded and had lost a hand, and the other was suffering from a severe systemic infection.

The county sheriff, Mr Weaver, reported that they buried five or six people a day, generally in shallow graves in a field near the old town graveyard. The local Catholic priest, Father Menendez, and the Baptist minister, Mr Harold, officiated at the brief ceremonies.

Our one overwhelming wish was to radio out and somehow get great loads of food and clothing and, above all, medicines for these people. But we knew exactly what would come: little, and too late. Instead we settled on a recommendation, which we presented to the sheriff and the two religious leaders the next day, that the whole population start moving north. A hundred miles closer to Dallas there were communities that were still very much intact. We also offered to send what supplies we could down from Dallas, but we couldn't provide much.

The situation was stark. If they stayed, all of these people were going to die. As the sheriff pointed out, a lot of them would also perish on the journey.

After we had dispensed all of our drugs and held as many information meetings as we could on every subject from personal hygiene to the three signs of terminal malnutrition, we took our leave of the people of Yoakum and returned to Dallas.

Eventually a column of these refugees did set out. Along the way they had lost about two thousand stragglers, with five thousand dead or unable to continue. Only six thousand people arrived in North Texas, of whom three thousand were placed in isolation due to their infectious-disease status. All three thousand of these eventually died.

Of the fifteen thousand people alive in Yoakum on the day we visited, approximately two thousand remain alive today.

Poll: What We Expect, What We Fear: American Opinion in 1993

About six weeks ago there arrived in the offices of the *Herald News* a familiar brown manila envelope that brought cheers when it was opened.

It was a production of the Consolidated American Polling Group, made up of former staff members of the Harris, Gallup, and Sindlinger organisations. After two years of reorganisation and preparation, they were finally beginning to distribute national polls once again. Two documents were enclosed, one a poll of attitudes about the present state of the country, and the other concerning future expectations.

We will be presenting sections of these two polls throughout the book at points where they seem germane.

The samples used in the surveys each consisted of more than 1,400 American adults eighteen years of age and older. The samples are statistically representative of the nation in terms of geographic and demographic design. For comparison purposes, 1992 data are given where appropriate.

Naturally, neither the polls nor our use of them in any way reflects the opinions of the Consolidated American Polling Group, Inc.

Do you think that the destiny of this country is presently in the hands of other nations?

	1993	1992
AGREE	46%	49%
DISAGREE	47	43
NO OPINION	7	8

When queried about which regions or nations of the world were most influential, the responses were:

Region	1993	1992
WESTERN EUROPE	45%	41%
JAPAN/ASIA	25	22
AFRICA	5	5
LATIN AMERICA	10	12
AUSTRALIA/PACIFIC	6	7
MIDDLE EAST	7	9
OTHER	2	4

When asked about specific nations, the responses were:

Nation	1993	1992
UNITED KINGDOM	32%	33%
WEST GERMANY	12	13
FRANCE	10	11
SWEDEN	7	6
JAPAN	26	21
SAUDI ARABIA	4	6
ARGENTINA	3	4
BRAZIL	4	4
OTHER	2	2

Will the United States ever again emerge as a world economic power?

	1993	1992
AGREE	37%	32%
DISAGREE	57	62
NO OPINION	6	6

Will the United States ever regain its status again as a military power?

	1993	1992
AGREE	32%	29%
DISAGREE	65	67
NO OPINION	3	4

Documents from the Emergency

There was no doubt that it was fire. They felt it
burn their skin, then their bones, then their brains.
– J. Hillyer,
Passion for War

THE BUREAUCRAT'S COLD EYE

The first test of my ability to get sensitive documents from official
sources came immediately. Both Whitley and I wanted to have a
selection of documents that had been produced in the months
following Warday.

Most people were too busy dealing with blown-out radios,
televisions, and telephones, and trying to understand what had
happened to us, to worry about bureaucrats and their pro-
nouncements.

But they were there, and they were pronouncing.

Many times since Warday I have imagined the places where
the postwar planning and thinking took place, the quiet offices at

the edge of the fire. I have wondered who the men – or the women – were who divided the doomed from the saved, who conceived of triage, who looked upon the rest of us with cold eyes.

Much of what I did to get documents was 'illegal' in the old sense of the word. I not only took things off desks, I opened files that were supposed to be sealed. But the documents in those files cannot be stolen, especially not the two collected here, which relate to the most fundamental of wartime experiences.

Like the people behind the numbers and the places in the radioactive zones, they belong to all of us.

ESTIMATED CASUALTIES ASSOCIATED WITH THE OCTOBER 1988 WAR

Deaths as a Result of October 28, 1988 Attack

New York City Area	2,961,881
San Antonio, Texas	1,081,961
Washington, DC Area	2,166,798
The Dakotas, Montana, and Wyoming	1,121,802
EMP-Related Accidents	8,106
Total Warday Deaths	7,340,548

Cumulative Deaths since October 28, 1988 Attack

Cincinnati Flu	21,600,000
Famine of 1988	26,200,000
Radiation-Related Illnesses	17,000,000
Other	3,000,000
Total Post-Warday Deaths	67,800,000

Total Deaths to Date

75,140,548

Total US Population Changes

1987 US Population	237,625,904
1992 US Population, Estimated	174,384,000

[Source: CDC, 1993]

Ø 14 15ØØ ZULU MARCH 89

TO ALL DIVISIONS OF THE UNITED STATES ARMED FORCES
FROM JOINT CHIEFS OF STAFF
COLORADO HDQ/JCS. 173.A888

UNTIL FURTHER NOTICE, THE FOLLOWING DESIGNATIONS WILL BE EMPLOYED
IN DESCRIBING RADIOACTIVE ZONES:

DEAD ZONE	BLAST CENTER. VIRTUALLY UNPASSABLE. RECON ONLY BY AIRPLANE. AVOID ALL CONTACT. NO ATTEMPT WARRANTED TO FOLLOW ILLEGAL ENTRIES.
RED ZONE	HIGH RADIOACTIVITY AREA. ADMITTANCE LIMITED TO 1Ø MINUTES WITH PROTECTIVE CLOTHING OR SUITABLE VEHICLE. ILLEGAL ENTRIES MAY BE SHOT ON SIGHT.
ORANGE ZONE	VARIABLE RADIOACTIVITY. SUSTAINED ENTRY WITH SUITABLE PROTECTION. VIOLATORS SHOULD BE GIVEN WARNING SHOT.
BLUE ZONE	VARIABLE LOW RADIATION. USE CAUTION AND PROTECTIVE CLOTHING WHENEVER POSSIBLE.
GREEN ZONE	PERIMETER AREAS. USE STANDARD MILITARY PROCEDURES FOR SECURITY IMPLEMENTATION.

ALL ROAD ENTRY TO ZONED AREAS SHOULD BE IDENTIFIED WITH APPROPRI-
ATE NOMENCLATURE. SECURITY PROCEDURES APPLICABLE EXCEPT WHERE
NOTED FOR CONTAMINATED AREAS.

THIS ORDER TO TAKE EFFECT 13ØØ ZULU 15 MARCH 1989.

Interview: Wilson T. Ackerman, Undersecretary of Defence (Ret.)

[THE CONDUCT OF THE WAR. Wilson Ackerman is well known in Dallas, in the same way that somebody with an exotic contagion might be well known. People glance at him in the streets, ask him questions. Sometimes, I suppose, they do more than that.

Ackerman was aboard the Doomsday Plane on Warday. His testimony seemed essential, and he was available.

The man is deeply afraid. His eyes never stop moving. Although I don't think he is more than forty-five, like so many of us he seems much older. His hands touch and caress his face as he talks, in a dry, quick voice that seems at times too precise, and at other times curiously rich.

There is an almost lyrical terror in this man. It is an emotional state, perhaps, beyond guilt. I do not think it has a name.

As Wilson Ackerman spoke in his careful tones I thought of a lover's murmuring, and the quarrels of children, and the voices of the night.]

I did not know that we were in a war situation until the Secretary telephoned my office and told me in a brusque tone to activate Case Quick Angel. I then set in motion the series of actions that were designed to disperse upper echelons of the Executive Branch during a nuclear war. This order was given by me at exactly 1530 on 28 October 1988.

Shortly after that I joined the Secretary, as per plan, on the helicopter pad. We left the Pentagon via helicopter at once, heading for Andrews Air Force Base. With Secretary Forrest was Air Force General Potter Dawes, who was carrying the backup codes. We reached Andrews at 1545 hours and found that the White House contingent had already entered the E-4B aircraft. Under the Quick Angel basing protocols, the E-4B had recently been returned to Andrews from a base in Indiana. Donald Meecham informed us that the President was aboard and the National Emergency Airborne Command Post (NEACP) was ready for takeoff.

We then entered the aircraft and proceeded directly to the Presidential suite. The President greeted us and we sat down to a briefing from SAC General Joe Point. General Point indicated that there had been a Soviet response to the Space Shuttle's deployment of the first satellite in the Spiderweb warhead-killer system. This response was to open the doors of a group of SS-18 silos in central Siberia. Altogether they were preparing a launch of twelve missiles containing a total of fifty-four warheads in the 5- to 10-megaton range. At that time they had not launched any missiles.

As our aircraft took off, we received telemetry from NORAD indicating that there had been an explosion, probably nuclear, in near space over the western Pacific Ocean. NASA then announced that the Space Shuttle had ceased to communicate with Houston due to this detonation, and had probably been destroyed.

As the Spiderweb satellites were radiation hardened, the one deployed remained operational, but it was far from its intended orbit, and we now had no means to transport it. It was effectively useless, and in any case, formed only a small part of the total system. At that point the President decided that it was probable that we would soon be in a hot war. He therefore authorised Defence to transmit a War Warning to all US military commands. I carried out that order at 1550 hours. Here is the text of the document:

The Space Shuttle *Enterprise* was destroyed by a nuclear device of
unknown origin at approximately 1545 hours US Eastern
Standard Time this day. It was engaged in a Defense Department
mission. Please consider this a War Warning, and proceed to
your designated alert level immediate.

This caused SAC and the US Navy Submarine Command to go
to One Alert status, and the other services to respond by entering
their highest states of readiness. It was at this point that war
became inevitable, but at the time there was still a sense of
control in the NEACP. The President activated the hot line to
Moscow. The telephone at their end was not answered. At last
the President put the instrument down. 'Gentlemen,' he said, 'I
am afraid that the Premier will not talk to me.' We then instructed
Ambassador Underwood in Moscow to call on the Premier at
once and inform him that the United States was willing to
negotiate a settlement of the question that had arisen between
us. We further attempted communication by the hot line tele-
type on the chance that the telephone system might be out of
order.

There had been a massive failure on the part of Western
intelligence to correctly evaluate the Soviet response to the
deployment of Spiderweb. This system, utilising ultra-
highpower particle beams, and which targeted and destroyed
warheads in space after they were ejected from their missile
bases, was intended to render the United States invulnerable to
land- or sea-based attacks. As the target acquisition system was
optical, the Soviet low-radar-profile systems were no defences.
We did not know at the time how far in advance of existing Soviet
weaponry this system was, or deployment would have been
evaluated differently.

It was our stated intention before the deployment to begin
dismantling the American offensive missile force once we were
protected by the Spiderweb system. The Soviet leadership had
given us no indication that they did not believe this, and had not
even protested the deployment of Spiderweb.

In retrospect it is obvious that they were so far behind technologically that they were afraid to so much as whisper a protest,
lest their weakness become known to us.

Although I was not a party to the decision to deploy

Spiderweb, I am trying to come to grips with the fact that I was
assisting in the management of a system of defence that had
drifted into a state of extreme brittleness, in the sense that our
own technological superiority was making our enemy in-
creasingly desperate, and thus was actually causing the very war
it was intended to prevent.

As per plan, the NEACP proceeded due south towards its
intended operational area, approximately 100 miles SSW of the
Cape Charles Lighthouse, over the Atlantic Ocean.

At 1555 the National Security Agency informed us that three
Soviet satellites had begun unusual orbital manoeuvres. NSA
said that these were designated as unusually large communications relay satellites, and that there had been optical and electronic surveillance confirming this. However, this remarkable man-
oeuvre capability made them highly suspect. The President then
ordered SAC to destroy these satellites, utilising the ground-
based Slingshot missiles, which are a classified weapons system.
The Slingshots were fired. Less than two minutes passed before
the threatening satellites were destroyed. But it was too late. We
were soon informed that they had successfully ejected four large
weapons, which were dropping to an altitude level of 100,000
feet over California, Nebraska, Pennsylvania, and Manitoba.
The President made a sighing sound, as if he had been struck in
the chest. We all knew what terrific damage the country was
soon going to sustain. It is far easier to create high-level electromagnetic energy in pulsed form than it is to shield against
it.

We were aware of the classified studies on this. We knew that a
vast number of electronic circuits in the United States would be
damaged, most of them beyond easy repair. Even those shielded
to resist a 50,000-volt pulse would be destroyed by the explosion
of such large bombs in near space, as the pulse each generated
would far exceed 50,000 volts.

At 1620, we watched our entire fighter escort, consisting of six
F-15s of the 113 TAC Group out of Andrews, corkscrew into the
sea. The Soviet EMP weapons had just detonated. The fighters'
shielding had clearly proved insufficient, and these aircraft had
undoubtedly lost their on-board computers, without which the
F-15 cannot fly. At the same time, most of the commercial
airliners in the air over the United States and Canada began to
crash or became dangerously disabled. Approximately three

hundred million radio and television sets, and most radio and television stations, ceased to function. All microwave relay stations in the United States and Canada ceased to function, meaning that long-distance telephone and telemetric communications were no longer possible. The ignitions of many automobiles built after 1977–78 were rendered inoperable. Many local power systems failed due to fused relays and subsequent overload. A staggering number of computers, and most of the automated factories used to manufacture them, were destroyed. Of course, repairs began at once, and some AM stations such as WOR in New York were on at low power within a week, but isolated cases of resiliency did little to ameliorate the overall effect of the pulse. Generally, the negative synergy of technological breakdown and economic chaos has meant very slow recovery from this damage. WOR, for example, ran for eight months, but was closed down when New York was abandoned.

Our NEACP aircraft was also damaged in a number of ways, and the pilot soon informed us that he would prefer to return to an overland situation.

SAC called, using the still-functional UHF communications channel, which was designed to be proof against any level of EMP. The President then ordered Case Dream Eagle to be activated. At 1625.12, six bomb-carrying satellites were armed to detonate automatically as they reached their target positions over the Soviet Union. To compensate for their greater state of EMP readiness, we generated an ambient voltage level of 120,000 volts with each bomb. This probably caused the destruction of ninety per cent of all electronic devices in the USSR, as even their best shielding was not effective past 100,000 volts. Our own decision to limit protection to the 50,000-volt level had been the classic wargame mistake of assuming that the other side would hit us with whatever maximum force we could conveniently defend against, and not with the maximum force they could muster.

We now went to our emergency communications systems, which consisted of the UHF channel to SAC, and an infrared laser communicator to keep us in touch with Washington. These were effective devices, and the NEACP maintained its essential communications despite the enemy's best efforts.

CIA came on the laser communicator with an evaluation to the effect that the Soviets would release their SS-18s within three to

five minutes. The President then opened the code boxes for
Minuteman and unlocked the switches. I remember that Mr
Forrest put his hands over the President's hands, because the
President was shaking.

The Defence Intelligence Agency then pulsed via UHF an
analysis of the targeting of the Soviet weapons that had been
rendered operational. While I was having this downloaded
to screen for the President, he activated Minuteman. There
were three flights containing a total of fifty-six warheads planned for the first wave. It was our intention to remove the
Soviet government without excessive loss of life in the population. We intended to destroy Moscow, Leningrad, and Sevasto-
pol, and hit the administrative capitals of all the republics.
This would result in destruction of only eight per cent of the
population, but would cause the USSR to lose the means of
government.

The NEACP System Commander then informed us that the
EMP damage had compromised the ability of the aircraft to
maintain trim, and it was now in a nose-low attitude, and was
unable to maintain altitude indefinitely. We could expect to be on
the ground, one way or another, within the half hour.

At that time the President again tried the hot line. It was
inoperative. An attempt to reach Mr Underwood in Moscow
failed.

The President was informed that the British Prime Minister
and the French President were both on the phone. The secret
NATO Omninet communications system had also survived
EMP. The President spoke briefly with each of them. The French
President told him that he and the Germans and the British had
informed the Soviets of the existence of a secret treaty between
the three nations, under which all American military installations in those countries were in the process of being entered by
local nationals. The treaty had been designed to go into effect
in the event that a nuclear exchange between the US and the
USSR occurred without the prior knowledge of NATO and
France.

So we found ourselves alone. Our European allies had abandoned us, or so it seemed then. I hope that the Treaty of
Coventry proves to have been a wise one. If it had not been
in place, the exchange of 28 October 1988 would undoubtedly
have escalated into at least four more salvos, two of them

against the NATO allies and France. Inasmuch as the eventual damage done by the limited war we did have was so very much greater than we imagined, an exchange on that scale would have rendered humankind a minor species, or perhaps an extinct one.

The President begged the European leaders to inform the Soviet Premier that we would in no case fire our missiles unless he first fired his, even at this late time. But the EMP exchange had caused them to lose contact with him. To this day his fate is not known.

The DIA targeting analysis had been downloaded, and I briefed the President. The indications were appalling. Washington, DC, was going to receive a total load of sixty megatons. New York would get seventy. This was enough to cause the land itself to melt, which is what actually did happen in Washington. The remaining missiles were all targeted for Minuteman, SAC, and the USAF refit and supply centre at Kelly Air Force Base in Texas.

So the Soviet first wave was primarily a military targeting. Even so, we were going to take a serious population hit. Nearly twelve million Americans lived in target areas. It was now 1630 hours.

I had an episode of angina pectoris at that time and was not present at the meeting with the NEACP Commander. When I returned to the Presidential suite, it was to find that the aircraft would have to land in fifteen minutes, and this landing would have to be accomplished on a beach off the coast of North Carolina, due to our inability to reach an airfield. If the NEACP was destroyed on landing, the United States would lose its ability to respond properly to a Soviet attack. If this plane was forced to keep the command, we would have to fire Minuteman before crash landing, whether or not the Soviets had fired. The vulnerability of this one aircraft could force us to use our missiles or risk their loss.

The President then ordered NEACP transferred to the alternate aircraft, which was operating out of Offutt AFB in Nebraska. This aircraft reported severe EMP damage and refused the command. The President then attempted to raise HQ NORAD/ADCOM Combat Operations Center in the Cheyenne Mountain Complex and transfer to them, but this communication was not encoded properly and was also refused. We could not find the proper coding card, and to this day I wonder if the war could have been averted if we had found it.

The President had a key to turn to fire Minuteman. He put his hand on this key and ordered the NEACP Commander to inform him when we were within one minute of touchdown. We commenced placing the command to Cheyenne Mountain every ten seconds, hoping against hope that the transfer of authority would eventually be accepted. We attempted to relay the transfer via the alternate airborne command post, but there was no protocol established for that, and the available chain of command did not have the authorisations necessary to create one. We began to try to communicate with the Vice-President, but he was en route to the US Government Emergency Command Control and Communications Center in Maryland, from which he was supposed to govern the country if the President became a casualty. We did not yet know that the EMP pulse had caused his helicopter to crash, with the loss of all aboard.

It was agreed that Secretary Forrest would replace the President at the key, should the President experience a physical problem in the next few minutes.

Soon we began to see a long, narrow island below us. We were informed that this was our destination, and we would be landing not far from Kitty Hawk.

The President ordered a check of the Minuteman communications system, and the arming of the proper missiles. We were told by SAC that fourteen B-52s were holding at their fail-safe points despite EMP damage, and could proceed with their mission. They were ordered to do so.

NSA then informed us that a suspicious satellite, also previously thought to be a communications device, was ejecting devices over South Dakota that, astonishingly, might be nuclear warheads. Without a word, the President then turned the key and initiated the Minuteman firing sequence. The time was 1636.28. At 1636.51 we received confirmation via UHF that the missiles were away. At 1637.06 Cheyenne Mountain told us that twenty-one nuclear devices had detonated in the missile fields in South Dakota. The Mountain then ceased to signal. The Soviet warheads had been fired from satellites. We had no knowledge of such weapons. Another few seconds and Minuteman would have been destroyed on the ground. Our alternative would then, as the Soviets well knew, have been to go to the city busters aboard our submarines and risk escalation to the destruction of our own population centres, or surrender.

At that point the President had to be attended by his physician, due to difficulty breathing.

At 1641.11 NORAD informed us that the Soviet SS-18s were launched from forward soils on the Kamchatka Peninsula. At 1642.40 we received a pulsed load showing the exact targets and throw times. Washington, San Antonio, New York. More for the Dakotas, Wyoming, and Montana. Oddly, Omaha was not on the list.

We were then told by the NEACP Commander to fasten our seatbelts, as the huge aircraft would be attempting a landing in the sand in two minutes. We left the command post and sat in the briefing room, where there were fewer sharp objects and access to the outside was quicker. We were given fire-resistant coveralls and breathing apparatus.

A few minutes later the pilot began counting down from twenty. There was a sort of soft, surging sensation, then a stronger and stronger pull to the left, then the sound of equipment breaking far below as the belly of the aircraft was torn out. I left my seat, thinking that the plane had stopped, only to find myself hurled against the ceiling. I then fell amid a cascade of ceiling panels. I was in the aisle beside the President. I was covered with blood. I got to my feet and began trying to make my way down the aisle, which was full of plastic ceiling panels. Then a hissing sound started, and foam fire-extinguishing chemicals began pouring out of nozzles in the front of the cabin. There was another abrupt shift of position and we were almost on our side. There was a strong smell of kerosene.

I reached up and attempted to rouse the President. He was lolling against his seatbelt. Two airmen came in and began cutting him loose. Others led me and Mr Forrest and the various other White House officials from the aircraft.

Moments later we found ourselves in a hospital tent that had been inflated by the plane's medical orderlies some yards from the aircraft, which lay on its side, its left wing bent and leaking kerosene, its right wing washed by the sea.

The President was brought in just behind us and laid on a tarpaulin. When his face mask was removed, it was discovered that he was dead, from a broken neck.

At 1654 we heard a long, crackling rumble from the north. I

knew that this was the sound of the Soviet weapons detonating over Washington, two hundred miles away.

I remember that a big crowd had gathered, and the local volunteer fire department soon arrived.

Zone of Nowhere

People change when they see a Dead Zone. Once observed, a Dead Zone becomes a kind of personal secret, like a private disfigurement. There is something awesome and terrible about the sheer power it takes to create such destruction. It is impossible not to change when you have the first-hand experience of seeing a vast wasteland where a city of a million people once existed.

One Dead Zone was San Antonio, the city where I was born and spent my youth and where my family lived before Warday.

In 1990 I pulled enough strings with the military to be granted a flyover of San Antonio. After two years, radiation levels were sufficiently low to permit aircraft to approach the cratered areas without much danger. The US Army–South Texas Military Area Command apparently makes such flyovers several times a week, sometimes for officials and foreign visitors, but also, I think, for a deeper reason. Even when the aircraft are empty of visitors, there remains the need to continue some human presence.

Entering a war zone – so called, I suppose, because it is a special place produced by war – is usually not possible overland. Radiation is only one problem; navigating rubble and half-collapsed buildings is by far the greater difficulty. Only the centremost circle of the blast area is smooth – the result of the vaporising effects of the explosion.

San Antonio is not going to be cleared. There is no need. No one wants to live there, and the potential for salvage is limited. Non-military visitors are confined to helicopter flyovers. To take the tour, I had to travel to Austin and then down to San Marcos, which is a combined Army and Air Force installation. It is the command headquarters for the San Antonio War Zone. After half a day of having my paperwork processed, signing waivers of liability, and undergoing low-level interrogation about my journalistic interests, I was put on a jeep and driven to the flight line. I boarded a six-passenger helicopter with Army markings.

My escort, the only other passenger on the flight, was a cheery captain who had made the trip dozens of times before. He kept up a mostly one-sided chatter all the way to the zone: 'You're not going to believe this place. It's a symbol of immense, total power. And the bombs used weren't even the largest the Soviets could have used.' He sounded like a schoolkid reciting from memory.

He made sure I was aware that no photographs were allowed. I knew that; my camera had been impounded before we left.

Why no pictures? Certainly there were no secrets to be revealed. The extent of the damage was well known. But I could understand the restriction. There is a pornography associated with such wanton, total destruction.

Since the war, a new terminology has emerged to describe the areas of nuclear destruction: Dead Zone, Red Zone, Orange Zone, Blue Zone, Green Zone. Painted signs, each with a skull at the centre, reflect the varying levels of invisible death.

What Army photographs the captain showed me were curiously bland. Each had apparently been taken at a high altitude and showed only a flat, empty San Antonio, devoid of detail. Emptiness says little. It is the remaining detail that reveals the devastation.

Just ten miles out I noticed the first signs of the war: huge areas of rolling land devoid of any standing vegetation, blackened by what must have been a massive fire. Another few miles and there were collapsed heaps of charcoaled rubble, the remains of houses and barns that had stood in the rural areas outside the city. Then, to the right of the aircraft, we could see in the distance the uninhabited town of New Braunfels, a burned jumble of structures. The captain told me that former residents often tried to return and resettle. They would go to the edges of the restricted zones and camp there, sometimes for months. I saw one such camp, a clutch of threadbare tents, and thought *they are the people at the edge of the ocean*.

As we headed for the first Ground Zero, or GZ as my guide called it, the last of the rubble passed beneath the helicopter. There were few buildings or houses left fully intact, though the contours of the land were varied enough to have made the destruction erratic. Closer to the centre of the city there was only rubble. The downtown area, which had consisted of twenty or so tall buildings, now looked like a forest that had been reduced to haggard stumps.

For the first time the impact of a Dead Zone struck me: there was incomprehensible madness here.

Scattered through the rubble were remote stations installed by the Army to monitor radiation and intruders. With their metal roofs painted bright orange, they looked like toys left by a child on a grey carpet.

We quickly came up on the first of three GZ craters which, even two years after the explosion, still shimmered in the sunlight from the fusion of soil, metal, concrete, and other melted materials. In the distance, perhaps eight miles away, we could see another GZ casting its own eerie dazzle.

'You should see them at night, under a full moon,' the captain said. 'You'll never forget the sight.'

We circled around and around, but I couldn't identify a single landmark. Where were the parks, the schools and universities, the shopping centres? And what about the Alamo?

Though I stared out the window of the helicopter, I saw nothing. Instead, a flood of memories came back to me. I remembered summers in San Antonio, the backyard cookouts with my family and drive-in movies on warm evenings. I remember thinking as a child, as children do, that nothing would ever change and that my parents would live for ever. Now I wondered what had happened to my bedroom, to the house I had lived in, to my old high school? Were the students and teachers vaporised on Warday, or merely crushed by flying stone and metal? What had happened to my family? What had happened to Whitley's?

My family and friends have stayed in my thoughts all these years. I lost my mother and a dozen other relatives in San Antonio on Warday; perhaps a dozen more disappeared or were lost in the postwar migrations to safer parts of the country. My wife, Vivian, disappeared in the exodus from Austin. I haven't given up my belief that she is alive somewhere, looking for me, as I have been looking for her all these years.

The fact that I had lost a home, a car, a career, and a thousand small possessions didn't even occur to me, especially as I looked at what was left of San Antonio. Instead, like most people in America, I thought of faces that were no longer there. And of family histories and small treasures burned away.

The landscape came back into view again. I could see the outlines of shopping centres, portions of streets, and enough of a building here and there to guess that it had been a school or a church or a store. One large shopping centre, at the edge of a blast area, was a flattened ruin surrounded by a vast field of congealed cars melted into the asphalt of the parking lot.

I had intended to take notes or record impressions as I flew, but I just sat there. My silence seemed to disappoint the captain. Without realising it, he had begun to take a certain pride in the drama of his tour. He asked if I wanted to see more. 'How about Kelly Air Force Base? You can see the shadows of twenty B-52s and four C-5As on the runway. Really weird.'

I shook my head.

Back in San Marcos I was given a colour enlargement of the San Antonio zone taken from three miles up. On the back in red letters was stamped, WARNING. NO PUBLICATION. There isn't much detail; it is a dark grey landscape.

'Sorry it's not from a lower altitude,' the captain apologised, 'but at least you have a memento of your visit.'

Rumours: The Road to Aztlan

Jim and I are on a train between Dallas and Austin, passing through Waco. I remember Waco as a small, intense city in the heart of the cotton-growing country. The parents of our friend Jay Westbrook lived there in the sixties, and the three of us used to be invited up for occasional weekends – usually after Jay's mother had been to the apartment we all shared in Austin and had become concerned that we were too thin.

The train rattles along at about forty-five. It's clean, but pretty worn. Twelve Amtrak chair cars and a baggage car. There is no diner and no snack bar, and air conditioning is provided by keeping the front and rear doors of the cars open. The windows cannot be opened, for these prewar cars were built with many assumptions that no longer hold true. The trip will take two hours and thirty minutes station to station, with four stops.

Most of our fellow passengers are business people. The cotton industry in Waco is booming. With the collapse of cotton imports from Egypt and other countries, the local growers are finding their product much in demand. Jim tells me that Governor Parker is hoping to make cotton and cotton products a net export item in the Texas economy soon.

We are asking our fellow passengers about Aztlan, the Hispanic Free State that stretches roughly along the Texas–

Mexico border from Piedras Negras to New Mexico. We intend to go there via Austin, San Angelo, and Odessa, with a stop in Austin to interview the Governor. But our fellow passengers are not encouraging.

MRS TOM MULLIN: 'I had a sister lived in El Paso and all of a sudden one day she turns up at our house in Waco with everything she owns in a shopping bag. She just got kicked out by the Mexicans, she says. And a lot of people weren't so lucky. They got hanged from street lights. And in Roswell – the Indians went in there and just about tore the place apart, the way I hear it.'

JODY PICKEREL: 'It's probably not really a separate country from Mexico. The way I see it, Mexico went in there and started something. We mighta forgot the Alamo, but they never did. They remember the Alamo and they want all of Texas back. Unless Parker gets on the stick, they'll be in Austin before too long, or maybe even up here in Waco.'

LIZ PICKEREL: 'He's right, it's a Mexican thing. You have to remember that they didn't get touched by the war. They still have an army and everything. They're in good shape down there, except for the money troubles and the food troubles and . . . well, I take that back, they're in bad shape. But that just makes them all the more dangerous.'

CARLOS GONZALEZ: 'I am on my way to Aztlan right now. You know what I am doing there? I am selling clothes. That's right, clothes I bought in Atlanta. I have them on this train. Seven hundred good, strong pairs of overalls. You think I'll get a nice price? You bet I will! Fifty Aztlan pesos each, and you know you can change them things for good Japanese yen. Americans don't want to trade with Aztlan. Everybody's scared. Like, this train doesn't go south of Odessa. You'll find out. I have to take a truck down from Odessa. The train goes on that old Sante Fe freight track up through to Albuquerque. They fixed up those tracks last year. Before that they ran buses.'

MINDY SCHWARTZ: 'I don't really know much about it. I live in Odessa, and we don't much go to El Paso any more. I really don't think about it.'

TOM LEGAN: 'You two gringos are going in there? Lemme tell you, they cleaned house last year. No gringos allowed. They hanged 'em if they stayed. You're a couple of assholes, you know that? They'll hang you if the bandidos don't get you first. Fifty miles south of Odessa the trouble starts. You try and stay on I-20 down there the other side of Monahans, and them bandidos are going to carve up your asses. That's all I got to say about it.'

The train pulls into the station in McGregor, which serves as the stop for Waco. There is a lot of bustle, people getting off and on, men wearing weathered jeans and straw hats, carrying duffles full of possessions, people pushing carts loaded with baggage, children crying, voices rising in joy or sorrow at the partings and returns.

About three-quarters of the passengers get out. We buy Cokes on the platform. We will eat out of our backpacks, to save money.

Five minutes later the train is full again, with a few people sitting in the aisles. We pull out exactly on time. Like many of the other passengers, Jim and I have our homemade lunches. The train is due in Austin at 4.07. It had better be on time, because our interview with Oliver Parker is scheduled for 4.30.

When the wind is from the south, I understand that the corrupt odour of San Antonio is sharp on the Austin air.

Interview: Oliver Parker, Governor of Texas

You know, Whitley, the fact is that some of the states are becoming separate countries. We have the beginnings of a military structure right here in Texas. I'm pushing a bill that will place the US Third Army, the Twelfth Air Force, the State National Guard, and the highway patrol under the overall authority of the Governor's office. I consider this the most important single thing I've done so far in my administration.

We are going to restore authority in the areas of Texas where there's a problem. Especially down in South Texas. Those people have suffered enough. They've really had it much worse than in most of the rest of the country, what with the destruction of San Antonio and the sickness and all. Plus there has been a tremendously high level of illegal immigration. All authority in Mexico has broken down. Without any significant oil income, with the collapse of trade and tourism, and our inability to export foodstuffs, I wouldn't be surprised if Mexico hasn't experienced a greater population decline than we have. I'd put it at forty to fifty per cent in five years. I know from personal friends that there have been eight revolutions in Mexico City, and when we were suffering from the famine here, they were absolutely and totally destitute. They had no corn, no bread, no soy products, only their own beans. They lacked cooking oil. In Mexico City there was no potable water because their US-made sewage treatment system failed. Mexico City was hit as bad by dysentery and cholera as it was by the Cincinnati Flu. You had whole huge areas of the city where there was nobody left alive at all.

If people wonder why in the world they're still coming north in spite of what we're going through, that's the reason.

You said you wanted me to say what I was doing on Warday. Well, I was in Dallas trying to get my campaign for the Senate together. I was going to get that seat from the Republicans. Mary was with me, and so was Elizabeth. The other kids were in San Antonio, I'm sorry to say.

After we're finished, we can go over to the house and you can see our war baby, Oliver Junior. Perfect formation. He looks just like his mother. I don't live in the Governor's Mansion, by the way. The state doesn't have the money to keep it up. We're just barely staying solvent as it is, so I live in a raised ranch over on Red River. Maybe next year we'll reopen the mansion.

I deal with real basic issues: defence, disease, food, shelter, crime. I classify this whole Aztlan thing as a crime. As far as I'm concerned they're rebels, no different from the Confederates. I consider Texas a part of the United States, and Aztlan a part of Texas. If there's ever a new Constitutional Convention, Texas will certainly be sending delegates.

Other crimes we have, mainly, are crimes of desperation. There is still a lot of hunger. Real, raw hunger. Hell, people are dying of hunger and a lot of other things down in South Texas every day. The area between Houston and San Antonio is blighted. I guess you could consider that whole area depopulated.

You know, from the roof of St Edwards University south of here – you remember St Edwards? Well, from the roof you can see the start of the San Antonio Dead Zone. The horizon to the south is charcoal grey. And the sky is brown. It's a weird sight. Like looking across to the surface of another planet.

You remember my house in San Antonio, Whitley? We finished that bathroom, and we were going to put in a pool.

I was meeting with the Dallas County Democrats at the Anatole Hotel when the war happened. The lights went out. That was because the EMP killed the hotel's computer. As it died, it turned off all the lights and sent the elevators to the lobby. I thought it was an internal thing. After a while we continued our meeting in the lobby, which is skylit.

Mary came in with the news that there were planes crashing all over the place. We went outside and looked up and there was this American Airlines jet wobbling around. It kept banking first one way and then the other. Then we found out my brand-new Lincoln wouldn't start. I had a lunch scheduled at the Adolphus with Bob Rossiter of Rossiter Industries. We tried to phone him and found out the phones didn't work. I said to Mary, 'Something big's happened.' We tried to find a working TV. Couldn't do it.

We ended up walking all the way from the Anatole to the Adolphus, only to find that Rossiter wasn't there.

It was in the Adolphus lobby that we first heard the rumour that San Antonio had been bombed. Mary burst into tears. We held each other. We didn't know what to believe. Finally we went back to the Anatole. It was almost a year before we left Dallas. We lived with the Clint Rossiters, and I did legal work to pay our board.

I've been Governor for three years now. The Senate campaign was cancelled, of course. When Mark White announced that he wasn't going to run for another term, Rossiter and the Dallas County Democrats got me to take it on. Mark's not at all well. He flew over San Antonio three days after the war and got a hell of a dose. I did it too, last year, at three thousand feet. The way I look at it, that's not a place any more. It's a hole in the world.

One of our problems in Texas is that we haven't got the banking technology available to run the state at a deficit. We're limited to straight-line budgeting. I've been thinking of issuing a Texas currency, but I don't see the underlying assets to do it. I could peg it to the state's proprietary oil holdings, but with oil at eleven cents a barrel, I wouldn't get very much out of it. And full faith and credit aren't going to wash, especially not overseas.

Look at this. Isn't this beautiful? A Texas dollar. It's an engraving, done for us by an outfit in Lubbock. For a while we were dreaming of Texas currency. We'd have bills denominated from a quarter to ten dollars. Sam Houston's on the one, Austin's on the two, Davy Crockett's on the five. We haven't had the others made up, because Texas hasn't got any underlying assets that would support a currency, as I said. Texas got hurt so bad in the war, sometimes I'm surprised that it's still here at all, that everybody didn't just move.

But we are still here. You travel around this state as much as I do, you'd end up with a deep feeling of confidence and reverence. Texas is the land of the strong. People are working to rebuild. You know who really runs this state? Volunteers. People see something that needs doing and they just do it. Fill a pothole. Pull down an abandoned house. You name it. When we censused in 1990, every single census taker was a volunteer. That project of mine, naming the dead – you must remember it, Jim, you wrote a thing about it in the Dallas paper – that was all volunteers. I know you didn't think it made sense, Jim, and maybe it didn't. But it means something to name the dead. I think it does. Here's what they did. There's over a million names in these books. Handwritten, every one. Over a million.

San Antonio was so pretty. God, I remember when I had my Austin Healey and we were running the Archdiocesan Council of Catholic Youth, right? We were a bunch. Who was that priest in charge of the thing? Oh yeah, Martin. Father Edwin Martin. I remember him well. He always had high hopes for us. We put on some pretty good things, really. For a bunch of overheated intellectuals we did a good job.

Is that thing running? Lemme see it. Sanyo. You got this from the paper? I've never seen one like it. Two hours of recording on that? It looks like a quarter. That's amazing. Well, let me get back to business. You'll have to edit this tape a little.

Another thing we're doing is working very intensively with some of the other states. California, Louisiana, Arkansas, Oklahoma, New Mexico, Arizona. We're going to form a sort of loose coalition. California will lead it. That's got to be. They're ten times the size of Texas. You know that California is almost like the old days? You been out there? Well, it's just beautiful. One thing, the Japanese are everywhere. And electronics are a good bit easier to get. I don't think there's any conspiracy to deprive America of electronic devices, by the way. That's a subject the Legislature's been farting about an awful lot lately. They don't want to debate Aztlan. Don't want to think about the rough stuff. Can't say as I blame 'em. But I'm going to have to get the Speaker to get the House off its ass on my military bill. Trask's got the Senate wrapped up tight. No problems there. I need an army to go after Aztlan. Or they'll come after us. I wouldn't be surprised at all to find them on their way to Midland–Odessa within a year if we don't take some very damn decisive action.

Anyway, getting back to the electronics. This thing is really beautiful. How big is it – let's see – yeah, I could put two of these inside a cigarette pack. Three of 'em. Nice to see a Japanese thing like this again. Beautifully made. Running flat out, the Japs can build fourteen million televisions a year. If we bought 'em all, we'd be back to prewar standards in about 2000. But we can't afford the foreign exchange. We imported six million last year and made eight hundred thousand here in the States. We managed to get a hundred and thirty thousand of those sets in Texas. That tells me we now have a million televisions in Texas. Here's a piece of sweet news. Starting next July, we are going to be getting HBO via the new communications satellite California sent up from Vandenberg in June. And NBC is starting up again in the autumn, broadcasting from Los Angeles. It's going to be all reruns at first, but who the hell cares? Maybe you ought to go back to writing, Whitley. Somebody told me you'd become a gardener. Well, I'll bet you could make some money in television. A growth industry all over again. We've got the Texas State Network, of course. I think the Hunt brothers bought two prints of every John Wayne picture ever made. I do a programme once a week, 'The Governor's Desk'. I think people need to feel that the governor's there. Without a President, the governors are that much more important.

You know, the amazing thing is, when we've polled the citizens, we've found that they aren't too interested in having a Presidential election. There just isn't all that much interest. Concerns telescope when people are having trouble. Somebody who has a sick kid or is facing cancer or NSD, or just living in these times, they don't care about the Israelis slaughtering the Arabs or the South Africans marching into Zimbabwe or the Poles into the Ukraine. They're indifferent to world affairs. And about all they remember of the US is the flag and taxes. We still have the flag, so they figure the hell with the taxes.

I just think one thing, though, and it's the message I want to leave at the end of this tape. Aztlan is a serious problem, and the only way Texas can deal with it is by going in there and establishing strict martial law. If we don't, Aztlan will get stronger and stronger, and we'll soon be facing an army. The Legislature has to act on my military bill. That's the key issue in Texas right now.

Documents on the Triage

Mother, mother, I feel sick,
Send for the doctor, quick, quick, quick.
Doctor, doctor, shall I die?
Yes, my dear, and so shall I.
— Skipping rhyme

FROM THE CENTERS FOR DISEASE CONTROL

The most feared and controversial medical decision of this century has been the CDC's triage recommendation.

Both Whitley and I have been especially eager to include as much information about the triage as we can, since it affects American life so profoundly.

I don't have any really good sources at the CDC headquarters in Dallas, so I was very glad for our stopover in Austin. It gave me a chance to visit a friend who works for the CDC here, and who was willing to give me the kind of documents that would be useful. I wanted information that few people had seen before.

I hit a vein of gold, as it turned out. My friend gave me the three documents reproduced here. For this I thank him and I guarantee his anonymity. It is ironic that more lives have been affected by these three short memoranda than by any number of critically important medical discoveries.

Because of these memos, millions of people have been denied even rudimentary medical care. But the triage has also guaranteed that those who can be helped are given what they need.

During the flu, twenty per cent of the population needed emergency help. This occurred against a background of chaotic supply problems, high doctor mortality in affected areas, and a tremendous demand for drugs at a time when the industry was having trouble even maintaining normal production levels.

Perhaps one in ten of the flu victims saw a doctor, one in a hundred entered a hospital.

There is no way to tell if triage saves lives. Not only the triage, but so many other things that we now take for granted – home care for the dying, euthanasia, black market and alternate medicine, the British Relief – came about because the demand for care simply overwhelmed the nation's medical system.

The existence of the triage means different things to different people. For me it means the constant, niggling fear that my lifedose will creep up and I'll find myself suddenly denied medicine for some small ailment that will therefore become large and finally kill. For Whitley, the triage means a shortened life. He cannot legally enter a hospital or consult a licenced physician.

Like so many triaged people, he has learned a great deal of medicine. Doctors who can't treat a triaged person can and do organise seminars for ten or twenty such individuals at a time. And then there are the underground medicals – the witches and the doctors who practice illegally.

And there is always the balance of hope.

These three short memoranda seem innocent enough. But they are not innocent. They are the foundations of postwar American medicine.

ATCEN/DC/35A. 1Ø88

VOICE TRANSMISSION FROM CENTERS FOR DISEASE CONTROL/ATLANTA
TO ALL REGIONAL OFFICES [CONFIRMATION BY COURIER]
FOR IMMEDIATE DISTRIBUTION TO STATE/MUNICIPAL GOVERNMENTS

3Ø OCTOBER 1988

Recent Soviet bombing of U.S. cities of San Antonio, Washington, D.C., New York area, and Upper Central and Western states created unprecedented numbers of dead and whole-body radiation-induced injuries.

Immediate burial and/or destruction of dead is imperative in order to contain spread of disease. Wherever possible, mass burial with suitable chemical agents is recommended. Civilian populations should be warned of disease potential.

Triage procedures must be implemented to assist individuals with radiation-related injuries. First-degree thermal radiation burns, i.e. 'flash burns,' are likely to occur to exposed individuals within 3Ø miles of detonation point given estimated Soviet weapon yield of 9–1Ø Megatons. Second- and third-degree burns are likely in unprotected individuals in 15–25-mile range. Appropriate medical treatments should be as prescribed for injuries of this type.

Nuclear radiation injuries caused by gamma rays and neutrons are most serious, and high dosage can be life-terminating. Populations in two-mile radii from detonation points might have received 1,ØØØ+ rems. Critical level is 4ØØ–5ØØ rems where radiation symptoms are strongly evident and casualty rate is 5Ø percent or higher. Exposures below 2ØØ are not believed life-threatening and little treatment is recommended. Death rate at 1ØØØ+ is almost 1ØØ percent.

You are requested to provide every assistance possible to medical authorities to facilitate treatment of victims. Further triage instructions will follow.

William T. Adcock, M.D.
Director

ATCEN/DC

TO: ALL MUNICIPAL GOVERNMENTS, SOUTHWEST AREA

FROM: U.S. DEPARTMENT OF HEALTH AND HUMAN SERVICES/
           CENTERS FOR DISEASE CONTROL/EMERGENCY TASK
           FORCE ON RADIATION INJURIES

DATE: VOICE TRANSMISSION 15 JANUARY 1989
           COURIER DELIVERY 16 JANUARY 1989

SUBJECT: EMERGENCY MEMORANDUM ON ACUTE WHOLE-BODY RADIATION
           INJURIES

You are being provided herein with guidelines for the identification of suspected radiation dosages based on readily observable physical symptoms. These guidelines are intended for municipal and/or county representatives enlisted to screen civilian populations for subsequent medical treatment or attention. The severe drain on surviving medical facilities requires operating knowledge by all government personnel in order to direct individuals or groups to appropriate medical services.

Most urban centers sufficiently distant from radioactive or zoned areas have created several 'screening areas' to process incoming refugees and native citizens: Level One areas are for those with no apparent radiation symptoms; Level Two areas are for those with limited hematopoietic or gastrointestinal symptoms; Level Three areas are for highly traumatized and ataxic victims. Some version of this system is urgently recommended to all municipalities. Refugee movement rates are still inordinately high and unpredictable; virtually all communities in this region have reported high levels of influxing populations. Similarly, these populations are demonstrating varying levels of whole-body radiation injuries. You have been notified previously of emergency steps necessary to screen physical objects and food supplies for potential radioactivity.

Because trained medical staff are limited and generally unavailable outside of central medical facilities, it is imperative that municipal staff, including police, fire department, civil servants, and temporaries, be aware of radiation-related illnesses. Because of many factors, but particularly because of proximity to bombed area and total radiation exposure, individuals may or may not be viable candidates for medical treatment. Large emergency treatment centers have been set up in key cities such as Lubbock, El Paso, Beaumont, Baton Rouge, Little Rock, Oklahoma City, New Orleans, and Albuquerque to treat individuals with medium to high levels of radiation dosages. Guidelines for treatment are under preparation and will be distributed to you as soon as available and approved by the Emergency War Recovery Administration.

Guidelines to be employed by municipal authorities in screening war victims are as follows:

LEVEL ONE SYMPTOMS: Ø to 1ØØ REMS

No apparent symptoms in this range. Internal blood changes will occur but are not apparent with superficial inspection. Care should be taken, however, to query all victims in order to determine point of origin, proximity to hit areas, and exposure to contaminated foodstuffs and objects from contaminated areas.

LEVEL TWO SYMPTOMS: 1ØØ to 2ØØ REMS

Short-term effects include fatigue and general malaise. Gastrointestinal effects may include nausea and vomiting on the first day. A two-week 'latent period' may ensue in which symptoms disappear but then reappear in milder form. Generally, the more severe the symptoms in the beginning, the slower the process of recovery. Individuals with these levels of radiation dosages are excellent candidates for recovery.

LEVEL THREE SYMPTOMS: 2ØØ to 6ØØ REMS

Individuals with dosages in this range can display symptoms ranging from mild to severe. Nausea, vomiting, diarrhea, lack of appetite, etc., are the most obvious characteristics. The more severe the symptoms, the higher the radiation dosage absorbed may be assumed. Again, there may be a latent period of a week or perhaps only several days. Higher dosages produce skin hemorrhages, bleeding in the mouth and urine, and, with dosages above 3ØØ rems, a loss of hair. A swelling of the throat is not uncommon. In the 6ØØ + rem stage, high uncontrollable fevers may be present, as well as emaciation. Death in these cases is probable in 8Ø to 1ØØ percent of the cases; judgments as to the extent of medical services to be provided are therefore advised.

LEVEL FOUR SYMPTOMS: 6ØØ to 1ØØØ+ rems

Gastrointestinal symptoms are the most obvious: extreme vomiting, diarrhea, nausea, prostration, ataxia (loss of motor control), and difficulty in breathing. Individuals displaying these symptoms will almost certainly die within several days to two weeks. You are not likely to see individuals with such severe symptoms. All subjects arriving in a coma or comalike state should immediately be referred to medical authorities for handling.

. Undoubtedly, these guidelines are not complete, nor are they intended to be inflexible. However, the immediate need to process large numbers of incoming civilians is crucial in order to assure adequate distribution of medical supplies and attention, food and clothing, shelter, and relocation services.

MESSAGE BY COURIER   SIGNED RECEIPT MANDATORY

TO ALL DIRECTORS, CIVILIAN AND MILITARY MEDICAL FACILITIES
    IN THE CONTINENTAL UNITED STATES
FROM U.S. DEPARTMENT OF HEALTH AND HUMAN SERVICES, CENTERS
    FOR DISEASE CONTROL (CDCHDQ) ATLANTA
REGARDING IMPLEMENTATION OF WAR EMERGENCY ACT AND
    EXECUTIVE ORDER 15

1Ø FEBRUARY 1989

Pursuant to the War Emergency Act (23 CFR 586, Sections 18–35) and
Executive Order 15, you are hereby instructed to implement at once the
emergency triage procedures necessary for the treatment of war victims. This
action is taken in view of the catastrophic numbers of victims requiring medical
attention and the overall burden on existing facilities. The unavailability of
adequate numbers of trained personnel and supplies, presently and for the
immediate future, poses a major health hazard. The unprecedented nature of
the emergency facing this nation mandates the immediate implementation of
selection procedures for treatment. Communities can expect severe resistance,
but you are reminded that the first task facing this nation is that of survival;
existing facilities, personnel, and supplies must be directed to those populations with the greatest probability of survival.

     Therefore, as of 12ØØ hours, 1Ø February 1989, you are instructed to
triage victims according to the following requirements:

1.Ø   GENERAL INJURIES (Non-radiation-induced)

       Mild to Severe: Injuries of this nature, such as burns,fractures,
                              contusions, etc., may be treated as conditions
                              allow.

       Severe to   Treatment should be limited to victims with
       Critical: greatest possibilities of recovery. Medical
                              supplies should be limited accordingly.

       Severely   No treatment desirable.
       Critical:

2.0 RADIATION-INDUCED INJURIES

Treatment should be accorded on the basis of radiation dosage absorbed. Whole-body measurements should be taken whenever possible: in cases where this cannot be done, interviews should attempt to ascertain proximity to radiation zones and duration of exposure. The following schedule should then be utilized:

0 to 100 REMS   No treatment necessary.

100 to 200 REMS   Treatment limited to radiation symptoms such as flash burns, nausea, vomiting, etc. No other treatment desirable.

200 to 450 REMS   Medical assistance most valuable here. At upper levels (350 +), chances of recovery with medical attention are 50 percent.

450 + REMS   No treatment desirable.

It is not known at this time whether radiation injuries are more severe in cases where radiation is absorbed all at once or cumulatively.

Your government is aware of the implications of this order. Steps are being taken by appropriate military authorities to provide assistance to you in implementation of triage instructions. You will be provided with further information as soon as it is available. You will be instructed as soon as possible regarding the cessation of triage requirements.

Signed: William T. Adcock, M.D.
                Director

                ATCEN/DC

Interview: Hector Espinoza, Aztlan Leader

[ENTRY INTO AZTLAN: RUMOUR TO REALITY. Officially, Aztlan starts in Monahans. The actual border, however, was not encountered until we reached the former town of Van Horn, now called Ciudad de Reforma.

The Texas & Western Bus Company stops on this side of the big white gate that has been erected across I-20. When we arrived at the border, we found that we were expected. Governor Parker had sent a special message to the Foreign Minister of Aztlan, apparently right after our interview.

Despite the differences between Texas and the new country, this letter smoothed our passage and enabled us to gain access to the highest Aztlan authorities. Once in El Paso, Aztlan's capital, we found that the real power in the country is centred around the Foreign Minister, who has obtained recognition from most of Latin America, Spain, and a number of African countries. Even more important, he has obtained much friendly help from Japan.

There is no reason, really, to introduce Señor Espinoza. He speaks very well for himself.]

We in Aztlan have created a new nation, stretching from Texas to
the California border. There is a constitution, and a national
government, the only one presently active in the former United
States. Aztlan is recognised by many countries. We have here in
El Paso ambassadors from Mexico, Brazil, Chile, Paraguay,
Nicaragua, El Salvador, Guatemala, Cuba, and Japan. Many
other nations are favourably inclined towards Aztlan. We have
received an agricultural team from the People's Republic of
China. Great Britain is providing medical help. Officially, Britain, France, and Germany have not recognised Aztlan. But we
are confident that they will one day do so.

Aztlan is a Hispanic country. The official language is Spanish.
This must be understood. As US citizens, you have the right to
enter and leave without showing a passport, but you do not have
the right to vote in our elections, or remain here more than thirty
days without a visa.

We have an army of four divisions, nearly forty thousand men.
We have a national police force, which is why, when you crossed
the border, there were suddenly no more bandits on the roads.
Also, the Japanese have sent road-repair teams to Aztlan, so we
have no more potholes in our interstates. And Japanese medicine
has kept our disease rate low. We have not been affected by
fallout. In fact, we drew the border through Fort Stockton rather
than including San Angelo and San Antonio, because of the
destruction and the radiation.

You must understand that, as a new nation, Aztlan has had its
share of growing pains. We have had to relocate many Anglos
across the border in Texas, and there has been a certain very
small amount of violence, inevitable when a new nation is
formed.

Aztlan is a strong, civilised, and free country. We have no
political prisoners in our prisons, and nobody has ever been
tortured in Aztlan. We do have a policy of encouraging Hispanic
and Indian settlement of the territory. We are very frank about
that. For five generations this land belonged to the Anglos, and
look at the result. For ten generations before that it was Hispanic
land, and before that, Indian for twenty generations.

We practice the same sort of enlightened socialism that is
found in progressive countries across the world. We follow the
Chinese example to some extent, but we also guarantee personal
freedom as the Swedes do. And we do not keep people in prison

because of their political views. There are many cooperative concerns in Aztlan, farms and factories and power establishments. When a farmer sells his holdings to the cooperative, he gets in return lifetime free medical care with no triage, an income based on his production capabilities, and the support that comes from being a part of our wonderful cooperative farm and ranch system.

The Japanese have provided us with millions of dollars' worth of advanced trickle-irrigation equipment, so we have been able to add many thousands of acres to the area cultivated in Aztlan. This acreage is planted with soybeans, which has become our largest export crop. We also sell oil and peanuts and wheat and corn and, of course, beef. Aztlan is a prosperous country. There is no unemployment here. If you want to work, you can work. If you don't want to work, you can go to Texas or California.

Officially, both of those states are part of Aztlan. But we do not want the part of Texas we don't already have, and we would have to fight a war to get California. We are not yet prepared to do that.

If we were ever to gain California, Aztlan would become one of the most powerful countries in the world. Not a superpower – we don't want that. But a great power, perhaps as economically powerful as, say, Sweden.

Do you know that we gave foreign aid last year? Can you imagine it? We sent five hundred thousand bushels of soybeans and two hundred thousand of corn to Mexico. Of course, you know that they are all dying down there. Officially, the border between Aztlan and Mexico is open. And in the past three years, perhaps a million immigrants have come here. Now we have an agreement with Mexico. They get our food aid, and in return they process all potential emigrants to Aztlan. Since we cannot take the sick and they will not let the able-bodied leave, the immigration from Mexico is presently very small. If they wish to enter North America, the Mexicans must cross the Rio Grande into Texas, not Aztlan.

I am myself the Foreign Minister and official spokesman for Aztlan. We have a full portfolio of ministers. Our present capital is the Marriott here in El Paso. It has been renamed La Capitola, and contains our administrative apparatus. Our government is not organised around a president or prime minister. Instead, the two parties run against one another, and the party that gets a simple majority forms the governing committee for the next four years. We have the State Socialists and the Social Democrats. The SD is part of the International Social Democratic Movement, and is the less radical of the two parties, as they believe that private ownership of national industries, such as power and transport, should be allowed. At the present time, my party, the State Socialists, is in power.

We believe in cooperatives but not in central planning. We do not want to repeat the disastrous mistakes of the Soviet Union and create a repressive and counterproductive bureaucracy. So we are not a rigidly planned community. Our socialism is strictly voluntary. If you join, you get the benefits of cooperative living. If not, then you go it alone, but nobody interferes with you. And the co-ops compete with one another in a free macromarket. Each co-op is autonomous. In soy farming, for example, there are sixty co-ops and fifty-one private farms, some owned by big international agricultural corporations, one by Central Soya, and eight by Japanese firms. The co-ops have an association that sets prices and provides a system of mutual assistance. Thus they are much more efficient than the private farms.

We have our own currency. The Far Eastern Bank Note Company in Hong Kong makes the notes. They are backed by an equivalent amount in Japanese yen. Of course, this makes the currency very valuable, as it is exchangeable at any bank in the world for yen. Ten Aztlan pesos to a thousand yen. Better than the dollar!

Our economy enjoys a balanced current account, which means that our exports pay for our imports. We have no inflation, as all prices are controlled. There is no hunger in Aztlan. And there is racial equality. Even Anglos, if they want to stay, are welcomed into the community of the Aztlan people!

Our Indian population is free to live and worship as it pleases. We have Hopi, Apache, Pueblo, and Navajo tribes living in Aztlan. Their tribal areas are self-governing. We do not keep records of their activities, nor do we have any sort of Bureau of Indian Affairs. We just let them do as they please in their own territories. But, unfortunately, we cannot grant you safe conduct into the Indian lands. Among the Indians there is, frankly, a good deal of hostility towards Anglos.

Now I suppose I ought to talk about what happened at Roswell, because you've probably heard about it from others.

You must understand that we view the Mescalero Apaches as a separate, sovereign nation within Aztlan, and Roswell is within the boundaries of their tribal state. They took over the town about six months after the war, as soon as it became clear that the central government had collapsed. When we declared Aztlan in 1989, we went to the Mescalero, they did not come to us. All I can tell you is that the incident was overblown. Those Anglos who were killed had formed an armed resistance movement. People were not tortured or burned. And nothing like a thousand were killed. It was no more than half or at most two-thirds of that number. And there were trials, you understand. The whole process took months. All of it was before Aztlan. If it happened now, we would try hard to persuade the Indians to let the Anglos leave Indian lands peacefully.

I am glad that you suggest that this book will be distributed in England. We have to get an awareness among the British people that Aztlan exists. British recognition would confirm us as a permanent nation, and a British guarantee of sovereignty would mean that our chief worry of war with California or Texas would never come true. If we had such a guarantee, even a reconstructed United States would have to think very carefully about invading us or destroying this serene and happy nation.

The territory we call Aztlan was originally part of the Spanish Empire and the Republic of Mexico. You must remember that Mexico was then a perfectly ordinary nineteenth-century republic, no more or less violent or repressive than the United States. But the United States first encouraged Anglo colonisation of Texas and California, then supported internal insurgencies. When the Anglos won the Battle of San Jacinto in 1836, less than one-third of the population of Texas was Anglo. And California was simply stolen. Mexico was forced to accede to the Treaty of Guadalupe Hidalgo in 1848 and give California to the United States. It was theft!

As a result of the loss of its territory north of the Rio Grande, Mexico was emasculated and her people lost their sense of personal pride. The image of the lazy 'Meskin' and the 'Frito Bandido' was born, but it was not laziness, it was sorrow. We Hispanics are *not* lazy and we are not bandidos and we are not stupid. If we are so stupid, how come we have the only happy, safe, and well-organised nation north of the Rio Grande? While the Anglos fight bitterly among themselves for the rancid bits of the old United States, we Hispanics have quietly created this beautiful country, this beloved Aztlan!

We even have our own poets, our own writers, our own film stars. Chito Hernandez, 'El Niño', Gabriela Jaime Nuñez, all names of which you know nothing. But they are our stars! We make ten films a year in Aztlan, and when you combine those with the ten made in Mexico and the twenty in Spain, you have a new Hispanic movie almost every week. And we have a television and radio industry. The Japanese sell us more radios than we can possibly use. They put up a new station right here in El Paso. Radio 'A', it is called.

We also have Japanese cars and a new Japanese train running on the Santa Fe tracks from Monahans all the way to Tucson, where it connects not only with the *Sunset Limited* but with the *El Costero*, which provides super-express service down the Pacific coast of Mexico. We are on the world map, I assure you. People want our soybeans and other farm goods, not to mention our oil and gas and uranium, even coal.

For many people in the old United States, the confusion that resulted from the obliteration of Washington was unbelievably destructive. But for us, the people of Aztlan, it was really almost a blessing. Of course, we are very sorry for all the death and suffering. But Warday also brought some good – our Aztlan.

I do not want to lie to you, though, nor seem too bombastic. I suppose I can't help it. I'm a natural enthusiast, and I'm excited by what we're accomplishing here. Still, the way has not been as easy as all that. And Aztlan is far from perfect. You might find things wrong here. But you will also find love and a powerful sense of community. This is the great Chicano state, this Aztlan, and I love it so much that sometimes it hurts my heart, you know, when things are not as I would wish.

We have to rely a great deal on the Japanese, and they are certainly exploiting us. But we have the brotherhood and sisterhood of our nation, and our great heritage. I trust our isolated little country to survive. Anyway, I hope it will.

El Paso

Hector Espinoza is afraid for his infant state, and so tries to hide its weakness behind bold words. But Espinoza does not know his own people. Whatever happens in Aztlan, the eager confidence of its citizens will not be utterly lost. They have created something new here, and it will have its effect. Obviously there have been excesses. There are no Anglo faces in the streets. The Mobil refinery that one sees on the way into town is closed. There are many Japanese soldiers about. Although we were not allowed to visit Fort Bliss, Jim and I both had the impression that it is now a Japanese enclave. No doubt they intend to protect the vast soya plantations that have sprung up in the desert, which must be providing essential foodstuffs to their homeland.

But these facts tell nothing of the feeling of this new El Paso. The streets are no more full of cars than Dallas or Austin, perhaps even less so. Yellow schoolbuses have been dragooned for street service. Each bus is apparently a small cooperative venture between its drivers and mechanics. At least, all are decorated differently, painted with flowers and slogans, loudspeakers blaring the music of Radio 'A' from their roofs.

We have been billeted at the Granada Royale on I-10, newly named Paseo de la Revolución. The hotel is a delight. Its large rooms surround an atrium garden full of flowers. There is an indoor-outdoor pool. The atmosphere is quiet and unhurried. Most of the other guests are Japanese, some of them obviously long-term residents. It is strange to hear somebody speaking Spanish with a thick Japanese accent. We were served breakfast in our suite and spent the next hour trying to arrange a tour of the city. First we used the old Yellow Pages to call Hertz, Avis, and the local car rental agencies. Hertz, now called Autocars Liberidad, was open. They were taking reservations for November. As this was August, we decided to give up on car rental.

There are no longer conventional taxis in El Paso. By law, they have all become 'pesetas', travelling fixed routes on the smaller thoroughfares, essentially supplementing the buses.

Our last option was to take a bus tour, but we soon found that both Gray Line and Golden Tours were booked for the day, or claimed to be.

Perhaps somebody didn't want us to tour the city.

We ended up spending the morning in the hotel. I observed the city from the rooftop restaurant, which commands a fine view of the whole area. I saw no planes take off from the airport, which is not far away. Here and there I could see sooty scars on a building, but beyond that there were no obvious signs of the revolution. Señor Espinoza appeared just before noon, his thin body swallowed by a seersucker suit. He was full of brightness and what I can only describe as punch. As soon as we saw him, we requested a tour of El Paso. He said that he would suggest something even better: we should have lunch with him. We could always see the town later, he assured us. He added that he had, by the liberal application of governmental authority, gotten us precious tickets on a 'Super Express' bus that left for Las Cruces at three. Tickets on another could not be guaranteed for weeks.

It was becoming clear that we were not intended to make any detailed reconnaissance of this community. Señor Espinoza was, in effect, throwing us out of his country. Given his position of power, we decided to let him do exactly as he pleased.

We were left to swallow our questions about such things as the condition of hospitals and prisons, and what was happening to the homes and property of the Anglos.

The Isabella penthouse restaurant in the Granada is now called Casa del Sol Norte. The food is Tex-Mex, what Señor Espinoza described as 'superb Aztlan cuisine'. Actually, his hyperbole was in this case not far from the truth. I used to enjoy Mi Tierra and La Fonda in San Antonio, and Casa Rio on the river. I can also recall going to this restaurant's namesake, the Casa del Sol in Juarez. When I lived in New York, I sought good Mexican food constantly, but what I found only increased my hunger for flavours like these.

I will repeat the menu in detail. We had cheese enchiladas, cabrito chili, chicken tacos, rice, and refried beans. The tacos were generously garnished with tomatoes, lettuce, and onions, and the seasonings were uniformly excellent. We drank Carta Blanca beer from Mexico. The menu showed that the meal was five pesos 'A' to *privatos*, two pesos to *comunistas*.

After lunch, we were not too surprised to find we had barely enough time to get the bus. Señor Espinoza claimed to have forgotten the time and left, pleading an urgent appointment. We soon found out the reason for the abrupt departure. Without the use of a private car, we were going to have to struggle to get to the station on time. Neither of us wanted to find out what would happen if we missed our connection.

Jim stood beside me outside the hotel as we waited for a bus. He was silent and withdrawn. Aztlan had saddened him, because it seemed to him a failure of the racial harmony that had been growing in Texas before the war, and yet another doomed ideological attempt to alter blood and land with words.

I felt much better about it. There was energy and optimism there, and the powerful spirit of cooperation was something that we would do well to import into the United States. I suspected that Aztlan was going to work, though not in the way foreseen by Señor Espinoza, nor in the way feared by Governor Parker. That beehive of little cooperative enterprises was going to grow, spreading its new economic ideas in all directions.

I also suspected that Señor Espinoza's caution was not based so much on a desire to hide his problems as it was on a fear that we might be spies for Governor Parker. After all, a letter from Parker preceded us here, probably by just a few hours. Espinoza was terrified of Parker, and probably also of us.

Before I went to Aztlan, the word *cooperative* suggested to me rural electric power on the one hand and vast, spiritless Soviet communes on the other. I was not prepared to meet such a strange new economy as the one we found: thousands of tiny co-ops, each dependent solely upon its own success to pay its members, none larger than the smallest economic unit necessary to perform its particular function.

This means that the motel where we stayed, for example, was run by two separate co-ops, the restaurant workers and the hotel staff. The state does not pay them, nor does it plan for them. They keep their own books and split their profits weekly. If there are no profits, nobody gets paid that week.

A brightly painted schoolbus jammed with people finally came down Paseo de la Revolución. Radio 'A' got louder as the bus got closer. Buses are supposed to stop whenever somebody hails them – there are no fixed stops in El Paso. But this one passed us by. It was full.

As we watched one jammed bus after another pass us by, we began to get nervous. The big purple Super Express tickets Señor Espinoza had given us were valueless if we couldn't make it to the bus station.

Finally a half-full peseta came along. We were almost surprised to see it stop when we hailed it. The fare is ten centavos 'A' for holders of yellow co-op cards, which most people wear pinned to their shirts and blouses. These cards identify their bearers as part of Aztlan's network of cooperatives. Capitalists must pay one peso 'A' to ride. We paid our pesos happily.

I got in the front seat of the massive old Buick station wagon, repainted many times, now the bright red of the flag of Aztlan. In fact, Aztlan's red flag with the gold radiant sun in the centre snapped from both front fenders and the radio antenna. Jim was jammed in the back with three other people, all wearing yellow cards. 'Estación de la autobúses del norte, por favor,' I said. My Spanish is less than minimal.

As we travelled into the centre of town, I collected these impressions of El Paso:

The cemetery beneath the complex tangle of the Spaghetti Bowl where I-10 intersects the Expressway is in prewar condition. Unlike the situation common in Dallas, new graves have not been dug in among the old. But there are many empty buildings, empty houses, and abandoned cars. Just before we turned on to Piedras, we saw along the side of I-10 the glittering aluminium ruins of a jet, cracked plastic windows in the few bits of intact fuselage, the plane's markings no longer readable.

Japanese soldiers passed us in squat Toyota military vehicles. Their light khaki uniforms were spotless, the Rising Sun on their shoulders. As they rode along they shot pictures of the distant Franklin Mountains with Minoltas as small and thin as credit cards. Earlier we had noticed a restaurant with the odd name 'Gunther's Lotus Blossom'. A closer look revealed that the sign had once read 'Gunther's Edelweiss'. Before Warday, the US Army used to train soldiers of the German Federal Republic at Fort Bliss, which is just up the road from here. We wondered if Gunther was still around, or if he had left only his name behind.

Japanese military planes flew low overhead. They were odd-looking things, with their wings canted forward instead of swept back, so that they appeared to be flying backwards. Instead of a jet's familiar scream, they made a low drumming noise that seemed almost to thump your chest. I recall the strange cant of the wings from NASA designs for future hypersonic aircraft.

We had ridden in silence for some time when the driver decided to try striking up a conversation.

'Hey, gringo,' he said with a big smile. 'Let's talk *norteamericano!* See if I can still do it!'

His name was Carlos León, and he was from San Antonio. 'I'm from there too,' I said. 'So is he.' I nodded towards Jim.

'Hey! *Compadres!* I grew up there. Left in '86 to get a job out here. Once the Mexican economy started to recover, there were lots of jobs here again. I was managing a McDonald's. Kept at it, too, until the meat stopped getting delivered. Then I said the hell with the franchise, sold the equipment, and signed up as a cooperator. They assigned me to pesetas and gave me a permit to buy a station wagon. Our co-op consists of me, my wife the bookkeeper, and my cousin the mechanic.'

'Where did you live in San Antonio?'

'West Side! I lived on South Zarzamora. My dad was a garbage man – but not in his own neighbourhood! We had to take our garbage to the dump ourselves until the fifties. My mom and dad died in San Antonio.'

'I lived in Terrell Hills,' I said.

'Rich, eh?'

'My dad was an oilman.'

'Oh boy! You're poor now, eh? I see you work with your hands!'

'I'm poor now.'

From one of the passengers: 'Good for you! Join the rest of the world.'

I laugh. 'No more oilmen.'

'Hey, that's good. No more oilmen! Just British and Israeli oil import agents, right?'

I did not mention that Texas oil was flowing again, and that refineries were opening up all over the United States. There was a razor edge of anger among these people. This was their place, their time at last, and these their days of sunshine.

Walls pockmarked with bullet holes were a common sight as we neared the centre of town.

'Jim and I went to Central,' I said, hoping Carlos might also be an alumnus. This is not as unlikely as it sounds: Central Catholic had a substantial Hispanic population when we attended.

The sudden silence tells me that my suspicion is correct. Carlos stops the car. 'Well, goddamn.'

'Brother Halaby?'

'Shit, yeah!'

'Brother Araña?'

'The Spider! I haven't thought about him in years!'

The Spider taught world history and his real name was Brother Gordon, but his thin, six-foot-four frame gained him the nick-name Brother Araña. So total was his identification with us that he was known to get mean when freshmen called him Brother Gordon. 'I'm Brother Araña,' he would snarl, 'and don't you forget it.'

Carlos had been five years ahead of us at Central. 'You remember Brother DeLoach?' he asked.

'He was principal our freshman year. He retired.'

'He taught me a hell of a lot. I was a real bad kid when I went there. Angry, you know? And so damn stupid. I'd been a year at Southton already! They hit me with a razor strap there. I was done for selling grass. Shining shoes and dealing grass to the soldiers on Alamo Plaza, then going to the Alameda to see Cantinflas movies. You know what we got for a joint – we called them Mary Janes – back in the fifties? We got a dollar. But they cost us eighty-five cents apiece. So we were risking years of freedom for fifteen cents! Sure enough, the next thing I knew I was down for a year and my mom and dad were thinking they had raised a rotten kid. When I got out I applied to Central. No way I'm gonna get in, my parents figure. I'm fourteen and already a jailbird. But DeLoach, he lets me in. "You stay away from the Mary Janes or I'll paddle your behind," he says. "You're a smart kid, that's your problem. We'll give you a little something to do with your mind, you'll stay out of trouble." '

'Did it work?'

'I loved that school! One of these days I'm gonna go back. I'm gonna see –'

Silence. We are suddenly very still, we alumni. Night has just touched us in the middle of the afternoon.

The Dream Bandidos

The Trailways sign had been taken off the walls of the station, and the newsstand carried papers with names like *Revolución* and *Viva Aztlan!* There were also Mexican and Spanish papers, *El Diario* and *La Nota*. The Japanese *Asahi Shimbun en Español* was prominently displayed, as was the London *Times* – in English, of course. I would have bought a copy, but it cost the equivalent of three dollars.

Jim was delighted to find that the candy counter was well stocked. Last year, M&Ms and Hershey bars reappeared in Dallas, but here in El Paso you can get all manner of colourful locally made confections as well. We stocked up on fresh pralines and other indigenous sweets in the fifteen minutes we had before the bus left.

It was a brand-new Japanese Hino, very comfortably appointed and efficiently air conditioned. In El Paso in August this is a definite plus. It was about ninety degrees, and would probably be a hundred before the end of the day. The driver was wearing a spiffy green uniform. He carried a .38 in a gleaming holster.

We settled into our plush tan seats and prepared for the one-hour journey to Las Cruces and the border. In the bus around us were well-dressed travellers, the men in light summer suits and dark glasses, some of the women even in silk dresses. These people were Aztlan's élite. Apparently the common folk go to Las Cruces in something other than Super Express buses, if they go at all.

Across the aisle from me sat a man in a magnificent suit, perhaps even a Savile Row creation. Beside him, his wife was wearing a designer dress of light blue silk. I tried to engage them in conversation, but they turned to each other and began to speak animatedly together.

The bus was soon on its way up the long, straight road to Las Cruces. There were trucks on the highway, many of them filled with farm produce. Sometimes we saw cars too, mostly the Toyota and Nissan limousines that are the modern hallmark of the Japanese businessman. A Chevy Consensus or two passed, and the usual sparse collection of prewar jalopies.

We were about twenty miles from Las Cruces, just south of the town of La Mesa, when the bus slowed and turned off the interstate. 'La Mesa,' the driver called, and a couple of passengers began to take their baggage down from the overhead racks. All along the roadside into town, there were makeshift dwellings. Derelict GM buses with Sun City Area Transit (SCAT) markings had been made over into shelters. There were tents and even geodesic domes. I saw some blond children toddling about, and an Anglo woman working on a truck. Anglos in Aztlan? Jim and I agreed at once: we would interrupt our trip in La Mesa. We'd take potluck on the final miles into La Cruces and just hope the nervous Señor Espinoza wasn't having us followed.

We got out at the brand-new La Mesa bus station and began walking back along the highway. A clump of Japanese in white coveralls came out of a restaurant and watched us for a time. 'Momento, por favor,' one of them called at last.

'Yes?'

'Ah. A moment, please.'

We stopped.

'You are – tourists?'

'We're writers. Doing research for a book about America.'

'Ah!' Bright smiles. 'You write about us?' Even brighter smiles.

'What do you do?'

The smiles became fixed. 'We agricultural specialists.'

'Helping out with the soya plantations, eh?'

'That's right. This is soya country!'

They let us walk on. When we passed the outskirts of La Mesa, it became obvious that there were no soya plantations in this area. You could see all the way to the Portrillos across the desert. 'They were uranium workers,' Jim said quietly.

'You're sure?'

'Those pouches at their waists – you saw them?'

'Yeah.'

'They contained face masks. I've seen people wearing them at Los Alamos. And those blue plastic strips on their collars. If they get a dose, those strips turn red.'

I looked back into the quiet town. The bus was long gone, and there wasn't a car in the street. In the distance, a motor rumbled. Cicadas screamed in the trees.

We caused an even greater stir in the tent community than we had among the Japanese. People began shouting, then running, and in a few minutes at least seventy or eighty had gathered along the roadside. A young woman came forward. She had an enormous .357 Magnum strapped to her belt. She was perhaps twenty-five, tall and sleek, her face weathered, her hands red from hard work. One hand rested firmly on the pistol.

'May we help you?' she asked. Her accent was familiar, the broad twang of West Texas.

Jim spoke, his eyes on the gun. 'We're writing a book about postwar America. We'd like to talk to you, if you don't mind.'

'Where you from?' a man asked from the crowd.

'Dallas. And we're on our way to California.'

Surprisingly, this revelation caused general laughter. 'You got entry permits?'

Jim frowned. 'We're writers. Surely they'll let us in.'

'Hey,' the man shouted, 'y'all hear that? All we gotta do is go up to the Yuma POE and say we're writers. We're in!'

This was not a friendly crowd. But I felt sure they had a story. 'Could we buy some supper?' I asked.

The girl with the Magnum nodded. 'You got pesos "A"?'

'Five. Will that do it?'

'Ought to, if you like rice. That's what we got. Rice and soybean soup.'

The group began to disperse back into the camp. The girl, our guard, stayed close. Her hand remained firmly planted on the pistol. She had a soft, open face, but the way she held her lips told me that she could be dangerous. The gun was serious.

Up close, the camp was a hodgepodge. There were L.L. Bean tents arranged with old cars to make shelters, the buses we had seen from the highway, trailers, and even a few portable buildings.

Why, in a nation of empty housing developments and abandoned apartment buildings, anybody would be living like this was beyond me.

'You don't have homes?'

'No, we don't have homes.'

'Go to Dallas. You can take over a couple of neighbourhoods.'

She snorted, tossed her head. 'We're on the wanted list in Texas. Don't you ever go to the post office?'

'A lot of wanted posters at the post office. I never saw one with your face on it.'

'It's there.'

I was afraid to ask why. Jim sat in the dust, very quiet, his eyes sharp. He did not speak.

'We're robbers,' the girl said. 'Espinoza let us stay here when we got chased out of Texas by the highway patrol.'

'Robbers?'

'We live by our wits,' an older woman said. 'You've heard of the Destructuralist Movement?'

I had indeed. They believed that there should be no social structure beyond the extended family. Even tribes were too much for them. 'Destructuralists tried to burn the Dallas Civic Centre.'

'That was us,' the girl said simply.

No wonder they had left Texas. 'People were outraged.'

'People are addicted to social structure. Warday has given us a historic opportunity to break the boundaries of social control. To be free.'

'We can't rebuild the economy without social structure,' Jim said.

The faces around him went hard. I wondered if we might not be arguing for our lives here. I hoped that he realised it. 'We don't need the damn economy,' a man said, his voice full of bitter sarcasm. 'The economy's worse than an addiction, it's a curse!'

'People are dying because the economy's in such a mess,' I said. 'At the rate of two hundred and fifty thousand a month, to be exact. That's about eight thousand a day. Nearly a hundred just since we started this conversation.'

'You're real smart,' the girl said.

'I'm a human being. I love other human beings.'

'People are dying because nature is rebalancing the earth's ecology.'

'They're dying because of Warday.'

Another voice intervened: 'Rice's ready!' This was a lean young man with bright grey eyes and a dusting of beard. People lined up before a big stainless-steel pot. They carried their own utensils. Each was given a smallish serving of rice topped with cooked soybeans. I thought of my lunch with Hector Espinoza. In fact, I longed for it. I still do. I would give a lot for another taco as crunchy and perfectly seasoned as that one, full of juice and chicken, just the other side of hot. The rice and soybeans were a pitiful meal. It reminded me of the famine, and made me feel frightened.

The sun was making long shadows when we were finished. I sensed that Jim was as eager as I to get away from this place. When I die, I want to be given the grace to go for a good reason. I didn't want to die to serve the frustrations of some very unhappy and confused people.

'We have a vision,' the girl said, 'of a true Jeffersonian society in America. This could be a nation of farmers, where everybody is self-sufficient and God-fearing, and the family is the centre of things.' Her voice rose. 'I had a family, you guys! I had a little girl. She was taken from me by heathens. She was taken for no good reason, and she was killed out in the backyard by people who had decided that my family no longer belonged in Roswell, New Mexico.'

A man put his hand on her shoulder. She turned and kissed him in what seemed to me a private way. 'We all lost people,' he said. 'That's why we come together. This is a family.'

Another voice was raised. 'If you're writers, write that another world like the world we had before Warday is going to mean another war. We have to change. We have to turn aside from the hypnosis of politics and the addiction of vast economic systems that eat this beautiful planet and spit out garbage. We need to turn to one another instead. What counts is the person in bed beside you, and your children, and the people next door. The rest is all addiction and hypnosis and more Wardays.'

My impulse was to try to comfort them, to make all the horror and the suffering of the past few years go away. But I couldn't do that. All I could do was eat their poor meal and look across their fire at them.

The girl with the gun sighed. 'Okay,' she said, 'here's what's gonna happen.' She nodded at Jim. 'You're gonna go wherever you're goin'. But you aren't sending anybody after us, like from Texas.' She put her free hand on my shoulder. 'You're stayin' here for a while, just to make sure he doesn't send anybody.'

I felt the blood drain out of my face. I really did not care to end up trapped in the worst place we had thus far encountered. What would they do with me? Lock me up in one of those stifling, filthy, derelict buses?

'Three months,' Jim said.

'Six.'

'Let him go in three months. If you don't, I'll assume he's dead and tell the Texas police where to find you.'

'Four months.'

'Four.'

With that, Jim got up. I was appalled. Apparently he proposed just to leave it like this. I was going to spend four months with this bunch. 'I'm triaged,' I shouted. 'I gave up precious time with my own family for the book we're writing. You can't take even more of my time, not if you love the family the way you say you do.'

'We didn't invite you here.'

Jim turned without a word and walked to the road. He soon disappeared towards La Mesa. At that moment I hated him. I screamed after him. I flung my empty plate at his departing shadow.

'You're lucky it didn't break,' the girl said. 'You'd have to figure out how to mend it. And we don't have a lot of glue.'

A great woe overcame me. I was facing four pointlessly wasted months. 'I swear to you, I'll keep your secret.'

'The Texans would kill us.'

'I'm not even going in that direction! I'm on my way west.'

'California's just as dangerous. Radical Destructuralists have been executed there.'

How odd that the terrorists of our time would hate authority but believe in what used to be its core symbol, the family. The old anarchists would have been very confused by these people. But, in a way, they made sense to me. I could understand their dream of a peaceful, agricultural America, where the horizon ended with the next farm.

I could see something more than violence and rage in these people. They weren't just inept terrorists or starving road people or fanatics. They had their wounds too, like all of us. And because of that, I could make a case for tolerance and under-standing.

As soon as night fell, the camp went to sleep. As we have all found out, it takes a high level of nutrition and lots of artificial light to keep human beings awake after sunset. They were still like the rest of us were during the famine – dead to the world as soon as the sun went down.

I heard the wet rhythm of sex in the shadows, and sensed stirring here and there in the silence. Birds made their evening calls as last light disappeared behind the Portrillos. Heat light-ning flickered. A young woman's voice, calm and pure, softened the murmuring of the children with a lullaby:

> 'Come and sit by my side if you love me
> Do not hasten to bid me adieu
> But remember the Red River Valley
> And the cowboy who loves you so true.'

When Jim woke me in the middle of the night, I was at first astonished. But not enough, fortunately, to cry out. He can move more quietly than a shadow; he learned his moves in Asia. We had gone together in the jungles of hate; escaping this camp of exhausted, sleeping people was not difficult.

'They might have killed us if they'd seen us,' he said, once we were out on the Las Cruces highway.

'I know it,' I said.

Desert nights are always cold, and that one was no exception. We walked north for hours. No cars passed. Towards morning we came into the little town of Mesquite. A neon sign and three pickup trucks identified an open diner. We had American-style eggs and bacon, and big mugs of coffee.

'Is this New Mexico or Aztlan?' I asked the waitress.

She laughed. 'You guys hitching up from 'Cruces?'

'El Paso.'

'Well, you're out of Aztlan. It peters out between La Mesa and here. Just past where the Japs are doin' their uranium mining.'

We had seconds of coffee and bought some salt beef and Cokes for the road.

Los Alamos

It was nearly dark when Whitley and I reached the outskirts of Santa Fe, in northern New Mexico. In the distance, beyond the thin line of awakening city lights, lay the Jemez Mountains. Hidden there, on the mesa, was the city of Los Alamos.

We felt that a visit there was essential.

It took a long time, however, to find a ride to the mesa. There was no bus service, and the Santa Fe taxis wouldn't take us out at any price. Finally we got a ride with a Los Alamos resident, in his gleaming new Toyota.

Los Alamos was always a company town, and the company was Uncle Sam. Warday would seem to have ended the need for all that. We really expected to come upon a scene of abandonment. Since the war, scientists have not been well treated in the United States, and this is especially true for nuclear scientists. And there isn't any funding for their work. We couldn't imagine the state of New Mexico, for example, spending money to keep Los Alamos in operation.

Our driver, whose name is best left unsaid, explained some fundamental truths of current life. The people of the mesa had been sealed off from the outside world on Warday. Units of the New Mexico National Guard had blocked all entrances and exits, followed by regular Army troops.

Then there was a black year, when the economy of Los Alamos failed due to the absence of government cheques. The Army guardianship was abandoned and the unpaid soldiers drifted away.

Most of the scientists and their families left, too, choosing to make their way in some less hostile environment. The others created a miniature farming community, using their technological skills to develop viable desert agriculture. We saw the results of this work – trickle-irrigated crops, strange-looking greenhouses made of plastic, and an elaborate hydroponic system.

We crossed the Rio Grande and made our way up on to a plateau called Parajito, which resembles a large hand divided into finger-like mesas. There had been rain earlier, and the air was heavily scented with fir and spruce. A peace lay on the land, almost as if it were uninhabited. But after a few miles we came upon the administrative complex. I felt an odd fear, seeing the absence of bustle among these familiar buildings. The library building and its classified papers archive were empty, doors swinging open, windows dark.

Our driver told us that there had been a serious attack by local residents right after the soldiers left, and some of the damage to the library had been done then. Local people had also talked of trials for the Los Alamos scientists, but there had been no arrests. Nevertheless, the scientists had been glad to leave when they could.

Which, it seems, is the central reality of Los Alamos. It is a place of leavings and departures, empty houses and abandoned lives. Nuclear science is a disliked religion in this area. Los Alamos people never spend the night in Santa Fe, and prefer to go in with Japanese guards when they can.

As we moved across the mesa, we saw that more buildings were gutted. I recognised these structures. On my last visit to Los Alamos, highly classified work on particle-beam weapons had been going on here. The labs have been moved in their entirety to Japan. And their scientists have gone with them. There is a new 'Atomic City', it seems, being built near Osaka. Los Alamos is a place of caretakers.

The plutonium fabrication plant was still standing, though hardly intact. It was aswarm with technicians who were dismantling it and crating its exotic innards as reverently as doctors might pack living hearts for transplant.

I wanted to go up to one of those Japanese workmen in his white coveralls and shake him and tell him that he was infecting himself and his people. I thought, Japan, Japan, surely you have learned. Let this place be a museum, and let these people be its caretakers.

We crossed the bridge that connected one mesa with the other and drove into what had been the main residential and commercial district of prewar Los Alamos. Most buildings were boarded up. But there was a lively open-air market and an astonishing atmosphere of prosperity. The families of the 'Japanese friends', as they call themselves, live in many of the houses vacated by American scientists who have already gone to Atomic City.

I asked whether they had any choice. Our guide smiled. 'We're going, that's all I know. The scientist is part of the laboratory.'

Were they paid?

'Listen. We're treated like gods. Paid? That isn't the word for it. You get cars, housing, schooling for your kids, all food and medical care free, and enough yen to buy the whole damn state of New Mexico. I don't know what would happen if anybody refused to go. Nobody does!'

I found in myself a kind of desperate urgency. Skill and intelligence are such valuable resources, and America needs them so badly now. I wanted to say to him, please don't go. Then I saw a gleam down in the canyon – a car that had been pushed off in the night by angry locals.

Can you blame them, though? This is the central station of the nuclear age.

Our guide sensed our discomfiture at what was happening here, and explained that scientific study had come to a standstill in America. Science was to some extent blamed for the war. But even where this wasn't true, there was no money, as he put it, for contemplation.

'That's what you need,' he added. 'Without contemplation there is no science.' I felt the vast silence around me and heard the wind whispering in the pines and realised the depth of that truth.

I thought about the friendships I had made in Los Alamos before the war, and the combination of awe and apprehension that I had felt when I first interviewed the scientists and first heard them tell of their work on weapons. I wondered then if it was possible to be divorced from the consequences of one's work. It seemed to me that no matter how subtle the problem a given weapon presented or how artful its contemplation might be, the ashes and the bones in the end would be the same.

It wasn't until we were returning across the Rio Grande, on the same bridge that brought Oppenheimer and his men here in 1940, that my mood began to lift. Despite all the thoughts that have hung electric in this air, the cottonwoods are still full and green. Across the way, the pueblos of San Ildefonso and Santa Clara gleamed in the sun. There were Indians working the land there, as they had for centuries. Los Alamos, for all its modern history, is returning to ancient ways.

PART TWO

CALIFORNIA DANGERS

You road I enter upon and look around, I believe
you are not all that is here,
I believe that much unseen is also here.
                              – Walt Whitman,
                    'Song of the Open Road'

California POE

The old *Superliner* clicks along the tracks. Jim and I are sitting in the observation car, staring out the wide picture windows at the desert. I haven't been to Los Angeles since 1983. In those days I used to do a certain amount of business with the film companies, and I made occasional trips west. I never cared much for Los Angeles; people who are consciously trying to be relaxed make me nervous. Jim has been to LA more recently, but not since the war. So we have no real way of knowing what to expect of the 1990 immigration controls. We've heard hard rumours of meticulous police searches and detention pens and people-smuggling out of Kingman, Arizona. Passing through there, as a matter of fact, we saw the largest hobo camp we've encountered so far. It made the little encampment outside of La Mesa seem positively orderly. It was a vast jumble of tents, abandoned vehicles of all types, and human beings. Its residents, the people on the train were saying, were all California rejectees. If so, the border controls must be brutal.

I know a few things about LA. First, with nearly nine million residents, it is by far the most populous city in the United States. Despite the general population decline, it has grown by nearly a million since 1987. It is more than four times the size of the second largest city, San Francisco, and larger than New York was before the war.

The conductor comes through, calling 'Needles, next stop Needles.' There is stirring in the car. Needles is one of the infamous California ports of entry. To get into the state, you've got to show twenty gold dollars or an equivalent amount in goods or paper currency, and a valid entry permit. The only way to get such a permit is to have business in the state or a job waiting for you there.

We do not have any permits. And between us we have eight hundred paper dollars, the equivalent of only eight gold.

None of our fellow passengers has talked about entry, but we sense that we are not alone. There are all kinds of stories about getting into California; few of them involve the possession of papers and astronomical sums of money.

'Needles,' the conductor shouts. 'Everybody stay in the train, stay in the train!'

We slow to a crawl and draw up to the platform. I'm shocked. There are soldiers armed with submachine guns every fifteen feet. Behind them are huge signs: ILLEGAL ALIENS LIABLE TO BE SHOT. STAY IN THE TRAIN. An amplified voice can be heard: 'Do not leave the train. Have your entry permits ready. Do not leave the train.'

We decide to obey. Around us a few people are pulling the precious green forms out of purses and wallets. But most are sitting passively, waiting. This is only the first step in their journey. They have timed their arrival carefully. There isn't an outgoing train for another six hours. For that much time they will be in the holding pen. They have staked their lives and their money on the possibility that they will be able to escape and somehow cross mountains and desert to the Los Angeles basin, there to disappear into the golden horde.

California State Police officers in white crash helmets, face masks, black leather boots, and khaki uniforms come across the platform in formation. They carry pistols in holsters. At a barked order, half of them draw their weapons. The other half have clipboards. These are some of California's notorious Processing Officers. When they catch people trying to escape the holding pens, they mark them with indelible green dye.

Suddenly a man in full radiation gear comes into the car from the side opposite the platform. He is carrying a small black device with a digital readout. It has a long, thin probe attached. He waves it back and forth as he moves down the aisle, touching some of the passengers with it, inserting it down the collars of others. He squirts a bright red aerosol on the back of one man's hand, and tells him that he's got to go take a detox shower and get an issue of paper clothing before he can even get port-of-entry processing.

Jim and I are examined without comment. Apparently this device only measures present radiation. My high lifedose is still my own business, unless I try to enter a hospital without a health card.

At the far end of the car he blows a whistle. Immediately, Processing Officers appear at both doors. Behind the man at the front is one of the clipboard carriers. 'California registered citizens,' he shouts, 'show your colours.' Four people pull out red plastic cards. Captain Clipboard runs them through a device like a credit-card verifier and reads something in the screen of a portable computer. One after another, the citizens are given the precious right to stay on the train.

One man is not as lucky as the others. 'You aren't computing,' Captain Clipboard says affably. 'You'll have to step over to the customs shack for manual verification.'

'What's the problem, officer?'

'You don't come up on the computer. Maybe your card's defective. Go over to customs – it's the yellow door.'

Uncertain, nervous, the young man rises from his seat. He goes to the rear of the car. As he is leaving, Captain Clipboard calls out, 'Arrest him, he's a jumper.'

The young man leaps down and dashes across the platform, heading for the chainlink fence that separates it from the parking lot. A voice calls in a blaring monotone, 'Stop, or we'll have to shoot.' Then, more gently: 'Come on, kid, take it easy.'

When he is three-quarters of the way up the fence, two of the US Army types raise their machine guns.

'Look, kid, you're going to die in ten seconds if you don't climb back down.'

The young man stops. He sags against the fence. Slowly he climbs down, into the arms of two other soldiers, who handcuff him, then connect the handcuffs to leg irons and lead him clanking away.

'Okay,' Captain Clipboard calls out, 'everybody hold up their entry permits.' Hands thrust up full of green paper. 'Hey, good car! This is gonna be a nice day.' He casts a frown at Jim and me.

From another car there rises the sound of female screaming. It goes on and on, trembling into the heat.

Captain Clipboard works his way along the aisle. One after another, he puts the green forms on his clipboard and goes over them with a lightpen. Two people are sent to the yellow door. They walk quickly across the platform, pointedly ignoring the chainlink fence, carrying their green forms and all of their belongings in their hands. Others, from other cars, straggle along as well. Finally there is nobody left in the car but us illegals.

'All right, now it's joker time! All of you displaced persons off the train, line up along the white line on the platform, and don't make sudden moves. You'd be surprised how nervous those dumb army boys get, standing out there in the sun. Let's go!'

Sixteen of us shuffle off the train, mostly threadbare, eyes hollow, about us all the furtive look of the new American wanderers. We are facing the toughest port-of-entry system in the United States. The odds are that all sixteen of us will be on the outbound train later this afternoon.

'Hey, Sally,' Captain Clipboard calls, 'you recycle fast, sweetheart.'

'I'm working on a tunnel,' one woman mutters in reply, her head down.

I wonder how many of us are repeaters. But, watching the soldiers across the platform watching us, I decide not to strike up any conversations. At a barked command, the soldiers move forward until they are facing us. 'All right, folks,' the giant voice says, 'single file to the pen, please. Move out. Double time!'

As we shamble away, the train gives a long blast on its horn and starts to roll. Not a few heads turn back, watching it pass the open track barrier. The lucky few inside are already reopening their newspapers and settling back for the run to LA.

We are herded into a fenced-off area about three acres square. There is a cyclone fence twenty feet high, topped by razor wire. At all four corners of the enclosure there are guard houses. Fifty feet beyond the fence there is another barrier: a run occupied by six huge hounds. I see light towers stretching off into the distance. I wonder if the whole California border could be lit. As we won't be here past 4.00 p.m., when the outbound train arrives, I'll never know.

'Bomb-out,' I say to Jim.

'Maybe. I think we ought to try to talk our way in.'

I assume that as a newsman, he's more practised at this sort of thing than I am. 'What do you suggest?'

'We can try the reporter gambit. I've got my *News Herald* ID.' We walk over to the gate.

A soldier, smoking a cigarette, closes his eyes for an instant and then regards us with a blank expression.

'I'm a reporter for –'

'No talking.'

'– the Dallas *News Herald*.' Jim holds up his press card.

The soldier stares, his eyes glazed with boredom.

'This man is also a writer. We're on our way to interview the Governor of California.'

There is a flicker of interest. 'You have any verifying documentation?'

'I'd have to make a call.'

The flicker dies. 'Then take the afternoon train to Kingman, which is the first place you can get off, and make your call from there. They'll mail you letters of entry and give you an access code for the border police.'

He starts to walk away. I decide to try another approach. 'How long have you been doing this?'

I can see him sigh. 'I was drafted in '91. Six weeks of basic and a month of crowd-control training and here I am.'

'You're with a US Army unit?'

'That's right. Regular Army, 144th Military Police, to be exact. And I ain't supposed to be talking to you.' Again, he starts to walk away.

'Look, is there any way out of here?'

'Sure. People get out all the time.' He laughs. 'Two, maybe three in the eighteen months I been here. And they were caught within the hour. I got to tell you, all those signs you see warning you about gettin' shot? They're for real. I've seen it happen. I'll tell you another thing. Captain says, soon as he sees you two, "We oughta just go ahead and paint those assholes. They're gonna be trouble." '

This time he does walk away, smartly. An officer is approaching, a tall, grey man with sparkling, sad eyes. On his chest is a nameplate that reads O'MALLEY. He wears the oak leaves of a major. 'Keep this area clear, Private,' he says. His voice is dry and quick.

'Yessir!' The private snaps to attention and salutes his superior

officer. There is a spit-and-polish about these men that I don't
remember from the prewar army. But under the surface, they're
still American. I suspect that I could get a laugh out of both of
them if I could remember a decent joke.

'You know what I think?' Jim says.

'What?'

'It's a pain in the neck to travel in this country. Frankly, I can't
see how we're going to get through this without illegal assistance. For which I guess we'll have to go back to Kingman.'

When the afternoon train comes in, we go along with the rest
of the thirsty, sweating mob that has been kept standing for
hours in the sun. For those who can't pay the price of a ticket,
there are two 'state cars' at the end of the train, ancient and filthy.
These people will be able to get to Kingman by train, but then
they're on their own. It's a tragedy for them. There is no more
romance to being a hobo in America. It means starvation, sometimes slow and sometimes fast.

We reach the outskirts of Kingman at eight o'clock at night.
The hobo city seems even larger, transformed as it is into an
ocean of flickering cookfires.

As the train stops, dirty children run up with cups of water,
shouting, 'Penny, penny, penny,' at the thirsty travellers. Their
shrill voices mingle with the barking of skeletal dogs.

It doesn't take long to find the people-smugglers. The moment
we jump down off the train to the dirt siding, we see a man in a
cap and dark glasses, far better dressed than most. We catch his
eye and he strolls up to us.

'Get you all the way, three golds apiece.'

Another man trots over, lean and quick, wearing a clean white
T-shirt, jeans, and hand-tooled boots. 'Five for both. And watch
out for that turkey, he flew right into an ambush last week.'

'Oh yeah? I'd be in prison camp if I'd done that. Why don't you
tell 'em the way you piled up that Tri-Pacer in June, asshole.'

Suddenly a woman's voice interrupts from behind us. 'One
gold each. And I'll take folding at a hundred to one.'

'Shit, Maggie, you can't even cover your gas!'

'Maggie – look, you guys, she's got a rotten plane and a worse
copilot. I don't wanna influence you, but as a professional
pilot –'

'I'm better'n no copilot at all, which is what you got, George,'
snarls a nine-year-old boy. He and the woman come closer. She

is pretty in the gloom, her eyes flashing, her lips edged with a smile. 'We fly a Cessna 182, gentlemen. It's clean and safe.' The smile develops. She nods towards a decrepit pickup parked just down the track. We bring out our money, then follow her and the boy.

'That's the last time you undercut us, Maggie,' one of the other smugglers says. 'Your prices ain't worth the risk.'

The truck is rusty and the engine sounds like it's only firing on about three cylinders, but it runs. 'You're lucky you didn't go with those two. Likely as not, they're California agents.' The airport is unlighted, just a dirt strip in the desert and a single ramshackle shed. The only sound, as we get out of the pickup, is the humming of a lighted Coke machine. 'How d'you like our runway light?' Maggie says as we pass it on the way to the flight line. I don't know about Jim, but I don't like it very much at all. For a nervous flyer like me, things are beginning to look kind of grim.

A coal-black Cessna 182 awaits us. Maggie and her boy start a flight check, walking around the plane, moving creaky flaps and rattling what seem to be loose propeller blades. Or maybe they're supposed to be that way.

'You guys ready? We want to get moving in case the competition informs on us. This is a cutthroat business.' She smiles. 'You got ID cards?'

We don't, of course, or we wouldn't be here. I get set to spend some more money.

'You got to be able to show IDs, or you'll be in the pen inside of twenty-four hours. All California citizens have them.' I remember as much from the train. 'We can give you fakes. They won't work in a computer, but they'll pass an eyeballing.'

'Is this part of the service?'

'No way. It's another sawbuck apiece. We had to pay fifteen hundred for the Polaroid machine. Them things are hard to get. Go in there without cards and you're wasting your plane fare. You don't want to have that happen.'

We pay our money and get our cards.

The plane bounces along the 'runway', at last shuddering into the air with a horrible popping from the engine. I almost wish it aloft, but it continues to stagger along at an altitude that could not be more than fifty feet. My heart begins to pound. The plane can't be working. It's going to crash.

Suddenly the kid starts counting backwards from ten. He has a stopwatch in his hand, just visible in the dim light from the dashboard. At the count of one, Maggie guns the motor and pulls her stick into her belly. We shoot upward, all except my stomach, which remains hanging, sickeningly, at our previous altitude.

'Power lines,' Maggie comments as we dive back to the altitude of my guts. I look at Jim. His eyes are wide.

'They're flying low,' he mutters, 'to avoid radar. Since they can't see, they're measuring ground speed against the stopwatch so they can tell when to climb over obstacles.'

'More or less.'

'If that's a question, the answer is less.'

We fly like this for what seems like hours. In fact, we go through the mountains literally at treetop level, with the boy counting and making check marks on a yellow pad, and the plane popping up and down almost continuously.

When I get airsick, the boy hands back a bag without ever missing his count.

Suddenly, just when it seems that the worst will never end, we are droning along straight and level, approaching the Los Angeles basin. 'Palm Springs off to the left,' Maggie comments. The lights of the town are beside us rather than below us. I decide to close my eyes until we land.

But there is no chance. I see LA then, and I almost burst into tears. Ahead and a little below are beads, strings, fountains of light. It is a vision from the past, wealthy and mysterious and wonderful.

'I'm gonna leave you near Colton airport. You know LA, either of you?'

'I don't,' I say, 'but I don't think we want to be left at an airport. We'll have to deal with customs, won't we?'

'I didn't say *at* Colton airport. Near it. We drop people various places. We ain't used this particular spot in a month. I'm gonna land on Interstate 10, just west of the airport. I'm not even gonna turn off the engine. You just pile out and I'll give 'er the gun and that's it. You're on your own. There's an interurban station right near the airport. Go there. There won't be anybody around this time of night. Last trolley comes through at midnight. It's a dime.'

Ten minutes later we are sitting in the brightly lit trolley stop. There is an ad on the back wall for Yamaha bicycles and a placard announcing, MARTIAL LAW AREA. OBEY LOCAL REGULATIONS. IF YOU VIOLATE A CURFEW, REMEMBER: SOLDIERS ARE REQUIRED TO SHOOT! Pencilled in below this are Colton's local laws: curfew is midnight or last trolley. The area commandant is Colonel William Piper, USA, address GPO Colton, phone number 213-880-1098. Suspicious persons should be reported at once.

Hello, sunshine.

Poll: Opinions from the Two Americas

There are really two Americas now, the first nation being California and its satellite Western states, the second being the rest of us folks – dirty, tired, and radioactive.

Out West, the public impression of the state of the rest of the country is very much worse than actual conditions would warrant. 'Outsiders' are looked upon as contagious at best, and probably downright lethal.

The West believes that

- America is recovering from the war.
- The West is helping the East as much as it can.
- The War Zones ought to be abandoned.

Naturally the East thinks otherwise, and though the War Zones are not broken out separately, they presumably feel that they should be rehabilitated.

Surprisingly, neither East nor West feels that long-term martial law in the War Zones is a threat to the Constitution, though the East has a stronger opinion in this matter than the West.

Do you believe that the United States is continuing to make a recovery from the 1988 war?

	1993	1992	1991
AGREE	49%	41%	30%
DISAGREE	46	57	67
NO OPINION	5	2	3

A significant East–West split is reflected in the response to this question. As first noted three years ago, marked differences appear between the states of the so-called War Zone and the remaining states. When asked this question in 1993, these two regions responded:

	East/War Zone	West
AGREE	30%	42%
DISAGREE	69	55
NO OPINION	1	3

In terms of assistance for recovery, do you believe that the federal government should abandon the War Zones permanently in order to concentrate resources on those marginally affected areas that could more fully benefit from the assistance?

	1993	1992
AGREE	47%	49%
DISAGREE	50	47
NO OPINION	3	4

As in last year's survey, there were sharp regional differences:

	East/War Zone	West
AGREE	25%	61%
DISAGREE	73	36
NO OPINION	2	3

Do you believe that the regions of the United States unaffected directly by the war are doing everything they can to assist in the full recovery of the War Zones?

	1993	1992	1991
AGREE	31%	27%	29%
DISAGREE	62	66	63
NO OPINION	7	7	8

Again, there were substantial differences between East and West:

	East/War Zones	West
AGREE	23%	51%
DISAGREE	71	47
NO OPINION	6	2

When asked what more the Western region could do to assist in recovery, or in what different ways it could do so, the responses were as follows:

	East/War Zones	West
DO THE SAME	13%	41%
DO LESS	2	22
PROVIDE GREATER CAPITAL ASSISTANCE	31	13
PROVIDE WORK TEAMS	12	10
ACCELERATE/INCREASE SUPPLIES AND MATERIEL	42	14

Are America's allies doing all they can to assist this nation to recover?

	1993	1992
AGREE	39%	34%
DISAGREE	57	61
NO OPINION	4	5

As in 1992, there were significant regional differences in response to this question:

	East/War Zone	West
AGREE	17%	39%
DISAGREE	79	57
NO OPINION	4	4

Does the continued use of the US Armed Forces to control the War Zones (approximately .7 million servicemen) pose a long-

term threat to the return of constitutional authority to state and
local governments in these areas?

	1993	1992	1991
AGREE	23%	21%	26%
DISAGREE	68	69	67
NO OPINION	9	10	7

Significant differences again appeared between regions:

	East/War Zones	West
AGREE	22%	35%
DISAGREE	71	55
NO OPINION	7	10

**Should the center of the national government once again be
reestablished on the East Coast, that is, moved from Los
Angeles?**

	1993	1992
AGREE	38%	39%
DISAGREE	45	42
NO OPINION	17	19

**Do you support the recent demands made by some groups for
dividing the United States into two permanent regions, e.g.,
West and East?**

	1993	1992
AGREE	47%	47%
DISAGREE	50	48
NO OPINION	3	5

Los Angeles

It is the greatest city in the United States. In size, San Francisco isn't even close.

Jim and I found it nostalgically complex, a vast mechanical toy full of buses and clanging trolleys and more cars than either of us have seen in one place in years.

It looks like fun, and the tension in the air reminds me a little of New York.

As much as there are things that are here from the past, there is something from the present that is missing. It is the sense of having suffered – the subtle tension that hangs between friends and strangers alike, everywhere else we have been so far. California didn't suffer too much from the famine, and few people here were weak enough to be killed by the Cincinnati Flu. Radiation sickness is almost unknown, except among refugees.

On our first night in the bright streets of Los Angeles, I found myself returning to my old metropolitan habits, moving with quick anonymity and never meeting anybody else's eyes.

There is a much stronger Japanese influence than ever before. The streets are packed not only with Japanese businessmen but also with clerks and factory workers and children with American nannies. And there are cars: new Nissans that whistle when they accelerate and get 130 miles to a gallon of gas, sporty Toyota

Z-90s, Isuzus and Mitsubishis and the occasional Mercedes-Benz. There are also a few Fords, big and beautifully made at the new plant in Fullerton, and a great improvement over the notorious Consensus with the plastic windows. Despite its size, the new Thunderbird gets sixty miles per gallon. It also has a sensor that sounds an alarm if any radioactive particles should be taken into the air-conditioning system.

More, though, than its prosperity, LA has the feeling of prewar America, the cheer, the confidence, the cheek that one associates with former days.

I indulged myself shamelessly. In Little Tokyo there are dozens of open-air fruit and vegetable stands where melons and tomatoes and lettuce and carrots and squash and dozens of other things are stacked in abundance. Little Tokyo, by the way, now extends all the way to Sixth Street. It must be four times its prewar size. In Little Tokyo I bought an enormous vine-ripened tomato for two cents and ate it like an apple. I have not eaten such a thing in years. It was rich beyond belief, dense with a flavour that swept through my nostrils, heavy with juice. If I could design hydroponics that would grow tomatoes that flavourful, I'd get rich.

For fifteen cents we spent half an hour at an open-air sushi bar, sampling the catch and burning our nostrils with Japanese horseradish. Then we strolled on, satiated, only to be tempted a few minutes later into a beautiful ice-cream store, which sold a new brand called Sweet Sue. I had a double-dip cone of cherry vanilla and, in honour of my son, pistachio.

I wish that my family could enjoy the life here. No wonder the POE is so strict. If immigration was free, California would be drowned in people.

As illegals, we were faced with a number of very serious problems. The first was transportation. There are ten long-distance trolley lines and many more buses than there were before the war, but a car is still a terrific convenience in LA. We did not have one and couldn't rent one without revealing that our IDs were bogus. So we were condemned to trying to figure out the intricate system of buses, minibuses, trolleys, and Aztlan-like pesetas.

Beyond transportation, we had the difficulty of finding a place to stay. I have enjoyed some extraordinary hotels in Los Angeles: the Beverly Hills, the Chateau Marmont, the Bonaventure.

But you can't register in a hotel without an ID that will pass the computer. In every bus and trolley, posted in stores and in post offices and pasted on every available public bulletin board, of which there must be thousands, is the following sign:

MARTIAL LAW ORDER 106: IMMIGRATION ORDER

PENALTIES

Illegal immigrants are liable to arrest and imprisonment for up to three years for the first offence, imprisonment for no less than ten years, without possibility of parole, for the second.

WARNING! There are severe penalties for failing to report an illegal! You may be imprisoned for no less than twenty years for this offence. So don't take chances, report!

REWARD

California will pay you for information leading to the capture of an illegal immigrant! You can make five gold dollars just for picking up the phone and dialling the Illegals Hot Line, 900-404-9999. So, if you get a bad ID or just see somebody who looks road-weary, give us a call. You never know when your suspicions might be worth their weight in gold!

We decided to assume a hostile population and made a few basic rules. First, we had to keep moving. Second, we had to sleep under the stars. We couldn't even risk a rooming house – assuming we could find one with a room to rent. Housing is a nightmare in LA. I saw ads in the *Times* offering small homes in the Valley for eight hundred in gold, no paper accepted and no mortgages given. Dallas has whole neighbourhoods where all you have to do is move in, bring your new house up to code, and it's yours.

Our third rule was that we had to look as happy and well fed as the rest of the Angelinos. Considering our other rules, this one was damned hard to keep. But we dared not look 'road-weary'. Angelinos know that overpopulation will strangle their prosperity, and they are generally avid to turn in illegals. We couldn't risk arousing suspicion, especially not among our interviewees and in the offices Jim was visiting to get government documents.

We spent our first night in a carport at the La Mirada apartments. Immediately after dawn the next day, we had our second taste of conflict between government and members of the Destructuralist movement. Shouting began echoing up and down La Mirada Avenue from the direction of El Centro. Then there were people running frantically through the carport, breathing hard, followed by battle-dressed officers on black mopeds.

One of the escapees dove under a car just beside us. Her gasping was so loud that we could hear it over the buzz of the passing mopeds.

One of the cops waved his pistol at us. 'You don't see this,' he called. Then he sped off.

'Halt,' echoed an amplified voice from the far end of the alley, 'you're all under arrest!'

Then there came the dismal mutter of capture, the gear-grinding approach of a small black schoolbus with bars welded across the windows, the quick disappearance of the little band of the desperate.

Then silence. Not a window opened in any of the houses that lined the alley, not a curious face appeared. We kept to the dim interior of the carport, listening to the breathing of the person under the car. We stayed like that for some little time. Once somebody came out of the La Mirada, got into a gleaming blue Consensus, and drove away.

'It's quiet,' Jim said at last. 'You can come out now.'

We then had our only contact with the Conspiracy of Angels, and learned a little more about the nature of Destructuralism.

A Statement by an Anonymous Member of the Conspiracy of Angels

People cannot continue to hide from the fact that this civilisation is totally bankrupt. Society needs a whole new way of doing and being if we are not going to build up all over again and wind up with an even worse war.

That is where the Destructuralist Movement comes in, and the Angels are militant Destructuralists.

What is Destructuralism, you might ask, and what's in it for me and my family? First off, Destructuralism says that your person and those you make your family are the only valid social unit, and the maintenance of that family is the only valid economic activity.

We say that the whole social edifice, from the Boy Scouts right up to the Army, is essentially an addiction, that it is more than unnecessary, it is dangerous. Social structures are the breeding ground of ideology, greed, and territorialism. Agricultural communities are peaceful communities, and families bound together by need and love do not go to war.

No matter how benign a given structure seems, it will inevitably lead to the same consequences all social structures lead to, namely, war and death. Real social harmony comes not from lawbooks but from the human heart.

If that is too high an ideal, then it is perfectly obvious that we are eternally condemned to the slavery of warfare, and probably also to extinction.

Government is institutionalised dehumanisation. People who deal with paper instead of other people lose the all-important thread of contact from heart to heart. Here's a story about a social structure that all of America loves, the British Relief. A man who joined our movement got eye cancer and the Relief did triage on him and sent him home. People wait in line for days, only to be told by some English nanny that they can't even get an aspirin. And if you go black market for medicine and get caught, it is not a jury of your peers that tries you, it is the Relief. And they forced you on to the black market in the first place. This man with eye cancer bought black market chemotherapy, got caught, and had to pay a fine, even though he was dying.

He became an Angel a month before he took henbane from a witch. He did not die of cancer, he died of structure, or at least suffered from it. There is no shortage of painkillers, for example. The Relief could have given him Brompton Mixture on an out-patient basis, but the rules reserve it for inpatients only, and he couldn't be an inpatient because he was triaged!

So the structure – simply because it was there – at the very least condemned him to unnecessary agony. If his family had been in control of his fate, instead of some bureaucrat in the Relief office down at the civic centre, he would have been spared the torment and indignity of the pain.

People say thank God Europe didn't get in the war, what would we do without them, but the Angels say we are just suffering more because of the structures that are now being imposed on us from the outside. When Washington was destroyed, we had a golden, historic opportunity to free ourselves from the age-old slavery of government. Instead, we are having both economic and political structure imposed on us from the outside – colonial exploitation, as a matter of fact, very similar to what the Europeans practised on the Chinese in the last century. The foreign presence on our shores is nothing more than a prescription for more structural enslavement, with the added problem that we don't even control the structure.

Also, they take crops from the few viable growing areas and allocate them *not only* to North America but also to themselves. Remember, if we weren't feeding Europe too, we wouldn't be starving ourselves. The story is that they have gone into Argentina and taken it over to make sure the crops are not held up for high prices. Argentina is no longer even a country. If you read the English papers, they always call it 'the Argentine' or some such thing. We believe that most of the population south of the border is dead of starvation, and the Europeans caused it by taking the only food our Latin sisters and brothers could get their hands on, the Argentine wheat. That is hundreds of millions of deaths.

We call ourselves Angels because we help people in need and because we remember the dishonoured dead of the world, those who died on Warday in the United States and the USSR, and the billions who have died since. We represent the living, the ordinary men and women and children who see that, in order to survive, mankind needs a whole new way of being.

There is inherent in Destructuralism the concept that people can remake their own hearts to include a new valuation of their fellow human beings. By refocusing our energies on our families we can learn never to forget for an instant how it feels to be the other person. For example, the American President and the Russian Premier could not have done what they did to the rest of us on Warday if they had been trained from birth never to forget for an instant that all human beings are partners in life and that everybody is as important to himself or herself as they were to themselves – that the death of the average Joe was going to be as much of a catastrophe for him and his family as the death of the great leader would be to his own precious self and his relatives. Instead, they sat in their command posts and talked numbers. To Destructuralists there are no numbers, there are only names and faces and hearts.

Only in a truly destructured, rehumanised social milieu can the kind of maturing growth that people need take place, because only if there are no distancing structures can the individual come to realise, through his identification with his own family, that every other life on earth is as precious and valuable as his own.

You might argue that Destructuralism is old-style anarchy all over again, but it isn't. Destructuralism is based on the caring of

Fugitives

As soon as she finished her statement, our friendly Angel got into the nearest American-made car, reached under the dashboard, and hot-wired it.

'You want a ride?'

We didn't. We just wanted to disappear. She backed out into the alley and was soon off down La Mirada. Not ten seconds after the car had disappeared, there came a roar from about thirty feet overhead and an ultralight aircraft darted past in the direction she had gone. There are large numbers of these planes in Los Angeles skies, used by police and fire departments to keep detailed tabs on rooftops and backyards. Soon, more of the moped cops shot past on La Mirada.

We were scared. The penalties for being an illegal immigrant in California are severe. Capture could mean years in a work camp. Maybe all the years I have left.

'Let's get out of here,' Jim said. 'Half the police department's in the neighbourhood this morning.'

I did not reply. I was thinking of Anne and Andrew, wondering what they were doing. It was a quarter to six in Dallas. I could imagine my family out in the henhouse, Anne collecting eggs while Andrew did the cleaning. I could hear the hens clucking and smell thick henhouse odours mixing with the aroma of morning coffee floating across from the kitchen.

Another ultralight appeared and began circling us as we walked along La Mirada. It was all I could do not to break and run as the damned thing soared round and round overhead, its engine whining like an angry wasp. Jim stopped and looked up, shielding his eyes from the sun.

'Don't do that!'

'It's more suspicious to ignore him.'

The policeman's amplified voice crackled down: 'IDs, please!'

We held up our red plastic cards. He peered down as he made another sweep, then flew off, talking into his radio.

'Do you think that did it, Jim?'

'No.'

'Neither do I.' We walked on, heading for the Santa Ana Freeway. If we could catch an interregional bus there, it just might take us all the way to Burbank.

Suddenly a black car pulled up, and behind the wheel was an unexpected but welcome sight: a priest in a Roman collar. 'Get in,' he said.

The thought crossed my mind that he might be a police agent. Then a siren began wailing. I could see the lights of a squad car far down La Mirada. 'Get in,' the priest repeated. 'Hurry up about it!'

We got into the old Buick. 'Down, down, you darned fools!' As the squad car roared past, we dropped to the floor of the back seat.

'They're on foot,' a voice rattled from the front seat. I was astonished to realise that the priest had a police radio. 'Two-four-two to Air Six. We do not, repeat, do not have them in our sight.'

The priest started his car. 'That's a relief, anyway.'

'Father –'

'Keep down!'

He drove us to his rectory, where we got a shave, a shower, and a much-needed change of clothing. He never referred to the Destructuralists, or why he had been in that particular neighbourhood at that time, or why he had so mercifully helped us.

He believed strongly in the value of human freedom, though, and in the old Bill of Rights. You can read that between the lines of the interview he gave us.

Interview: Reverend Michael Dougherty, Catholic Priest

I was afraid we wouldn't have time to do this, but I think you're probably safe here for another half hour or so. I'm glad to get the chance to speak for publication. We've forgotten a few basic human freedoms out here in sunny California. We need to rediscover ourselves as Americans – as people, really. As children of God. Sometimes I think of the world – is that thing on? I don't see the red light. Ah, okay. Sometimes I think of the world as a little lost bit of dust in the middle of nowhere, and it is deathly ill, and there is nobody to help us. But then I feel the presence of Christ, as if He had taken the world in His arms and was hugging us to Himself the way a father might hug a hurt child.

I think that we Americans are feeling terribly guilty about ourselves. Especially the older generation. I see the effects. One of them is that priests like me have gotten incredibly busy, and one of the things that keeps me busiest is ministering to the sad and the guilty. We've got three priests here at St Francis, me and two newly ordained, as well as three deacons and four nuns. I've been a priest since 1975, so I'm an old hand. That rarity, the prewar religious. The rest are all new. Since Warday, my parish has more than quadrupled in size. In the past five years, I can hardly remember a Mass that wasn't full. Even at six o'clock on Saturday morning, it's full. Many, many kids. The children of secularised parents, rebelling against the indifference of their elders. And the elders too, now, fumbling with the St Joseph's missals we have in the church, saying their prayers as best they can.

But it's in the confessional that I hear the motives people have for returning to the Church. It isn't piety or love of God, not among the older folks. People are coming back to the Church because they feel that their own indifference, just letting things happen, was a big part of what caused the war. Remember, back in those days it just seemed like there was nothing you personally could do. The solutions *now* to our problems *then* seem obvious. But in those days we were all very different people. We were dulled by living under the Sword of Damocles for nearly half a century. We had done the worst possible thing – gotten used to an incredible and immediate danger. The nuclear mechanism was far more hazardous to each one of us individually than, say, pouring gasoline on our clothes would have been. But it didn't feel that way, not in those sunny, treacherous days.

We understood how absolutely deadly the bomb was, but we did not understand how helpless we were in the face of the mechanism of war. The mechanism began to run quite mysteriously, and went on until it broke down. It could as easily have destroyed the world. Only faulty design prevented that. We thought that people dickering about arms control in Geneva mattered, when what we really needed all along was a massive change of heart. How absurdly outmoded the elaborate diplomacy of the prewar period now seems. There could have been a massive shift of heart, towards acceptance and understanding and away from hostile competitiveness and ideological obsession.

The whole business of the United States and the USSR squandering their resources on territorialism seems incredibly silly now. Our prewar mistake was to believe in rubble. We visualised ourselves as crawling out of the basement and putting brick back on brick. Places don't just cease to exist.

You know, they say that a person set down in the middle of the Washington Dead Zone would have died within hours. Just keeled over and died. Birds died flying across it. That was in the

LA *Times* after the war. It's a forty-square-mile desert of black glass dotted with the carcasses of sparrows and larks and the occasional duck.

Before the war there weren't even intellectual references for such things. No comprehension. The message of Hiroshima wasn't understood. We thought that it meant devastation. But ruins have to do with the past. Modern nuclear war means life being replaced by black, empty space. It means ancient seats of government evaporating in a second. The moral question is almost beyond asking. What are we, that we can do this? What is evil, that it can speak with such a voice? We no longer know what we are, we of the Holocaust and Stalin and Warday. We unleashed hell on ourselves by pretending that diplomacy, of all things, could control its fires. The heart, and the heart alone, is more powerful than hell.

Am I preaching? Excuse me. I run so fast, give so much advice, quite frankly I think I've forgotten how to talk without a degree of pontification. Sometimes I wish I had a wife to have a private life with. Someone who would say, 'You're preaching, Mike,' or 'You're talking through your hat.' But I don't have time for a wife. Or children. I couldn't raise kids in a life that doesn't have ten free minutes a day. So I'm no longer uptight about the celibacy rule.

Before Warday I was well on my way to losing my vocation. I wanted to get married. I think I might have become an Episcopalian. But then came Warday and, afterwards, the Reunion with the Anglicans and the Episcopals. Then, most of all, the tremendous upsurge of need for my services. I got the feeling that Christ was very close to us religious people, full of forgiveness and need, asking for our help. I want to be Christ's servant. Now when I'm feeling alone I take my soul to Mary, who is His mother and therefore the mother of all mankind. She's what the witches call the Mother Goddess! I just kneel before her altar and say the rosary. She never fails me, Mary. The rosary is far better for me than, say, meditation. It's not only meditation, with all the repetition, it's humble and it's a request for help. She was once a human being. She knows what we suffer. She is always there, anytime, for anybody. Mary doesn't care a fig about the details. She loves and respects you because you exist.

The witchcraft movement talks about taking personal, individual responsibility for the condition of planet Earth as if they invented the idea. But it's also a Christian and very specifically Catholic notion. At least I think it is. My saddest, guiltiest parishioners say that they sinned terribly by not taking some kind of personal action on behalf of peace between the United States and the Soviet Union. They say they should have demonstrated against this or in favour of that. But I tell them no, the sin was that we did not accept one another in our hearts, neither side. Our leaders hardly even knew each other. The two greatest nations on earth, with almost total responsibility for the fate of planet and species, and they hardly even spoke! They should have made it their business to be close personal friends. And there should have been as much commonality of policymaking and government as possible. Instead the two countries were separate islands, distant from, and mysterious to, each other. That was the sin of pride, doing that.

What a price has been paid for the pleasure of such indulgence.

When I think of what our generation did, I pray very, very hard that the future will somehow accept us and find in the Body of Christ the love and understanding that will enable them to say, 'Our ancestors chose foolishness over wisdom and hostility over acceptance, but we understand and we forgive.'

Now I'm not your deep thinker. But I do try. I've read the Catholic philosophers, and the Greeks, and most of the moderns. I mean to say, I've read my Whitehead and my Hegel, my Aristotle and my Plotinus.

You know, throughout history, philosophy centred on the concept of being rather than the ethics. That was fine until recent years, when we began to try on some pretty bizarre concepts, and to hell with the ethics of it all. Nazism and so forth, I mean. And the concept of nationhood that allowed us to think we had the right to build such things as nuclear bombs.

The American and Russian peoples should never have allowed their leaders to play the game of overstating the threat to justify exorbitant military expenditures. We were supposed to be seeking a balance of terror, weren't we? But the United States *in fact* got so far ahead of the Russians technologically that we were about to send up a satellite that would have made their missiles useless against us. And they had no similarly effective weapon. So they were forced to start the war. They were backed up against the wall.

I'm just a priest in a medium-sized parish. Nobody on high

would ever have listened to me. Before the war I had eight hundred in my parish. Now I've got close to ten thousand frightened and suffering people. In some ways I'd rather have had eight hundred and the old world than ten thousand and the new.

Let's see now, you asked me for an idea about how my day goes. What I do. Well, I get up at five-thirty and I run like a madman until midnight, then I sleep like the dead until five-thirty the next morning. I've got my schedule for last Wednesday. I'll read it into the record:

5.30 a.m. Arose and said breviary.

5.45 a.m. Breakfast of corn soup and milk.

6.00 a.m. Said Mass. Gave out communion to 230 people.

6.30 a.m. Meeting with my staff. Discussed the reroofing project. Looked over Father Moore's report to the bishop on the feasibility of splitting St Francis into two parishes. I hope that this is done!

7.00 a.m. Met a parishioner who has just been diagnosed as having stage-three Hodgkin's and has been triaged. Has a wife and three teenage children. Is fifty-two. We prayed together and he cried. He paced like a trapped lion. Prayed for him and put him in the Mass list for Sunday.

7.20 a.m. CCD leaders met in my office to plan a bake sale. They have thirty pounds of flour, six pounds of sugar, some apples, some molasses, and so we are very excited. Thank God they also have Sister Euphrasia, who is one good baker.

7.45 a.m. Had coffee and listened to the Vatican US Service on the shortwave.

8.00 a.m. Went to Holy Cross Hospital for my visitations. I'm glad I took Father Moore, as my list was sixty names long! I had an hour there, and because he took half my people, I was able to spend two minutes with each patient. I blessed, I prayed, I heard eighteen confessions and gave out thirty Holy Communions. I gave the Last Rites to twelve patients on the critical list.

9.15 a.m. Returned to the rectory. Did youth counselling until noon. We have seventy young people who are converting, and an active Sodality and CYO. But these were all special cases. I gave each kid half an hour. Saw six troubled kids. A girl who is pregnant. A boy who is in love with a younger boy. A girl who says she sees visions of the Virgin, and indeed may. Another girl who has beaten her mother and father so badly that they want her out of the house. Where does a petite girl of sixteen get such titanic anger? Two boys who steal. I warned them very sternly. They must remember, these children, that we have a looting law here in California, and they are liable to be shot on sight if they're caught. It isn't like the old days. There is no due process at the end of a gunsight.

12.15 p.m. Lunch of soybean soup, lettuce and vinegar and oil, and a delicious Budweiser.

12.30 p.m. Met with Parish Council. We are going to try to expand our food programme this winter. Last year we distributed 31,280 meals to the hungry. This year we are going to try for fifty thousand. Mrs Cox said that the baby boy found behind the rectory last week was just fine, normal in every way, and has been placed with the Tucker family. They are at risk for having children, so they are terribly grateful.

1.00 p.m. Met with Joe O'Donnell, who is thinking about running for chief of police. The most powerful job in the Valley. Will he do it? He'd do a very creditable job, I feel sure. I promised to call the bishop on his behalf. There is certainly nothing wrong with having a Catholic in that job, and Joe is a good man.

1.15 p.m. Back to the church for fifteen minutes of prayer. Spent it with Mary and had wonderful, intimate communication with her. Has our need somehow made our connection with deity stronger? Sometimes I feel as if Christ and Mary are here, alive, almost in the flesh. This, I suppose, is faith.

1.30 p.m. Catechism with my eighth-graders. Fifty kids. What a bunch of jokers! I love that class. We might be in hell, but kids are kids, always. What did I find in the question box? 'Father, if you couldn't consummate marriage any other way, would it be permissible to use an Erector Set?' Kid's humour. We are into sex education. Some of these children are sterile.

2.30 p.m. Adult counselling for two hours. I took a Charismatic study group for half an hour, then a disturbed couple, then a woman who has bone cancer and is contemplating euthanasia. Personally I detest the practice, but I can see if I get a really rough cancer I might want to turn to it myself. His Holiness and the Archbishop of Canterbury have agreed that it's no sin to withdraw life support if the person is beyond hope. I promised to attend her.

4.30 p.m. Spent ten minutes with my breviary.

4.40 p.m. Went to the church and said Benediction. Our choir is just wonderful. Who would have thought ten years ago that I would have a full choir for weekday afternoon service? Not to mention two hundred people in the church. Christ has not failed us. He is awakening our hearts.

5.00 p.m. Heard confessions for an hour. 'Bless me, Father, for I have sinned.' How I love them, my dear parishioners. I will not speak of their sins, except to say that they are good people, and I know they are forgiven their little transgressions. I tell them to make penance a sacrament of self-discovery. Confession should be a joy.

6.00 p.m. Supper. Vegetable goulash with nice big pieces of sausage. Another Bud. Much laughter and joking around our big table of men and women. We have a lot of fun together.

7.00 p.m. BBC Overseas Service News. The UK has recognised the Kingdom of Azerbaijan. We looked and looked on the map, but we couldn't find it. Somewhere in the former Soviet Union, but where?

7.30 p.m. 'Moon Over Morocco', a cigarette, and a cup of coffee. My half hour of indulgence! That's a delightful radio show. I must admit that I miss TV. Boy, what I wouldn't give to feast my eyes on 'M*A*S*H' just one more time. As a semipublic institution, we have some chance of getting a TV before too much longer. The BBC is already beaming shows over here by satellite, and Ted Turner is getting organised again in Atlanta and LA. Also, HBO and the networks are coming back. Soon, please, and don't neglect the half-hour format, because that's all I have time for!

8.00 p.m. Meeting of the Charismatics in the basement of the church. I'm glad that Sister Euphrasia and Father Booth are both members of this movement! I can't begin to speak in tongues. I can't keep up with their intensity. Their faith is like fire. These are God's people, these Charismatics. We are going to have to move our group upstairs. Three hundred people are too many for the basement. Might even be a fire hazard.

9.00 p.m. Meeting of the Knights of Columbus in the school cafetorium. Full-dress affair. I led prayers. We are making elaborate plans for the Christ the King procession upcoming.

10.00 p.m. A call from the man who was diagnosed as terminal Hodgkin's yesterday. Met him in the church and we said the rosary together. He told his family over supper. He says they spent the evening singing and talking about how close the Lord is to them now. I suggested they go to the Charismatic meeting tomorrow night. They heal each other all the time, maybe they'll heal him. But I didn't say that to him. I said, if he feels Christ in him so strongly, he belongs among them, and so does his family.

11.00 p.m. Breviary for fifteen minutes, and another fifteen reading the new Mailer book. *Ghost Dance* is a great statement on our lives now.

11.30 p.m. My five minutes in the shower. Father Moore snapped me with a towel. How I would like to be twenty-three years old again! These old bones . . .

12.00 a.m. Lights out at the St Francis rectory. Silence. My cross, a darker shadow on my dark wall. The wind moaning past the eaves. Sleep, and a dream of long ago.

Documents from the Civil Defence

There goes the night brigade
They got no steady trade . . .
                    – Ezra Pound

HELPFUL HINTS FOR THE UNAFFECTED: BLUEGRAMS

You probably don't know about Bluegrams. I certainly didn't see any in Texas during the war, and Whitley doesn't remember them from New York.

They are apparently called Bluegrams because they are printed on light-green paper.

There is an element of practicality about Bluegrams. Their distribution, however, appears to be limited to areas where they aren't needed.

So, in case you might find them useful, I include here the two most practical ones we picked up.

One sees Bluegrams in all sorts of places, pinned to community bulletin boards or left in stacks on the counters of luncheonettes. We could have included Bluegrams on control of radioactive roaches or on the washing of hot cars with sponges attached to fishing poles, but we decided to limit ourselves to material of at least some interest to people who live in the communities for which they were obviously intended in the first place.

Why don't areas of genuine need get Bluegrams! Maybe the Civil Defence officials responsible don't want to upset us, or – more likely – they'd rather stay in California than set out with their little blue trucks to that softly glowing world beyond the Sierras.

CIVIL DEFENSE BULLETIN
December 13, 1988

HOME OR BUSINESS PROTECTION FROM RADIATION

In the event that the United States sustains another nuclear attack, you are advised to seek the best protection possible for yourself and your family.

If you live in or near a city, you should receive advance warning of an attack. It is possible, however, with the current emergency conditions, and with only partially repaired communications, that an attack warning will not be given or will be brief at best. In some cases, you will learn of an attack only after it has occurred.

IN EITHER CASE, YOU MUST TAKE PROTECTIVE ACTION IMMEDIATELY AND IN THE STRUCTURE WITH THE HIGHEST PROTECTIVE LEVEL AVAILABLE TO YOU AT THE TIME.

Different buildings and structures vary in the level of radiation protection offered. In general, basements or rooms underground offer the best protection. In an emergency, however, you and members of your family may have to make quick judgments as to the best and most accessible place available to you at the time.

The following examples list structures along with their respective protection factors. The higher the factor, the better the protection.

TYPICAL BUILDINGS AND THEIR PROTECTIVE VALUE

Type of Building	Factor
Underground shelters covered by 3 feet or more of dirt, or sub-basements of buildings with more than 5 stories	1000+
Basement fallout shelters, basements without exposed walls, and central areas of upper floors (not top 3) with heavy exterior walls	250 to 1000
Basements of buildings with frame and brick veneers, central area of basements with partially exposed walls, and central areas of upper floors (not top floor) in multistory buildings with heavy floors and exterior walls	50 to 250

TYPICAL BUILDINGS AND THEIR PROTECTIVE VALUE

Type of Building	Factor
Basements without exposed walls of 1–2 story buildings and central areas of upper floors (not top) of multistory buildings with light floors and walls	10 to 50
Partially exposed basements of 1–2 story buildings and central areas on ground floor of similar buildings with heavy masonry walls	2 to 10
Aboveground rooms of light residential homes or apartments	2 or Less

REMEMBER, SOME PROTECTION IS BETTER THAN NONE.
GOOD PROTECTION WILL SAVE LIVES!

FOR LOCAL DISTRIBUTION

CIVIL DEFENSE DIRECTIVE A-25
December 15, 1988

EMERGENCY INSTRUCTIONS FOR
RADIOLOGIC DECONTAMINATION

THE FOLLOWING EMERGENCY GUIDELINES SHOULD BE
FOLLOWED UNTIL FULL-SCALE GOVERNMENT
DECONTAMINATION EFFORTS CAN BE UNDERTAKEN.

If you live near a War Zone, or if you are being billeted temporarily by military or local government, you may be in considerable danger through contact with materials that have been made radioactive by the bomb explosion itself, or from fallout.

Radioactivity cannot be seen. The only sure way to know if radioactivity is present is to use electronic detectors that measure radioactivity. These devices are available from your local government, or from the military units assigned to your area.

BUT WHAT DO YOU DO IF YOU DON'T HAVE ACCESS IMMEDIATELY TO RADIATION DETECTORS?

It's best to be safe. If you live within 100 miles of a designated War Zone, it is highly likely that you will have at least some objects or surfaces affected with radioactivity. Or, if you live within any of the areas where fallout has occurred, you probably have some degree of contamination.

MOST RADIATION WILL DISAPPEAR WITHIN 60–90 DAYS. HOWEVER, DEPENDING UPON YOUR LOCATION AND PROXIMITY TO A BOMBED AREA, YOU COULD HAVE SUFFICIENT RADIOACTIVITY PRESENT TO CAUSE SERIOUS ILLNESS.

IF POSSIBLE, YOU SHOULD CHECK WITH YOUR LOCAL GOVERNMENT OR WITH MILITARY AUTHORITIES TO DETERMINE THE LIKELIHOOD OF RADIOACTIVITY IN YOUR HOME OR BILLETING AREA.

If you know some radioactivity is present, or you suspect this to be the case, then you should utilize the following methods for decontaminating common materials and surfaces.

1. CLOTHING

Clothing that is heavily contaminated, e.g., that which has been outside and unprotected, should be discarded at once and buried in a location that will not affect water supplies.

Other clothing can be brushed or washed, though you should be careful to control the runoff in order to prevent further contamination. Using a detergent will help. All washing should be done in one area and the runoff directed to the same collector, which later can be covered up.

Always use gloves if you can, and wash yourself thoroughly afterwards.

2. FOOD

Packaged food can be brushed or washed, though you should watch out for dust particles. Unprotected food should be disposed of as soon as possible. You should not plan to hunt for wild game for another four months; the possibility that wildlife has ingested radioactive particles is still dangerously high.

3. METAL AND PAINTED SURFACES

Metal or painted surfaces, including cars and trucks, can be washed or scrubbed, with or without detergents or cleansing agents. Again, you should control the runoff. The use of complexing agents – oxalates, carbonates, acids or oxidizing agents – can be useful for porous surfaces but chemically dangerous; care should be taken in using chemicals.

4. LARGE STRUCTURES

Large structures, such as houses, buildings, barns, etc., are most quickly cleaned with water sprays. Structures that are heavily contaminated, however, will need more intensive treatment. Chemical treatment may be necessary; abrasion or sandblasting may be necessary with concrete and brick. Runoff can be a major problem, and all cleaning personnel should wear protective clothing and masks.

5. TERRAIN

Earth surfaces that are radioactive can be removed, though disposal can be a problem. For farming areas, plowing under may be the most expedient action, but the ground remains radioactive for some time and may not be readily usable again. You should consult your local authorities about any substantial earth-moving activity you propose. Protective clothing should be worn at all times, and face masks, such as those worn by medical personnel, should be used.

6. WATER

Standing water, such as that in pools or tanks, should not be used and little can be done to purify the water, short of using complex ion-exchange equipment. Water from streams or rivers may have surface contamination as a result of having passed through radioactive areas. Water for personal consumption should be purified using available equipment or homemade devices, such as natural filtration through buckets filled with stones, clay, and other filtrating materials. Filtered water should then be treated with iodine tablets to remove any trace of radioactive iodine. Water from deep ground wells should be usable without treatment.

WARNING: IF YOU ARE UNCERTAIN ABOUT THE LEVEL OF RADIOACTIVITY OF ANY OBJECT OR SURFACE, USE CARE AND DECONTAMINATE! DO NOT HESITATE TO CONSULT YOUR LOCAL GOVERNMENT OR MILITARY AUTHORITIES FOR ASSISTANCE.

Rumours: Mutants and Super-Beasts

Jim and I heard our first rumour on the trolley into LA. Since then, we've found that rumours run in the blood of this city.

RUMOUR: There is a gigantic beast with bat wings and red, burning eyes that has attacked adults and carried off children. The creature stands seven feet tall and makes a soft whistling noise. It is often seen on roofs in populated areas, but only at night.

FACT: Of all the rumours we heard, this was the most persistent. Claiming that we were LA *Times* reporters, we called Dr Edward Wagner of UCLA, a biologist, and asked him to comment on the possibility that some sort of radiation-induced mutation could have produced a new species of giant bat. Dr Wagner stated that giantism is a fairly well understood evolutionary phenomenon that is caused by space-competition among species. He doubted that something as fully developed as this could have come about in the thirty-odd bat generations that have elapsed since the war.

A Glendale resident, who was attacked in August of '91, recorded his experience in the weekly *Glendale Courier*:

I had just gotten off the Glendale trolley when I heard this soft sort of cooing noise coming from the roof of a house. The sound was repeated and I turned to look towards the house. Standing on the roof was what looked like a man wrapped in a cloak. Then it spread its wings and *whoosh!* it was right on top of me! I remember it smelled awful, like something dead. It was working at my face with these long, probing fingers. It got them around my neck and it started snapping its teeth and hissing. Its wings were wrapped around me. I was smothering in there, in the stink of the thing. When I saw its eyes, red and glaring, hideous, I thought it was the devil come for me and I gave out a scream. Just like that, it spread its wings and started flying, its fingers still around my head. I was dragged halfway down the block, then it let me go and took off into the sky, cooing and hissing. I saw the moonlight glint off its wings, then it was gone.

The individual who told this story to the paper was also reported to have extensive scars on his neck and head, of the type that long fingernails or talons might make.

We have no further information about this story.

RUMOUR: Radiation has caused many terrible mutations, such as babies who claw their way out of the mother's womb just as the first contractions of labour start. Also, babies who are born with the genitals of adults, or women having animal children, usually monkeys or pigs.

FACT: We have great difficulty getting used to the high level of mutation that is an inevitable side-effect of high ambient radiation. Naturally, mutations occur with greatest frequency in areas most seriously radiated. A mother in California, for example, has little more chance of bearing a mutant child than before the war, but a mother in Dallas is many times more likely to bear a mutant.

Mutations take two basic forms, degenerative and progressive. Ninety-nine out of a hundred degenerative mutations involve some sort of destruction or malformation of the foetus. They *never* involve atavism, such as a woman giving birth to an animal child. Such a mutation is probably not possible. Nor are they likely to involve such farfetched nonsense as babies with claws or babies with fully developed genitals. The truth is much more prosaic, and much sadder. Common mutations are mal-

formed limbs, bones, or eyes, brain disorders, and malfunction-
ing organs, such as improperly formed hearts. In cases where the
mutant is declared non-viable on the Hexler Function Scale, the
parents may elect euthanasia.

Progressive mutations are much more rare, but they are not
unknown. The most usual progressive mutation we are aware of
is so-called hyperintelligence syndrome (HIS). Babies displaying
this syndrome exhibit certain common characteristics: they are
extremely aware even at birth and are generally capable of lifting
their heads, smiling, and making organised sounds within a few
hours of being born. This initial precociousness is not followed
up, however, at least not evenly. There are HIS children three
years old who can read Shakespeare but are still mastering the art
of walking. A common problem in HIS children is difficulty
acclimatising to extreme stimuli such as loud sounds or bright
colours. HIS children generally learn reading and mathematics
by passive assimilation by the age of two or three. The oldest
known HIS child, Charlie B., is now four. He was born in
Philadelphia eleven months after Warday, six months before that
city was temporarily evacuated due to high radiation levels
caused by the Washington and New York strikes. Charlie B. is
physically developed to the size of a normal four-year-old. He is
the clear intellectual superior of all adults who work with him.
He has no formal education; indeed, there is no educational
system yet devised that can help him. He reads four languages, is
conversant in the most abstruse mathematics and physics, and
has what his parents describe as a 'vast' memory. He is often
despondent. His family has plans to move from its present home
in Los Angeles to England if Charlie is accepted, at the age of
seven, by Oxford.

There are eighteen identified HIS children in the United States.
Twenty-four are known to have been born, but one was killed in
a home fire and five have died for other reasons. Poor reporting
and record-keeping may mean that there are undiagnosed HIS
children.

These two are the basic 'mutant/super-beast' rumours that
are current in California. Variations are many, including the
Hopping Devil rumour that seems to be a variant of the Giant Bat
story, and the story of the secret think-tank at Cal Tech where
Japanese scientists exploit HIS children in the development of

ever more extraordinary technologies, which they do not share with the Americans.

Since there cannot be any HIS children older than four, this last rumour appears to be without real substance, though the exploitation of HIS children is something that the Relief or some responsible US agencies should certainly examine very closely.

The Immigrant Quickstep

Father Dougherty explained to us that the only way to evade the
California authorities was to keep moving from city to city or,
even better, to leave the state at once. He warned us that we were
taking great risks staying in LA even long enough to go downtown so Jim could gather documents from the remains of the old
federal government, which has its offices in the LA Federal
Complex. When it became clear to him that we weren't going to
change our minds, he insisted on driving us. He felt that,
without help, we had no chance of staying out of the hands of the
police.

On the way into the centre of the city, Father Dougherty told
us that, like it or not, he was leaving us at Union Station after Jim
got his documents. He briefed us about how to contend with the
various travel zones.

'You have Red Zones, Yellow Zones, Blue Zones, and Green
Zones. Stick to the Greens. They lead to the intrastate tracks,
which will be on your left as you pass through the main waiting
room. Yellow Zones are for incoming trains from our sister
restricted-immigration states, Washington and Oregon. Red
Zones are for trains arriving from abroad, which means the rest
of the United States. Don't even look as if you might be interested
in them. Remember that the IPs are just dying to check you out.

Need I add that there is also a White Zone in the waiting room? It's for the outgoing *Southwest* and *Sunset Limited*s, and the *Desert Wind*. Nobody will bother you in the White Zone.'

We arrived at the Federal Complex and parked. There were plenty of empty spaces. Father Dougherty and I would wait while Jim looked up a few likely parties in the government. He had some contacts he had met during the years he researched and wrote about atomic weapons and the community of men around them.

The federal government takes up only the lower floors of the federal building. Most of the structure is given over to the California State Department of Small-Scale Agricultural Control (Southern Region), an organisation devoted to the licensing and regulation of private gardens.

According to Father Dougherty, Jim had at all costs to avoid straying into any part of the complex controlled by the state. 'The President and the Governor aren't friends,' was the way he put it. 'This is a state in name only. Within five years it's going to be accrediting ambassadors. Already there's an Embassy Row in Sacramento. But as far as the Feds are concerned, you'll be subject to their laws on their territory – which means you'll have full constitutional rights below the eighth floor of the building. If somebody on the federal floors asks for your ID, ask for his warrant. But, for God's sake, don't go upstairs.'

As he crossed the parking lot, I could see that Jim was edgy. I did not envy him this duty. We hoped for the chance of an interview with the President, or at least with some senior officials. So little is known nowadays about the federal government, we felt that anything we could get would be of enormous value.

The silence of waiting settled into the car. Father Dougherty turned on the radio, a new Sony. There were about ten stations up and down the dial. Twisting it, I heard the Beach Boys. Their voices, the tone and feel of the music, evoked the past, summer weather. How anybody can bear to listen to the Beach Boys for very long these days, I cannot imagine.

It is interesting that the past has come to seem so beautiful. I wish we could remember it clearly enough to avoid its mistakes. But I am coming to recall it more for its laughter than its danger. I remember how Anne and I used to enjoy SoHo, and the East Village galleries that were gaining a foothold by about '84.

Extremes in art spoke to us then, though I cannot now remember why. America was sunshine, wasn't it?

It was also excitement. I remember, for example, space exploration. At the time I took at most mild interest, but now I'm fascinated. What wonders we accomplished: the moon landings and Viking, and the Space Shuttle. Most of all, the confirmation by the Infrared Astronomy Satellite in '85 of the planetary system around Barnard's Star, with a fifth planet that might be very like Earth.

Suddenly Father Dougherty started the car. Jim was hurrying towards us, a thick manila envelope under his arm.

'I didn't manage to see the President,' he said as he got in, 'but I got good stuff. Some Presidential papers on radiation, and a report on the state of the upper atmosphere.'

'Meaning you two will finally do the sensible thing and leave Los Angeles?'

Jim nodded. 'I still don't have many California state documents, but maybe I'll pick some up in San Francisco.'

'So you still intend to remain in California, do you? I can't bear the thought of people getting arrested for nothing. I wish you'd reconsider. The moment you buy a White Zone ticket, the IPs will leave you alone.'

We had been through this at the rectory. We didn't need him to convince us of how poor our odds were. But the book could not be complete without a visit to San Francisco.

'We've got to try, Father.'

He sighed, then got out of the car and opened the trunk. He brought out a small suitcase, opened it on the front seat. 'These are clerics' suits. Get into the darned things and God go with you.'

I am not sure how convincing we were as priests, but the collars and jackets certainly changed our attitudes. To cops we would now seem a lot more confident, a lot more normal.

My black suit fitted well. Jim's was a bit too short. 'Well now, Fathers,' Father Dougherty said, 'you look like a couple of rascals if ever I saw them.' He showed us the priestly blessing. 'People will ask for it, so be ready to give it. God will forgive you for this little impersonation, since it's in a good cause,' he said. Then he drove us to Union Station and blessed us himself. 'Take my advice and buy your tickets on the White Zone trains.' He laughed. 'I sound like a broken record, I know. But please. For your own sakes.'

We thanked him and said goodbye.

There was an atmosphere of subdued intensity in Union Station. Along one wall of the waiting room, a high cyclone fence enclosed a makeshift holding area. In it, the morning's suspects sat on benches, most of them going through their purses and wallets before they appeared before the examiners to verify their right to be in California. These were people who had gotten through the POE nets, only to be tripped up just when they must have thought they were free.

It does not take long for such scenes to seem normal.

We bought tickets on the *Coast Daylight*, which was leaving for Oakland in thirty minutes, and sat ourselves down in the Green Zone waiting area with our tickets showing from our top pockets, like everybody else. The economy sections of the train were already full, so we were forced to buy First Class Ultras, which are four times as expensive as normal coach seats. We consoled ourselves with the thought that a police spot check of two priests in the VIP cars was unlikely.

Documents from the Acting Presidency

I believe we must adjourn this meeting to some
other place.
                                    – Last words of Adam Smith, 1790

ON THE ROAD

The federal government has been in transit since Warday.

Though diminished in size, it is still a complex institution.
Because the current President has not been legitimised by the
ballot, he considers himself more a caretaker than a leader.

For example, he would not grant me an interview on the
premise that it would not be in keeping with his 'custodial' role,
as he described it. Acting President White is in office simply
because he was vacationing at Key Largo on Warday, and had
the good sense to stay there for a month rather than attempting
to return to Washington. He was Undersecretary of the Treas-
ury, and as such was the highest federal official both to survive
the war and agree to serve as President.

I have collected here a sampling of the sort of documents that might cross the President's desk on a given day. They reflect, more than anything, a government trying to grapple with what happened to it, and to identify the direction of the future.

There was resistance to my getting these documents. Even some recently appointed federal officials are nervous that there will eventually be trials. I think not. I suspect that the people are beyond placing the details of blame.

When I found resistance to my requests, I reminded my contacts that the government has a long tradition of disclosure. The present bureaucracy is very concerned with traditions, right down to the painting of the few government cars with the exact LA motor-pool designations they would have had before the war, and the meticulous use of the old bureaucratic forms for every functional detail.

These three documents are about the one effect of Warday that is hardest to grapple with – in a way, the most consistently surprising effect: radioactivity.

It is what worries the acting President the most.

MEMORANDUM

TO: CHARLES F. DURRELL, JR.
        Assistant to the President for Emergency War Affairs

FROM: Winston Sajid
        Chairman, Committee on Long-Term Effects
        National Security Agency

DATE: 30 March 1992

SUBJ: 12th Report on Atmospheric Effects

Concurrent studies by U.S. and United Kingdom task forces suggest a continuing deterioration of stratospheric conditions. Specifically, there has been an observed depletion or thinning of the ozone layer of the upper atmosphere. Studies conducted in the summer of 1988 have been used as a baseline measure. A full report on all aspects of atmospheric deterioration is complex, but for purposes of summary it can be reported that an overall depletion of approximately 14 percent has occurred in four years.

It must be emphasized that while a further depletion might be expected in future years, it is not possible at this time to project a statistical trend with any certitude. Such a trend is difficult to predict because (1) little data were collected for approximately 18 months following the war, until atmospheric studies were resumed by the U.K. and other Western European nations; and (2) such a dramatic change in ozone levels is unprecedented and existing mathematical models are not sophisticated enough to consider all the variables.

Data are presently being gathered to document the observed increases in skin cancers, increased propensities to skin 'burns' and rashes, and the most significant ecological effects, such as the warming trends at the North and South poles, the disappearance of some subtropical vegetation, and the global depression in crop production.

At this time, the American-based U.K. atmospheric teams are preparing a series of high-altitude rocket surveys, as well as completing, with the University of Tokyo's Atmospheric Research Laboratory, a multivariate computer model designed to calculate long-term ozonal changes.

The President will be informed as soon as this Agency has had a chance in the next six months to review the results of these studies.

CONFIDENTIAL

REPORT TO THE PRESIDENT

PROJECTED LONG-TERM RADIATION EFFECTS AS A RESULT
OF THE OCTOBER 1988 WAR
PREPARED BY THE LIVERMORE NATIONAL LABORATORY
DECEMBER 7, 1992

EXECUTIVE SUMMARY

On December 1, 1992, the Livermore National Laboratory completed a six-month effort to assess existing studies on the long-term radiation effects of the October 1988 war. Data from this study were then used to calculate the somatic and genetic effects that can be expected over the next 35 to 40 years. Using information from European and Japanese sources, the study was also able to assess long-term radiation effects on areas (1) outside of the United States affected by fallout, and (2) within the Soviet Union as a result of the American counterattack.

BACKGROUND OF THE ATTACK

The Soviet attack in October 1988 was directed against three urban centers in (New York, Washington, D.C., and San Antonio, Texas) and against the operational SAC bomber base and ICBM fields located in four upper Central and Western states (Montana, Wyoming, North Dakota, and South Dakota). It is believed that some 300+ megatons (MT) of effective yield were realized in this attack. The Soviets employed a strategy against urban centers of detonating their weapons at a height of some 7,000 feet, which was clearly intended to heighten the range of destruction. Against military targets they employed a mixed strategy of airbursts against airbases and groundbursts against hardened missile silos. Airbursts and groundbursts above cities appear to have averaged some 10 MT each.

It should be remembered that impacted areas remain highly radioactive for a period of time, although considerable radioactive decay will occur within the first 30 days. Fallout, however, continues over an extended period of time. While lethal doses of radiation may not occur, sublethal doses have been common; most of this fallout, sufficient to have caused considerable injury, was material deposited in the troposphere and brought down to earth over a period of weeks, largely by rain. Some fallout was placed into the stratosphere, where it will continue to fall to earth over a period of years. Radioactive elements such as strontium 9Ø and carbon 14 have particularly long lives and pose the greatest danger over the long term.

Our projections for long-term radiation effects are perhaps most affected by the fallout of these dangerous elements.

PROJECTED LONG-TERM EFFECTS FROM RADIATION

Given the nature of the Soviet attack, the targets, calculated MT yield, and existent and projected fallout, the following somatic and genetic effects can be anticipated in the United States alone over the next 35–4Ø years:

SOMATIC EFFECTS

Cancer deaths	3,000,000
Thyroid cancers	2,000,000
Thyroid nodules	3,000,000

GENETIC EFFECTS

Abortions due to chromosomal damage	1,500,000
Other genetic effects	4,500,000

These same effects, considered for the Northern Hemisphere (concentrated between 30 degrees and 60 degrees North Latitude) for the same time period, are as follows:

SOMATIC EFFECTS

Cancer deaths	1,500,000
Thyroid cancers	1,400,000
Thyroid nodules	2,000,000

GENETIC EFFECTS

Abortions due to chromosomal damage	850,000
Other genetic effects	3,000,000

The estimated effects on the Soviet Union as a result of the American attack, over the same time period, are as follows:

SOMATIC EFFECTS

Cancer deaths	1,500,000
Thyroid cancers	2,500,000
Thyroid nodules	3,600,000

GENETIC EFFECTS

| Abortions due to chromosomal damage | 1,750,000 |
| Other genetic effects | 2,000,000 |

These projections, of course, do not include those individuals killed either during the attack or shortly thereafter.

PRESIDENTIAL BRIEFING PAPER

National Security Council
Committee on Long-Term Radiation Effects
August 27 1992

The Committee on Long-Term Radiation Effects was asked by the Executive Office on August 1, 1992, to prepare a summary of information available on the physiological and related socio-psychological effects observed to date in victims of the nuclear bombings of 1988, especially on those effects caused by or related to radiation. Further, we were asked to report wherever possible on data for both the United States and the Soviet Union. Unfortunately, scientific information is largely unavailable from the Soviet Union. Secondary observations from visiting European teams suggest, however, that long-term trends observed here in the United States are generally comparable to trends believed to exist in the USSR. It is not the intention of this summary report to describe political developments, as more complete studies of the subject are available from other government agencies.

The Committee wishes to stress from the outset that while this report summarizes a considerable body of evidence, based on classic prewar studies as well as on American and British studies undertaken since 1988, only major trends are reported here. Contemporary studies, for example, have been conducted only during the last three years, although some five years have passed since Warday. It must be noted that the full, long-term consequences of massive radiation dosages cannot be known completely at this time; this is particularly true of genetic effects.

As requested, this report will address presently observed trends in physiological/genetic injuries caused by war-related radiation exposure. Where appropriate, however, related socio-psychological effects also will be described. It is important to note that these data describe only survivors of the attack.

1.1 NEOPLASMS

The single most dramatic trend observed to date is in the inordinate number of radiation-induced neoplasms, or cancers, from some 30 percent nationwide before the war to almost 60 percent today. Studies conducted by the National Centers for Disease Control in the Washington,

D.C., zone, and by the joint American–British Radiation Effects Teams in the South Texas zone, provide the most comprehensive evidence to date that perhaps as much as 90 percent of the affected populations in both zones suffer to some degree from radiation-induced cancers. Of this population, depending upon radiation dosage (both short and cumulative), more than 60 percent have experienced malignant neoplastic diseases. Skin tumors are perhaps the most common, followed by lung, stomach, breast, and ovary/reproductive organs. The prewar cancer rate for the entire population, excluding cancer of the skin, was perhaps 30 percent; of that population, some 15–18 percent died. Exposure to radiation at the 150–200-rem level, however, effectively doubles the rate of cancer. Studies conducted after Warday suggest that more than half of the population in or near bombed areas suffered rem exposures at the 350–500 level. Aerial surveys of the Texas and New York zones suggest that individuals as far away as 2.5 miles from GZ [Ground Zero] experienced exposure levels of 100–150 rems. Those individuals two miles from GZ probably received exposures in the 500-rem level. Demographic correlates, therefore, suggest that in these two urban zones alone, more than 35 million persons experienced radiation levels sufficient to cause cancer. Correcting for those killed instantly and those who died within the first six months, some 15 million persons have now, or can be expected to have, malignancies.

Related to the dramatic rise in cancer rates is the substantial rise in leukemia, of which granulocytic leukemia is perhaps the most frequently observed. Consequently, there has been a dramatic rise in related blood diseases.

While cancer and leukemia represent the most dramatic radiation-disease trends, it must be remembered that radiation fundamentally attacks the cellular system of the body. This occurs because ionizing radiation creates changes in individual cells. When sufficient changes occur, the individual organ ceases to function properly. Cells of different types, and therefore different organs, have varying levels of radiosensitivity. Consequently, all of the following organs are susceptible, in descending order of sensitivity:

- lymphoid tissue and bone marrow
- epithelial tissues, such as the ovaries and testes and the skin
- blood vessels
- smooth and striated muscles
- differentiated nerve cells

Nerves in general are the most resistant to radioactivity, although the nerves of embryos and of the adult cerebellum are exceptions and are quite sensitive.

1.2 CATARACTS

The incidence of non-vision-disturbing lens opacities, or cataracts, also has increased markedly. These cataracts are similar to those reported in cases where individuals have experienced an overexposure to X-rays or gamma radiation. Fast neutrons are generally regarded as the primary source of this disease. It is suspected that cataracts of the type observed are caused by exposure to radiation dosages of 300 rems or more. Although firm data are not available, extrapolations of observed sample populations suggest that between 12 and 15 percent of the population, or ten million persons, have or will develop radiation-induced cataracts. It is not known at this time what percentage will require surgical treatment.

1.3 SKIN DISEASES

Skin diseases, in addition to the neoplasms described above, are largely related to radiation burns, usually caused by beta particles. Skin diseases caused by fallout can be from beta and/or gamma radiation. Diseases of this sort range from sensations of 'burning' to skin discoloration, lesions, ulcers, formation of keloids, or overgrowths of scar tissue, epilation or baldness, and atrophied limbs or whole portions of body surfaces.

Again, although hard data are not available, statistical projections based on observed samples suggest that some 75 million persons are or can be expected to be infected with varying degrees of skin diseases.

It is important to note that the substantial areas of the United States still designated Dead, Red, or Orange Zones for their varying radiation levels almost certainly guarantee a continuing population of afflicted individuals. Those populations located adjacent to radioactive zones come into contact regularly with objects or contaminants of one kind or another that either engender first-time exposures or form part of the cumulative exposure so frequently reported by local and regional medical centers. Radioactive foodstuffs are a continuing source of contamination, as are objects 'looted' from restricted or forbidden areas. The greatest single source of 'new' radiation, however, is that dropped by atmospheric fallout. Fission products such as cesium 137 (half-life of 30.5 years), strontium 90 (half-life of 27.7 years), and carbon 14 (half-life of 5,760 years) are perhaps the most important contributors to long-term radioactive exposures. Their effect upon skin diseases is more ascertainable; their effects on internal systems are unknown and therefore merit close medical study.

1.4 GENETIC ALTERATIONS

It is well documented that exposure to radiation in measurable amounts causes changes in the hereditary components of reproductive cells. Observations of nuclear industry workers, as well as of the victims of World War II atomic bombings, confirm these effects in future generations. However, none of these prewar populations was exposed to such high and continuing levels of radiation as have been the populations of the United States and the Soviet Union. Genetic mutations have been noted in both countries and in adjacent countries where radioactivity is present through fallout in abnormal counts.

The process of genetic alteration is very complex and beyond the scope of this report. Full implications of genetic changes are not known and will not be known for multiple generations, although some ten million people in the United States are expected to be affected during the next 25–35 years. The following observations, however, serve to illustrate the extreme changes that have already occurred. Until extensive studies are completed, it is impossible to differentiate between those genetic changes caused by minor radiation exposures (Ø to 25Ø rems, for example) and changes caused by higher levels of exposure (25Ø to 5ØØ rems). Also, it is presently impossible to understand the different effects of radiation absorbed all at once or cumulatively, in terms of resultant generatic alterations.

In summary, then, the following genetic trends have been observed in individuals exposed to varying levels of radiation:

- increased rates of sterility of 65 percent
- increased rates of abortions caused by chromosomal damage of 27 percent
- increased rates of stillbirths to 35 out of every 1ØØ births
- increased rates of children born with physical handicaps of 57 percent
- specific increase of 32 percent in frequency of children born with varying levels of mental retardation
- increased rate of 28 percent in infant deaths
- increased rates of 25–3Ø percent of chronic susceptibility to disease in young children born after Warday, especially to respiratory and cardiac diseases

1.5 NONSPECIFIC SCLEROSING SYNDROME

While not necessarily induced by radiation exposure, Nonspecific Sclerosing Disease, or NSD, is noted more frequently in individuals, and in populations as a whole, that have been exposed to radioactivity, especially in populations adjacent to contaminated areas. Early symptoms include parched skin, mostly on the chest or abdomen, and the development of lumpy swellings over the surface of the body. Lack of appetite or anorexia follows, often complicated by difficulty in breathing. Eventually there is a collapse of the internal organs. Very little is known about NSD. The origin of the disease and its etiology are little understood. It is perhaps trauma-related, although individuals almost always have had exposure to radiation above 100 rems. There appears to be no treatment at this time, and the fatality rate varies between 70 and 100 percent among those who contract it.

1.6 GENERAL

There is a whole family of medical conditions related to the shock and trauma associated with nuclear war. Much has been written about the broad sociological changes that have occurred in the last four years, especially regarding individual and societal perceptions of national and international government, long-term security, possibilities for international accord, and fundamental changes in relationships between individuals at all levels of society. This report, however, is concerned with effects of a more physiological nature.

In both child and adult populations there is a marked increase in general susceptibility to disease. No doubt this susceptibility is influenced by stress, lack of suitable diet or caloric intake, and depressed metabolic levels. Continuing unsanitary conditions in or near War Zones are another major contributor to high levels of illnesses such as influenza and dysentery.

There is an increase in the number of persons displaying high levels of depression, dysphoria, unprovoked fears, etc.

Also, there is an increase in the number of persons exhibiting pronounced and chronic shock and disorientation. In some cases this condition, if severe enough, produces abnormal and often violent reactions to ordinary stimuli. It is estimated that some 10–15 million persons exhibit permanent disorientation. It is believed that this condition is a major factor in the large nomadic sub-populations that live on the fringes of the War Zones.

It should be mentioned here that a considerable portion of the population demonstrates varying degrees of phobic reactions to real or imagined radiation. There is a very pervasive fear of radioactive contamination, which has led to excessive countermeasures, such as over-strict local or regional laws. This abnormal fear is present even in 'safe' areas such as California and the Northwestern states.

Other conditions, also believed to be trauma-induced, include marked increases in the reported rates of impotence, baldness, and a range of 'sympathetic' ailments in individuals with little or no exposure to radiation.

SUMMARY

Less than four years have passed since Warday. While the full long-term implications of radioactivity are not known with certainty, sufficient trends have emerged to provide a disturbing portrait of surviving American society. The Committee recognizes that while the full effects of nuclear war are many, it is clear that the United States will have as a major concern, for many decades to come, the treatment of radiation-related diseases.

Both the Executive and Legislative branches of government should place their highest priority on the care and treatment of those members of the population who have suffered, or will suffer, the lasting effects of this war. The evidence is sufficient to document the alarming rise in human systemic illnesses; the effects upon the newly born and upon generations to come are even more disturbing.

SIGNED: Charles Wilson, M.D.
Everett Simkin, M.D.
Mary Louise Amadden, Ph.D.
William Lloyd, M.D.
Mario de los Santos, Ph.D.
Trevett Cole, Jr., Ph.D.

Coast Daylight to San Francisco

The *Super Chief*, the *Broadway Limited*, the *Twentieth Century* – these legendary trains came to mind as the sparkling *Coast Daylight* left Union Station and picked up speed past the Los Angeles County Jail. Soon we were heading towards Santa Barbara and the north.

We were on a super deluxe train – or at least in the super deluxe part of it, in a beautifully refurbished Superliner observation car. It was decorated in tan, with luxurious club-style seating and a view of the California coast so spectacular that we almost missed the appetiser tray.

'Father,' the tan-uniformed waiter said, leaning forward to present me with an array of shrimp, oysters, crab claws, and raw vegetables to go with my Bloody Mary.

These wonders were part of the ticket price – a hefty eleven dollars. Lunch in the spacious and spotless dining car behind us was included as well. I suppose we could even have taken the roses on the table, had we wanted them.

Also included, as it turned out, was conversation with Mr Tanaka, a Japanese rail official, who happened to be sitting beside us, watching the passing view of the ocean.

On our train trip to Needles, people had not been willing to talk much. But that was another world. Those were refugees;

here in the first-class section of the *Coast Daylight* were the new prime movers, and they were not afraid to speak their minds.

'This train's barely doing sixty,' Mr Tanaka scoffed, apparently his way of starting a conversation.

'How do you know that?' Jim asked. I saw him turn on his recorder.

'Simple. Each rail is thirty-three feet long. Each "click" you hear means one rail. I count the number of clicks every sixty seconds and thus calculate the train's speed.'

'Are you a trainman?'

Mr Tanaka gave Jim a card that read H. TANAKA, TECHNICAL DIRECTOR, NIPPON-AMERICA INTERNATIONAL RAIL CORP., 1130 SUNLAND BUILDING, LOS ANGELES.

'I'm Father William,' Jim said. 'This is Father Brown.'

We exchanged handshakes. 'What's a Japanese railroad man doing here in California?' I asked.

'Ah, a great deal. This is the land of opportunity. Things need to be done here! We're working with your government to create the most modern train system in North America. LA to Oakland in an hour and twenty minutes, and that includes a five-minute stop in Bakersfield. How do you like that?'

'Extraordinary.'

'It's because of a revolutionary new transport system we call a magnetic-cushion tube train. Top cruising speed potential of five hundred miles an hour. Of course, this run is too short to reach that speed. But one day we'll be going all the way to Seattle. Then you'll see some speed.'

'What about air travel? Aren't planes coming back?'

'Don't talk to me about the competition! I'm telling you, we can move more people faster and with greater efficiency than the best airline in the world. Our energy costs are thirty per cent less than the most efficient jet engines now under development back home. Planes can never compete.'

'But all those miles of track –'

'Prefabricated aboveground tunnel segments with magnetic cushions inside. Built in Japan very cheaply and shipped here for easy installation. The roadbed is a circular magnetic field in the tunnel. The train floats in it. Our cost per mile is about three million gold, and if California can't get the money directly, it can find a way to obtain it from the Feds.'

It seemed a lot to me.

'This thing is creeping,' Tanaka scoffed. 'Bullet trains do better at home with dead birds on the windshields.'

'How long have you been in the United States?'

'Since 1990. I've got my whole family here now. We bought a house in Beverly Hills last year. Lovely house. Pola Negri used to live there. Or maybe Theda Bara, we're not sure. We are redoing the gardens and installing a complete computerised home security system. It's lots of fun, because such huge houses are unobtainable in Japan.'

'How do you find working here?'

'I love it! There's so much to be done. A whole new world is being built in this country, and it's starting with California.'

'Do you approve of California's immigration policies?'

'Not my business. I'm a foreigner. My interest is in getting people from place to place fast. I don't care why they make their journeys.'

'How about the rest of the country? Have you done any travelling?'

'Well, Japan Air Lines operates an all-America tour, but we haven't taken it. I don't want to fool around with radiation.' He lifted his left hand. Two of the fingers were grown together, a thick stump. 'My mother was at Nagasaki.' There came silence between us. 'The road can be very hard,' he said at last. 'This we Japanese have learned.'

After a moment he settled back, contemplating the black cliffs and the slow blue sea.

Golden City

The *Daylight* reached Oakland at 8.36 in the evening. As soon as we got off the train I went to a phone booth and called my one contact in the area, a writer named Quinn Yarbro, whom I had known before the war.

Quinn wrote historical novels back when such things were popular. I haven't seen her name on anything in the Doubleday bookstore in Dallas in years, so I had no idea what had happened to her. There seemed to me a risk in using long distance in California, so I had delayed trying to call her until we were actually here. I dialled the last number I had for her.

After five rings an older woman answered. 'Yarbro Locators,' she said.

'May I speak to Quinn, please?'

'This is she. May I help you?'

'Quinn? This is Whitley.'

'Oh God, where are you calling from?'

'Oakland. I just came up from LA. I have a friend with me. We're doing a book on America together. We're here to see San Francisco.'

'Whitley, this is – I mean, I'm in the locating business, so I guess I shouldn't be surprised – but –'

'I lived, Quinn.'

'Oh God, Whitley, I assumed – with you in New York and all.'

'We've been living in Dallas. Anne and Andrew too.'

She told us to take the BART to Market and Powell in San Francisco. 'I – well, I'll wear something recognisable. If I must, a blue fedora.'

'Quinn, we're dressed like priests.'

'Ah. Okay. Shall I expect to pray?'

'Just look for two middle-aged priests with backpacks.'

'I'm sure I won't have any trouble. And you can forget the darned fedora. I'll find you.'

We travelled on BART for fifteen cents. The highest fare is a quarter, the lowest a penny. The trains are jammed and not particularly frequent, but they work. Like so many things in California, much EMP-related damage sustained by BART has been repaired. There are ticket clerks, however, instead of computerised machines, and my impression was that the trains were directly controlled by their motormen rather than by a central computer. I noticed signal lights along the tracks much like those in the old New York subway system.

Even past nine at night, the Powell Street station resounded with the footsteps of a swarming crowd. Like Los Angeles, the San Francisco area has sustained a massive population influx in the past few years – despite the efforts of the immigration police.

'Hello, Father Whitley.'

She was older, very much older. 'Quinn.' There were tears at the corners of her eyes. Finding old friends alive hurts. It is a pain one at once seeks and fears. I embraced Quinn. I touched her hair, which was still red but struck with grey. Her eyes, looking at me, were wide. Jim stood nearby, silent, not intruding, waiting. 'Quinn, this is Jim Kunetka.'

'Father Jim?'

'Simply Jim. This is a disguise.'

'I'm glad. You both look too thin to be priests. I'd peg you as robbers.'

'Is there much crime in California?' Jim asked, ever the newsman.

'More than before the war. People are so desperate. We have rich and poor and not much in between.'

'It looks so good.'

'It's still got the best weather in the world, anyway.'

'Quinn, we're fugitives.'

She laughed. 'I gathered that. You want to get off the street?'
'Exactly.'

She offered to put us up at her apartment on Russian Hill. We rode the Powell–Hyde cable car for two cents each. There was an 'I Stop at the St Francis' sign on the front of the car, and the familiar yellow destination sign: Powell & Market, Hyde & Beach. We had to hang on all the way. The gripman was a master with his bell, and he needed to be – the streets were jammed with pedestrians. On the way, Quinn asked if we'd eaten dinner. We had not. Lunch on the train had seemed sufficient for a month. I can remember very long periods of my life without so much food. And the freshness of it was unforgettable, as was the menu: lima beans cooked in real butter, a thick lamb chop with the juice running in the plate, mashed potatoes with pan gravy, an endive salad, two different wines, and, for dessert, frozen pecan balls.

It is no wonder that people are willing to risk prison to come to California.

Despite the danger of the streets, we could not resist seeing if we could tuck in a dinner in Chinatown. I thought at once of a certain restaurant. 'Dare I ask if Kan's is still there?'

'Kan's is still there.'

We hopped off the cable car and went looking. Kan's had not changed at all. The restaurant had opened in 1936, and it retains the comfortable spaciousness of former times. If I was impressed by lunch on the train, I was delighted by dinner here, even though I couldn't eat much. A stomach used to a simpler diet cannot adjust quickly to the richness of California food.

In a way, being at Kan's made me sad. Anne and I had taken five days in San Francisco in the summer of '87. Andrew was at camp and we flew out for the chance to be alone together, to see a few good friends, to enjoy the city. It was our last vacation, and we had our last meal in San Francisco at Kan's.

Over dinner, the three of us traded lives. As soon as Quinn understood what we were doing, she had an idea. 'I know a man you'll want to interview. If you're trying to understand things, he's somebody who probably knows. He's an economist, and he teaches at Berkeley. He's also somebody I love. He'll be over to the apartment in the morning. You can meet him then.'

Neither of us had heard of Dr Walter Tevis. I doubt, however, that we will ever forget him.

I asked her what she was doing. 'I'm a gumshoe,' she said.

'A what?'

'A detective.'

Jim went pale. I was stunned. It wasn't possible that we were in the hands of the police.

'I'm not a cop,' she said, 'so you can redirect some blood into your faces. I find lost people. I'll try to locate anybody you're missing. If I succeed, I get a fee.'

'You must be incredibly busy,' I said.

'Very.'

Jim leaned forward. 'My wife – I lost her in Austin right after Warday.' His face was suddenly sharp, his eyes boring into Quinn's.

'Give me her name and description and last known address. I'll see what I can do. It might take some time, you understand.'

Jim gave her the information.

After dinner she took us to her apartment, on a hidden Russian Hill byway called Keys Alley. 'I warn you, I still have cats,' she said as she let us into the single cluttered room. A huge red furball came up and began protesting.

The room was jammed with the tools of her trade. There were stacks of old telephone books from dozens of cities, city directories, maps, old newspapers, census tracts, Zip Code directories, copies of birth certificates in lettered stacks, card files and Rolodexes identified by coloured tags, and hundreds and hundreds of photographs in thick black albums.

I could see how she carried out her trade, working from the telephone and through the mails. It must have been a frustrating and difficult job.

'Sorry about the mess.' She sat down. She looked, then, very small and tired and somewhat lost herself. 'A lot of people are missing,' she said.

Jim and I slept on the floor. Just as I was dropping off, the cat woke me by flopping down on my face. I moved it aside and sat up. The little room was quiet. Quinn was a shadow on her couch. On the table beside her was a Princess telephone attached to an answering machine whose power lamp glowed red. I wondered how she managed. She must be besieged with clients. Names and names and names.

A trapped feeling came upon me and made me get up and put on my collar and my black suit and go out to get some night air.

Keys Alley was silent, lit through the leaves of trees lining the street. Music drifted in the dark, a radio playing an old, old song I could not name, but which drew me back to childhood summer nights, watching my bedroom curtains make shadows on the walls and listening to my parents and their friends talking in low voices under the trees outside, talking of the cares of forty years ago, Truman and the cost of the Marshall Plan and Stalin's health.

I stepped softly as I left the silent alley. I went up Pacific Street to the crest, then turned and looked down across the roofs of Chinatown to the Bay. The view is not one of San Francisco's most spectacular, but it satisfied me. Far out in the Bay I heard foghorns beginning to sound above the subdued rumble of the city. The hour was late; midnight had come and gone.

Slowly, nearer horns started sounding. A fog was coming through the Golden Gate. Soon I could see it slipping up the streets and across the roofs, dulling lights, drawing the dark close around me.

When it swirled up Pacific, cold and damp, transforming crisp night sounds to whispers and making me shudder with the cold of it, I returned to the stuffy little flat and the sounds of Quinn and Jim sleeping, and the cat purring.

Sometime in the night the phone gave half a ring and the answering machine clicked. I heard a voice talking quickly into the recorder, quickly and endlessly, droning, filling my sleep with a tale of loss I no longer remember.

Interview: Walter Tevis, Economist

What happened to the economy on Warday was quite simple. Six out of every ten dollars disappeared. The Great Depression of the thirties was caused by the stock market crash of 1929, when three out of ten dollars ceased to exist. Simultaneously, we lost the ability to communicate. We lost all our current records. Chaos was inevitable. We're fortunate that the continuing deflationary process hasn't been worse.

All the money that was somehow in process in the computer systems of the government and private banks simply ceased to exist because of electromagnetic disruption or, in the case of Washington, permanent and total destruction. That was about one dollar in ten, but it was all hypercritical money, because it was in motion. It was the liquid cash, what people were using to pay other people.

The other thing that happened was that records were thrown into chaos. Records that had survived, but only on magnetic media, might as well have been destroyed because they couldn't be read. The destruction of the computers was exactly like the failure of a nervous system in a body. All of a sudden there were no messages getting through. The body lost contact with itself.

Storage companies such as the Iron Mountain Group preserved a great deal of data in underground facilities. Without the machines stored underground, as a matter of fact, there wouldn't have been a single functional computer left in the United States after Warday. The wisdom of those storage and preservation programmes is now obvious. Without them, for example, there couldn't have been the gold distribution of '90. Even so, most people had only about fourteen per cent of the dollar value of their prewar cash holdings restored.

Between the cash lost in transit and the inaccessible records, we were out about three dollars in ten. The collapse of Social Security, Medicaid, and the whole federal entitlement system meant another two dollars gone when those cheques stopped arriving from Washington. The loss of the rest of the federal budget was another dollar gone. In a few hours the cash economy of this country was more than cut in half.

And there was more to come, of course. This sudden loss of cash meant that thousands of banks and businesses were bankrupt. But they were also without the means to communicate, or the records to communicate about. So people didn't get paid, or if they did, the banks couldn't cash their cheques, and the next thing we knew, most nonessential businesses were shutting down.

Add to that the complete anarchy that reigned in the stock market, with people frantic to escape New York City and the electronic records in mayhem and the sell orders roaring in – it meant the end of Wall Street, essentially.

The next thing was the calling in of loans by foreign banks. In the mad scramble to leave the dollar, the whole delicate Eurocurrency market trembled and then collapsed.

By this point the state of the world monetary system made the Great Depression look positively healthy.

It will take years to recover. It's a funny thing that before the war the great economic bugaboo was inflation. God knows, deflation can be worse. Money's so damned hard to get because there's so little of it around. I'd rather work an hour for twenty inflated dollars than a day for fifty deflated cents! And in terms of buying power per hour worked, we Americans are operating at about a sixth of the prewar efficiency level, meaning it takes six times as long as it did before the war to earn the same amount of buying power.

You'd better believe that goes for economists, too!

I was vacationing on St Bart's on Warday. I'd been there for three days and planned to stay another eleven. A few days after the war, the police rounded up all the tourists and put us aboard a passing cruise ship, the *Canberra*. There was a great deal of trouble. The *Canberra* wasn't prepared to take on over a thousand extra passengers. The first thing that happened that made this feel like a war was that a man refused to leave the police launch he was in. He said he had rights; he had prepaid his vacation. The police threw him into the water and sailed off.

That, more than anything, brought home to me the fact that the world had changed. We were not affected by EMP, so we still had radios. We were glued to them, listening mostly to the BBC. There was this curious, terrifying silence across most of the dial. The United States was silent. Cuba was silent. The BBC reported massive fires in New York and Washington, and said that flights from England had been forced to return without landing because of unsettled conditions in other American cities.

My daughter was in school at Colgate. My wife was at our home in New York. At that time I was working for the Chase Econometric Institute, forecasting flow of money, which is my speciality. I had taken some time off to be alone and to think about the consequences of the massive IMF refunding that had been proposed the week before by the Saudis. This was critical to Chase because it affected the viability of our Nigerian loans, and thus our whole African exposure. Not only that, our failure to support the proposal could call into question our relationship with the Saudis. But with free-market oil soft at twenty-two dollars, and the Mexican and Brazilian debt moratoriums creating cash-flow problems for the bank, we were concerned that we would not be able to sustain the additional loan demand the refunding would create.

So I was alone on an island with my computer and all the data I needed, quietly developing flow analyses and projections based on various cash/loan levels.

I never dreamed that the bank I worked for was about to become a part of history, and the computer I worked with worth considerably more than its weight in gold. My initial concern was just to get home. I kept thinking, standing at the rail of the *Canberra* on that warm October afternoon, feeling the reassuring hum of the ship beneath my feet, of my wife and daughter and that measured BBC voice saying, 'New York is burning.'

For some reason I just assumed the Russians had won. I felt that as an employee of a capitalist bank, I would not have much of a future.

I don't want to go into my whole life story over the past five years. Suffice to say that it has been sad in some ways, but in others lucky. I have been preserved from the suffering and upheaval that have blighted so many lives. Of course, I lost my wife and daughter, but since I met Quinn here in San Francisco, I have found that I can contend with the hollowness inside me, and the awful sense of having deserted them. Quinn hasn't been successful in finding them. In looking for them I found her, I guess.

The *Canberra* eventually docked at New Orleans. Since the war, I have not gone north of Atlanta. I put my name in the Red Cross National Finders, but nothing ever came of it. And of course, Quinn's scoured the earth. Even so, I still look at the lists every month, when they post them in the Student Union. But Berkeley is a world away from the war.

Hell. I'm a goddamn coward, is what I am. My little girl could be anywhere and I'm afraid to go look for her. I'm so scared of radiation. Even while it's killing you, you don't know it's there. I wake up in the night when the wind blows down from the mountains, thinking maybe some microscopic bit of plutonium from the Dakotas has found its way here, and is aiming for my lungs. I get these weird, nonspecific sicknesses. So I go to the Medical Centre and they tell me I'm fine. Once I heard them showing a man on triage how to manage lung cancer by breathing steam!

I went to a psychologist. I went to an osteopath. I went to a witch.

Now listen, I'm really getting off on a personal tangent. I think in a sense that I've developed the habit of being a patient. Half the world is starving and I'm worried about my own damn guilt trip.

This interview method is cunning. You guys find the people who *want* to talk, don't you, and then just let 'em rip. Get a man's secrets right on disc.

What are you, a couple of State Intelligence or MI-5 types? We've got both around Berkeley, believe me. The British are good friends to this country. The best friends. But they are also very interested in using the current crisis to solidify their international position, shall we say.

One thing I'm sure of. There will never be another United States as free, as powerful, as magnificent as there was before. From a statistical standpoint, we regressed too far. Now outsiders can control how much reconstruction we do of our technological base industries, and thus make sure we stay just far enough behind not to be a threat. The tendency of Japan and Europe is to look upon the US and Russia as two countries that went kind of mad. By 1980 or '81, both nations were effectively insane. The accession of Reagan the actor and Andropov the human computer were the first sure symptoms of the war madness, according to the poolside theories of my friend Dr Hideo Hayakawa, who is a psychopolitical theorist.

We have about a hundred and seventy-five million people in this country, and the death rate still exceeds the viable birth rate by two to one. So we've had a net loss of fifty-five million people. That's twenty million births and seventy-five million actual deaths. We have *lost* as many people as there are in England. Yet look at the English. They're all over the place. Two thousand British bureaucrats are running this country through the blind of the Relief, which is really a colonial government disguised as a sort of Red Cross with teeth. The provisional US government in LA is gaining strength every day, but so far it's mostly paperwork and planning.

The Capital Replacement Program, where the government prints money to replace the capital of corporations that lost it in the banking catastrophe, has been effective here in California, but so far it hasn't spread beyond the borders. Thus we're dealing with a three per cent inflation rate out here, which is really only reflation of the deflated currency, while the rest of the country is still deflating.

I recall my own personal sense of panic when I discovered that I had no money. None. Even my MasterCard was meaningless. My bank account was simply another lost record among billions of lost records. Our economy was electronically erased, really.

One of the great acts of economic heroism – which, as usual, nobody outside the profession understands at all – was the creation of the Gold Tier in the currency. Barker Findlay, the chairman of the Federal Reserve, is responsible for that idea. If he

hadn't been in Atlanta on Warday – if he had been in Washington – I hate to think about it.

We have experienced an economic situation with no known
parallels. We've been in uncharted territory. At home we had
dollar deflation due to scarcity, while abroad our currency was
becoming as worthless as if it had inflated itself out of existence.
So you had a situation where a house in the States might cost
a thousand dollars, while in Italy, say, a thousand dollars
wouldn't buy a cup of coffee. This has hurt trade very badly. If it
weren't for the gold, we'd be dead in the water as a trading
nation. But we're doing pretty well – and out here on the Coast
we're beginning actually to thrive – because we've been able to
pay in gold for foreign products. By the time the gold gives out,
it's to be hoped that we'll have enough independent production
to be able to offer goods for trade.

What we are doing is supporting ourselves on gold transfers to
foreign companies. The National Mint in Atlanta makes all those
beautiful double eagles we send abroad in return for the few and
astronomically overpriced televisions and radios and computers
the colonial powers will send us.

Around the economics faculty here, it's popular to say that the
undamaged powers need our markets. The hell they do. You
didn't see Belgium developing the Congo. They do not need our
markets, they need our resources, and they will encourage
American economic development just enough to get our agricultural system running on a stable base, and then they will put
the brakes on.

Our First World friends want to develop their own technological economy *without reference* to us. They want America to be
an agricultural nation. We supply the corn and wheat and
soybeans and they give us an occasional stripped Toyota. And
yet, we *have* the plant and equipment here. Detroit is three-
fourths idle, but it didn't get bombed. And EMP did not damage
it that much. You can build cars without computers. Hell, we did
just fine at it, right up until the seventies. So why aren't the
plants in Detroit running? Oh, I'll grant the flow from American
plants out here on the Coast, but look at the cars – a mess. Plastic
doors, for God's sake. Look at the difference between a Chevy
Consensus and, for example, a Leyland Star or a Toyota. It's
ridiculous. We don't even have any chrome! And yet a Consensus costs more than a Toyota! You can get a Toyota 4xD Timbre

for thirty gold dollars, but no paper currency accepted. A Consensus costs three thousand one hundred paper. With a hundred paper to one gold, that's still a hundred dollars more for far less car. Of course, if you're like most people, you can't *get* gold to buy a Toyota, so you end up with the Consensus.

Now let's see. What haven't I covered? Ah yes, debt. The federal debt, of course, has ceased to exist, largely because of the failure of so many records. And the moratorium on remaining prewar debt will be made permanent within the year, in my opinion. Or at least restructured to new dollars. I mean, you can't expect a man who earns a thousand dollars a year to pay off a hundred-thousand-dollar mortgage, can you? That would have to be pared down at least ten times. Besides, it's unfair to a man whose debt records survived to penalise him with responsibility for them when another man, whose records were lost, gets off scot-free.

I wish you guys would talk to me. I know I agreed to do this solo, but I'm really very uncomfortable with two heavily disguised roadies sitting across from me with a very expensive-looking disk recorder, no matter if you're Quinn's friends or not. I don't know what I've been saying. Maybe I've been a bit subversive. The British have been a tremendous help to us. So have the other Europeans. And the Japanese. I think we would have gone back to the barter level without access to their technology and services, and our economic efficiency would have declined too far to enable us to adjust to the continuing condemnation of farmland in the Midwest. Famine would have become a permanent institution. And, just for the record, I adore California and if anything I may have said implied otherwise, it was a mis-statement.

I think I can lay my hands on some figures. Yes – these come from the US Census Bureau, by the way, the Statistical Abstract of the United States, extrapolated to 1991 from original 1987 data, and taking into account war damage.

First, to say that nobody understood the effects of EMP would be superfluous now. We lost, in about three seconds, approximately a hundred and fifty million television sets; five hundred million radios; ten million computers; three hundred million electronic calculating devices; fifty-six million electronic telephones; all television, radio, and microwave relay stations; all electronic business exchanges, such as stock and commodity exchanges; millions of electronic automobile ignitions; most electronically dependent aircraft, either crashed or permanently disabled; all communications satellites, either traversing or in geostationary orbit above the United States, Canada, and the USSR; and something in the order of two hundred trillion pieces of information held in computers.

The war burned down the electronic village, is what it did. What we had not understood was that our financial system depended on that village. All of our destinies were contained in fragile electronic superbrains, and so we have been deprived of destinies. I guess that's the real point of war, isn't it? To create intolerable deprivations and induce deaths.

Since the war we've been like a great lobotomised beast, flopping and struggling in the trackless void, unable to control or comprehend even the smallest shred of its own destiny.

After 1983 the government and many private companies began shielding against the highest level of EMP pulse they could, without spending intolerable sums. That was fifty to a hundred thousand megavolts, depending on the type of system being shielded.

So the Russians simply used larger bombs and tripled the power of the EMP pulse generated. A few extra warheads made billions and billions of dollars' worth of shielding useless.

Because of the ease with which the pulse strength can be increased, EMP shielding is essentially impossible without a vast amount of investment and effort.

Before Warday, we were living in a dream world.

Christ, sometimes I think I'll get up and just walk into the river. Thinking about what mayhem our little bitty nuclear war caused makes me crazy. For example, there's this extraordinary place down the Coast. I know people who've been there. Undreamed-of technologies! A European preserve of ultimate luxury. Shuttles to luxurious space stations we are told nothing about. A new world, and we are being left out of it. I know people who say they've seen that port. Somewhere between here and Baja, I don't know where. They want to send us back to the Stone Age so they can have the stars to themselves.

Oh no, that's paranoia. Rumours. I doubt that the Europeans even have any space shuttles. They suffered too, economically.

I hear about this European plan to create zones in the United States. A British Zone, a German Zone, and so forth. I know that the federal government in LA is opposed to that sort of thing. But there's *never* anything about forming a second Continental Congress and appointing a new electoral college. Or elections. They say we're too electronically disorganised. The last time this nation had a population of a hundred and seventy-five million was 1955, and we managed to vote quite well then without computers. We had no four-lane interstate highway system then, but we travelled freely, and we had a thriving steel industry, a thriving auto industry, a powerful military, a strong and effective government, and a reasonably content population. Remember the Eisenhower years? You guys must have been kids then. There was no sense of dislocation. Not like now.

Of course, there's the fact that we've had a war. But now these little European states are trying to tie down the giant with a million threads! After World War II, Germany and Japan were far more devastated than we are now, but we poured on the aid and they revived.

Oh, what the hell. You can't blame them for being fed up with superpowers. All they probably want is to see the US broken up into a number of small, independent nations. Can't blame them, damn it.

You know, the problem with being a person like me, at the centre of a big university economics department, is that I get too much low-grade information. Although I must say one thing, the British have been very free and open with their statistics. Also, we are beginning to see real bureaucratic reorganisation in the US government.

Now that I think of it, perhaps I've painted too black a picture. I'm overwrought because I need facts in my profession, and I never get facts any more. Conjecture. Rumour. Estimate. That's my problem.

I think there is a panic state in this country so deep that people don't even acknowledge it. Subconsciously we're panicked, all of us, and some of us are worse than that. Some of us seem fine on the surface, but inside ourselves we are insane. Take that quack medical group, the Radiant Exercise people, the ones who expose themselves to radiation to acclimatise themselves. They're mad. Mad as hatters. And the Positive Extinctionists. And above all the Destructuralist Movement. That one's really dangerous, because it's so darned seductive. Give up. Live hand to mouth.

Become a goddamn caveman. That's what the Destructuralists are saying. Despite all that has happened, I don't think humanity would do a service to the planet by voluntarily rejoining the apes, which is what Destructuralism is really all about.

Another thing that's mad is the movement in Europe to make us pay reparations. For what? Both combatant powers lost the war. By staying out, Europe won it. Now it turns out that the whole European peace movement, the Greens and such, were secretly supported by the very governments they were opposing, to give the Soviet Union the impression that Europe was too divided to be dangerous. Meanwhile, the Secret Treaties – you've heard about those? Don't look at me with such blank faces! What are you, a couple of idiots? I'm not a political science professor. The English and the Germans and the French and probably the Italians and the Japanese all had secret treaties to the effect that in the event of a sudden and unexpected nuclear war between the two superpowers, they would seize American nuclear components on their soil. So the Russians had us isolated and didn't even know it. It's pitiful. If they had but known, they wouldn't have felt nearly so cornered by Spiderweb.

Let me tell you something. There's a school of thought that the Europeans tempted the Soviets into getting trigger-happy by revealing those treaties to them and making the Western Alliance seem disastrously split. Their real purpose was to trick the superpowers into crushing one another. And they succeeded brilliantly. We're in a state of advanced confusion. And the Soviets! My God, from what I've heard, they've dissolved. We got a report from the London School of Economics to the effect that the Soviet's Eastern European empire is gone. Poland, Rumania, Hungary renounced COMECON. Czechoslovakia broke off diplomatic relations with the Russians. Now the Czechs are under United German protection, whatever that means. Russia lost Moscow just the way we lost Washington. And there were those purple bombs in the Ukraine. Nobody knows what they were, but they killed every stalk of wheat, and now nothing will grow there. The LSE report estimates that the USSR has lost close to half of its population. It's divided into republics, military areas, communist states, even a White Russian enclave. A madhouse of starving, diseased inmates that nobody can help. Then there's China, India, Bangladesh. Do you know about them? About the fate of the world, my friends?

There has been a great reduction in the numbers of humanity on this planet.

When the fallout blew south and east out of the Dakotas, we lost most of the stored grain in the Midwest. And we had to abandon crops on about twenty-eight per cent of our grain-planted acres. Smoke blotted out the sun for so long the temperature dropped in the Midwest. Add to that the cash crisis, the collapse of the banking system, the disruption of transport, and you have a net farm output down fifty-five per cent by 1989. And in 1990 we dropped to thirty-eight per cent of 1987 levels. Farm machinery broke down and spare parts were hard to get. People couldn't get their land tested for radiation, and they abandoned it rather than breathe the dust of their own soil. You had hundreds of thousands of good acres abandoned, and then the great dust storms. That's not over yet. That's going to be a problem. If we don't get in there and at least reseed the land with grass, we're going to see the bare topsoil in the Midwest blowing all the way to the Atlantic and the Gulf. Of course, that would be the end of this country as a farming entity. We'd then have another famine.

The Agriculture Department is pushing hard to do this reseeding from the air. The trouble is, we can't get enough grass seed! There isn't enough, not in all the world, to get cover on all the fallow acres before next spring. The past few years we've had long, wet winters. We've had dry springs, but not dry enough to cause more than local dust problems. But time is against us.

Let's see now, which of my peeves and beefs haven't I covered? Well, there's the state of the industrial economy. The fact that most Americans are travelling in trains when we could easily be flying. The fact that the Japanese will *not* provide us with the equipment to build microchips on our own. Short-term, that's a sensible policy for them, but in the long run the vision of America as an agricultural society, industrially backward and politically castrated, just isn't going to work.

We're seeing one good thing, though, and so far it hasn't been interrupted, except by Japan. This is the return of American technology from abroad. We've recently seen RCA's whole Singapore and Taiwan manufacturing facilities returned. They're in Los Angeles now, in twelve bonded warehouses, the equipment we need to start producing a whole new generation of computers on American soil. And we've kept our intellectual base intact. Our schools are still damn good. We've had IBM equipment returned from Europe, Pan Am and TWA planes from all over the world, US military equipment coming back, all sorts of things like that.

But we could easily absorb millions of small computers, and hundreds of thousands of large ones. Not to mention radios and televisions in the hundreds of millions. Net import of televisions in 1991 was exactly six million units. You know what a Sony TV costs, of course. Ridiculous, that the average American would have to put in six months' work to buy a television set – if he can convert his paper to gold. Of course, I understand the Japanese problem. They can't possibly produce enough electronic equipment to satisfy US needs. What's more, we can't afford it. All the gold we've got won't be enough to rewire the electronic village.

By the end of this century, either Britain or Japan will be the most powerful nation on earth. I was taken to England last year. The London School of Economics offered me a chair, with about triple my current salary, free medical care, and the same kind of life we were used to here before the war. Hell, I would have taken it if I hadn't been such a stubborn old curmudgeon. I like these goddamn United States. My family emigrated from England to get work. The Golden Door. I am not going back, it's as simple as that.

But my trip there was a hell of a surprise. First off, you have the Conservative Party and the Social Democrats. Labour is dead. The Liberals are a strong third. That is one vital, alive, active country. The Thames is jammed with shipping. The airports are full of planes. They've built a high-speed, magnetic-cushion train system between London and their various other cities. Planes, trains, cars. I never saw so many Rolls-Royces and Bentleys in my life. My God, London is like some kind of a high-tech jewel. You can talk to your goddamn TV set to order goods and services. Talk to it!

I was shown the Royal Space Centre, where they're planning for eventual interstellar travel. They hope to reach Barnard's Star, which they believe has an Earthlike planet.

I came home on *Concorde II*. Seven hours, London to San Francisco, and no sonic boom, not flying as high as it does. I came back to Berkeley. Back to my damned Consensus with the

Documents: California Dreams

The enumeration in the Constitution of certain rights shall not be construed to deny or disparage others retained by the people.
— Ninth Amendment, the Constitution of the United States

THE DAZZLE OF THE WEST

Long cars on long roads; restaurants and bars open round the clock; supermarkets that sell everything from toothbrushes to pasta machines to mountains of food; bars where piña coladas and pink silks compete with Coors and Steam Beer; enormous flounders served in light, bright, Muzaked restaurants; Pinot Chardonnay and Cabernet Sauvignon; sun-bleached hair and the thick scent of Ray-Ban Coconut 'n' Aloe.

America, in other words, ten years ago.

California today. But also: illegal immigration warnings posted on every wall and in every bus and trolley; Whitley and I on the run; holding camps and returnee camps and prison camps and

four new gas chambers in San Quentin; military uniforms everywhere; black market Sony and Panasonic televisions; meatless
Fridays and the wonderful red interurban trolleys; 'finder' columns in the *Los Angeles Times* and the *San Francisco Chronicle*; the
Beach Boys; Meryl Streep defying the police by producing and
acting in the banned play *Chained*.

I am dazed by California. Sometimes, walking the streets with
Whitley, I get a joy in me, and I think to myself that the past is
returning like a tide, and soon all will again be well. There is
energy and movement here – danger too, of course – but there
is a little of something else that I think is also an important
component of the American spirit – frivolity. Not much, I'll
grant you, but it isn't dead yet.

Of course, the place is also tension-ridden. In Los Angeles,
militant Asian Returnists whose native countries won't let them
come back compete for barrio space with Chicanos and hundreds
of thousands of illegal immigrants from the other states. The
American illegals are by far the worst off. Because they are de
facto criminals, they are helpless and are ruthlessly exploited.
The division between rich and poor is exceedingly sharp. Beverly
Hills and Nob Hill glitter with Rolls-Royces and Mercedes-
Benzes.

In California, the rest of the United States is thought of as a
foreign country, poverty-stricken and potentially dangerous.
The local press reports it only incidentally. A bus plunge killing a
hundred in Illinois will appear at the bottom of page forty of a
Times that headlines the discovery of strontium 90 in Anaheim.

It is possible to be greedy here. It is possible to be blind.
Impressions:

A movie is being made at the corner of Market and Powell as
we leave San Francisco – massive reflectors, Brooke Shields
looking like a goddess as she steps from her air-conditioned
trailer.

There are casting calls in *Billboard West* and *The Hollywood
Reporter*.

Street-corner newsstands, which used to line up the porno
papers, now feature half a dozen small-time political journals,
state and Chicano separatist papers, the Aztlan *Revolución*, and
Westworld and *Ecotopia*, the journals of two geographical separatist movements.

In California, more than anywhere else, you hear talk of

dividing the United States. 'California First' and 'Forget the Rest' are common T-shirt slogans.

There is also a lot of radiation paranoia. Vendors commonly advertise their fruits as 'radiation-free'. There are walk-in clinics where for fifteen cents you can get a whole-body scan or have objects checked. The government regularly warns people to avoid the black market because of the danger of contaminated goods from 'abroad' – which must mean the rest of the United States.

Immensely wealthy Japanese move about in tremendous Nissan limousines with curtains on the windows.

You can buy all the Japanese and English papers: *Asahi Shimbun* in Japanese, English, and Spanish editions; the London *Times* and *Express* in English, and something called *The Overseas Journal* for British residents. It's all about where to get English cars fixed in California, and how to avoid the embarrassment of old-fashioned American hairstyles by going to local branches of chic London salons.

I found it difficult and dangerous to get into state government offices to obtain documents. In fact, I couldn't do it. But there were vast files of them at Berkeley, in the archives of university departments that shall go nameless. They reveal something about the inner structure of California's immigration policies.

They say more than their authors realize.

Ø 9 15ØØ ZULU OCTOBER 89

FROM: CG U.S. ARMY COMMAND, Fort McPherson, Georgia
TO: 6th ARMY COMMANDER, The Presidio, San Francisco
CLASS: Confidential

Personal for CG Only

1.   You are hereby authorized to deploy 7th Army personnel up to a strength of 7,6ØØ as the Task Force for Civilian Migration Control.

2.   This task force will assist federal and state governments in the control of civilian movement in Arizona, California, Colorado, Idaho, Nevada, New Mexico, and Utah.

3.   This task force will be under military command but under the general jurisdiction of federal authorities associated with migration control as per the War Emergency Act. You are to establish appropriate interorganizational mechanisms for coordination purposes between military and government units.

4.   You are reminded that the purpose of this command is to assist state governments in maintaining order and providing assistance in the distribution of food rations and other resources as part of the national recovery plan. The primary concern at present is the prevention of overpopulation of Western area states, but particularly California. You are further reminded of the temporary martial-law powers granted to the military under the Emergency War Act.

5.   Task force personnel are to be deployed at critical points at your discretion, but including highway and rail traffic points and additional points where personnel and vehicular traffic require military control. Primary traffic centers should include the following:

5.1 ARIZONA
    Yuma, Highway IH-1Ø
    Junction IH-1Ø and H-6Ø
    Kingman, IH-4Ø and H-93

5.2 COLORADO
    Fruita, IH-7Ø
    Cortez, H-666 and H-789
    H-4Ø at Colorado–Utah border
    Sterling, IH-76

5.3 IDAHO
Ashton, H-2Ø
Coeur d'Alene, IH-9Ø
Lewiston, H-12
Nampa, IH-8ØN

5.4 NEVADA
Boulder City, H-93
H-95 at California–Nevada border
Reno, IH-8Ø
Wells, IH-8Ø
Bridgeport, H-31

5.5 NEW MEXICO
Tucumcari, IH-4Ø and H-54
Gallup, IH-4Ø and H-66
Lordsburg, IH-1Ø, H-7Ø, and H-9Ø

5.6 UTAH
Thompson, IH-7Ø
Wendover, IH-8Ø
St. George, IH-15
H-73 and H-5Ø at Nevada–Utah border

6.   Personnel under your command should be instructed as to the nature and provisions of the present civilian relocation plan. This instruction should remain current at all times as to appropriate federal/state documentation approving movement, including: (1) civilian mobility, including (1a) authorized travel for individuals and/or families; (1b) relocation for same; and (1c) emergency movement authorizations; (2) military movement; and (3) U.S. government and/or foreign government movement. Considerable falsification and misuse of stolen documentation permits is occurring. Wherever possible, cross-verification via [TelNET] should be utilized. This is particularly true of permits issued to government personnel.

7.   You should assist in the confiscation and/or disposal of contraband and/or quarantined materials. Relevant provisions regarding these items and materials are as per DOD 5Ø2Ø.17.

8.   Task force personnel will be in place by 13ØØ ZULU 12 October 1989.

9.   This order is in effect until further notice.

END OF MESSAGE

CONFIDENTIAL BY COURIER

STATE OF CALIFORNIA

TO: GOVERNOR MARK B. CAMPBELL

FROM: Harold White, Special Assistant

DATE: 21 March 1990

SUBJECT: Current Status of Illegal Immigration

As per your request of 15 March, I have reviewed all current migration statistics from the California Highway Department, the War Recovery Commission, and the U.S. Department of Transportation. All data suggest that California is exceeding its current immigration quotas from other parts of the U.S. by almost 550 percent!

Our best estimates are that some 1,500–1,800 persons a day enter the State, most of whom do so illegally. Our present monthly quotas, as you know, have been set by agreement with the federal government at 7,500 per month through the remainder of 1990. This figure does not include exempt positions in the technological fields, nor the temporary residence 'visas' issued to federal government and military personnel and foreign government staff.

The Highway Department Special Study Group believes that most illegals enter through the Arizona and Nevada corridors, which, because of their comparative uninhabited status, remain difficult to patrol. Highway Department figures project that some 40–60 percent of illegals enter through these corridors. Another 10 percent enter by low-flying night aircraft from multiple directions.

As a result of this influx, there is an enormous drain on all city and county services throughout the State, including water, sewers, police, and power. It has been impossible to reduce (and certainly to eliminate) the size and number of 'tent cities' within the State. You will recall that the troop strength for the Highway Patrol is five times its prewar size.

Despite federal objections, the states of Oregon and Washington have implemented far-reaching statutes to reduce immigration. They are presumably acting within the provisions of the Emergency War Act, which, while it does not permit states to refuse settlement, does provide for 'control' and 'regulation'. I am continuing conversations with the California Attorney General's Office in order to draft proposed legislation on this matter for the upcoming special session of the State legislature.

In the meantime, you may want to consider the following 'emergency' steps authorized by the legislature and apparently permissible under the EWA:

Recommendation One: Authorize an immediate increase in State Highway Patrol troop strength by 3,000 for purposes of reinforcing border control.

Recommendation Two: Immediately authorize an investigation of special-entry permits. You should issue a concomitant order to 'freeze' such permits except as approved by you.

Recommendation Three: Direct the California National Guard to increase migration support. You may want to authorize some temporary visa control.

Recommendation Four: Place a request before the legislature asking for an additional $11 million for war relief. As permitted by the EWA, some of these monies can be used for migration control as well as for intrastate relocation.

Recommendation Five: Accelerate deportation activities by eliminating second- and third-stage appeal steps. This will no doubt produce some outcry, although it might be offset by the reduced drain on utilities and services.

Your request for recommendations for control/reduction of displaced illegals in the State will be ready by the end of the month.

The Prison Bus

Jim had noticed that San Francisco International had flights by the dozens to every imaginable destination. The idea of getting a closer look at that airport fascinated us. Quinn objected so strenuously that we had to give her the slip. But we couldn't very well visit the West Coast without obtaining a first-hand report of the condition of air travel in the area.

To make a long story short, if an illegal goes to the airport, said illegal is going to be caught.

The Immigration Police are a fearsome crew, especially when they appear out of nowhere, their dark glasses glittering, their scorpion faces expressionless, and say, 'ID, please.'

We were on the concourse, passing an exhibit of new Ford Americars when it happened. We hardly even had our wallets out before there were two military police trotting over, and another three cops.

The reason? We didn't have stamped airline tickets 'visible on our persons at all times,' to quote the regulation.

The cop put our cards into a processor about the size of a recorder. The alarm flashed green (no doubt to con the criminal into thinking he'd passed the test and thus prevent a struggle). We were made to stand against the wall and searched. Jim's recorder and his precious box of diskettes were left alone. California actually *wanted* us to keep our possessions. They don't want potential deportees to leave so much as a used toothpick behind to give them a possible reason to return to the state after they have served their sentences and been ejected.

We were marched out of the airport, past the long rows of ticket counters. Japan Air Lines, All-Nippon Airways, Singapore Airlines, Cathay-Pacific, Philippine Airlines, Thai Airlines, British Airways, Caledonian, Lufthansa, Alitalia, Aer Lingus, Air France, South African Airways, Pan Am, TWA, Delta.

You can fly from San Francisco to Tokyo ten times a week, to London, Singapore, or Paris eight times, to Bonn five times, to Taiwan four times, to Milan twice.

There is no American city except LA with near the service.

New York, Washington, and San Antonio are not on the schedules, of course, and most other American cities are barely there. You cannot fly from San Francisco to Minneapolis at all, but you can go nonstop to Buenos Aires on British Airways or Pan Am, twice a week.

Just being in that airport – despite the cops and the handcuffs – made me long for the magnificent ease of jet travel as I remember it. I even have dim recollections of flying in pre-jet days from San Antonio to Corpus Christi with my father, and the hostess handing out mint Chiclets in cellophane packets. I remember my amazement on learning we were a mile high. I feel equally amazed now that I am earthbound.

Things one took for granted never quite seem lost. I suppose it's a defence mechanism, but somewhere in the back of my mind I always assume that things will one day return to normal, which means life as it was in about 1984.

I remember when Hershey bars got bigger.

And the Ford Tempo, and Chinese restaurants with menus ten pages long, and they had it all.

I remember inflation, and how happy everybody was when it ended – and how unhappy when it started up again, right after the '84 election.

And OPEC. I wonder if it still meets, and if the Israelis send representatives or allow their Arab client-states to continue the pretence of independent participation.

Walking along in that spit-and-polish gaggle of officers, I considered the idea of just breaking and running.

But I want to live. Badly.

Ticket clerks glanced curiously at us as we passed, and I

thought of light on wings and how small the ocean seems from a jet.

I thought of the magical land of Somewhere Else.

They don't have Immigration Police Somewhere Else.

They don't have Red Zones and Dead Zones and British civil servants.

Somewhere Else the corn is always safe to eat and you don't see cattle vomiting in their pens.

They never triage Somewhere Else, and they don't write Bluegrams.

They don't love each other as Anne and I do, either, not Somewhere Else, where the sky is clean and death is a hobby of the old.

Somewhere Else they assume that they have a right to exist and do not stop to consider that it may be a privilege.

California needs the rest of America. It must not be allowed to become a separate nation. If there is such a thing as a geopolitical imperative in our present society, it is to prevent this from happening. The current California immigration laws are an affront to the very memory of the Bill of Rights – and in most parts of this country it is much more than a memory.

We were taken to a holding pen right in the airport, an airless, windowless room jammed with miserable people and booming with fluorescent light.

We remained there, without food or water or access to counsel, for fifty hours. We slept as best we could on the black linoleum floor, entwined with the other captured.

I was the first to appear before the magistrate. He was a cheerful young man in a blue Palm Beach suit and one of the raffish grey panamas that California's affluent class wear nowadays. They are grey because they are dusted with lead.

He was perhaps thirty. 'Let's see, you're one of the ones dressed as a priest. Funny. This is funny too: By the power vested in me by the state of California, I sentence you to two years at hard labour, to be followed by transportation out of the state.' He banged a gavel. 'Next case,' he said, absently shuffling papers.

My mouth was dry. I was too shocked to make a sound. Two years in prison, just like that. No jury, not even a chance to ask a question. And where was my lawyer? What the hell happened to my side?

I didn't hear Jim's sentencing, but I could see by his expression when we entered the prison bus, which was waiting at the far end of the main building, that he had been hit too. I held up my hand, indicating the number two. He nodded and held up first one finger and then another, then another.

Jim had done worse than I had; he was in for three years. Why the stiffer sentence? I found out later that he had asked the judge for a jury trial.

The bus was an old model with cyclone fencing welded into the windows. It rattled and shook along. There were ten of us, men as well as women, all handcuffed, seated on narrow steel benches. When I realised that no guards were back here in the un-air-conditioned part of the bus, I began to talk.

'Maybe we can get word to someone in the federal government,' I said. 'Perhaps they can help.'

Jim stared at me as if I had gone completely mad. 'Look,' he said, 'I've still got my recorder and my disks. Once we get to the prison, they're going to be locked in a property room. Maybe stolen or erased.'

Obviously there was no time to fool around with government officials. 'So we break out of the bus. How?'

'Not too hard, it isn't very secure. I think they expect illegals to be passive. You remember how to fall?'

My mind went back to basic training. I had fallen then, often enough. 'I guess so.'

'We're gonna jump and hope for the best.'

'Jim, we're wearing handcuffs.'

'That's not much more of a problem than that door.'

The rear door of the bus, once the fire exit, was welded closed. 'How can we possibly jump?'

With an angelic expression, Jim raised his eyes.

Right above us was a ventilator. It was pushed open. Jim passed the word that he and I were going out on the roof if we got the chance, and we'd pull anybody up who cared to follow.

We waited, then, for the bus to leave San Francisco proper. We had no idea of our destination, but we were soon across the Bay Bridge and going through Oakland on Route 80, heading towards Richmond.

We passed Richmond, moving at about forty miles an hour. The bus slowed as we reached the Hercules exit. We turned off and took a right beneath the railroad tracks on to a two-lane blacktop called Crow Canyon Road. It was 9.15 a.m. The *Zephyr* would be leaving San Francisco at noon.

I prayed that I would see Anne again.

We passed the Crow Canyon golf course and a big truck depot, then began climbing a hill. Soon our speed was dropping and the gears were making a lovely racket. Jim wasted no time. He raised his cuffed hands above his head and grabbed the edge of the ventilator. In a moment he had pulled himself up and hooked one arm over the edge. With his free hand he unsnapped the plastic armature that held the vent in place. It began to bang against his arm and I heard him stifle a scream. Then his legs were up to his chest and he had rolled out on to the roof. A second later he opened the vent for me.

Now we were passing an abandoned kennel. People don't keep many dogs these days, not even in California. The road cut the edge of the hill, which rose steeply to our right. On the left was a horse farm and open countryside and a chance to get to Richmond and intercept the *Zephyr*.

We jumped and rolled into the grass at the roadside.

All up the hill, that bus leaked prisoners. By the time it got to the top, I don't think there were three left inside.

'Maybe we can find something to cut these cuffs at that truck depot back down the road,' Jim said. 'If we don't get them off, we might as well forget the train.'

We moved quickly. A lot of people were going to be trying to break into that depot today, all wearing handcuffs, all looking for shears. The place was open, so after the first ones came, the workers there would be on their guard.

The depot stood on the roadside in the heat, a broken semi blocking one driveway. In the other driveway, a new Mercedes truck was parked, getting diesel fuel. Behind it, an ancient eighteen-wheeler awaited its turn.

We went far up the hillside that backed the depot, and came around behind it. There was a door into the rear of one of the metal buildings. Inside, two men were working on a magnificent '87 Thunderbird, a sleek red dream of a car with gleaming black leather upholstery. It was a breathtaking joy to see, that prewar car, and judging from the polished beauty of the engine compartment, we weren't the only ones smitten by it.

I am a law-abiding man, but when Jim found those big metal shears and cut my cuffs, and I cut his, and I realised that we were both fugitives, it occurred to me that it would be an awful lot of fun to steal the T-bird.

'Too conspicuous,' Jim muttered. Just then, three more prisoners came in the rear door. I thought I heard a siren off in the mountains. It was time to leave.

We crossed the road and headed out into the countryside, moving back towards Route 80. It was eleven-thirty by the time we saw 80 in the distance. We had come about five miles. All during this time we had heard sirens, and seen an occasional police vehicle back on Crow Canyon Road.

There was a bus stop in the little town of Pinole. The schedule on the wall indicated that we should see the next Richmond bus at 12.10.

According to our timetable, the *Zephyr* would pull out of Richmond at 12.22.

If the bus was right on time, we would make our connection with exactly one minute to spare – assuming that the Immigration Police had not thought to extend their dragnet to cover the Richmond depot. Our Roman collars had become advertisements of fugitive status.

The bus came, and wheezed up on to Route 80. We would be in Richmond in a few minutes. The depot was the first stop. When I told the driver we were trying to make the train, he nodded and promised to do his best.

We sat there sweating, reading the aisle cards: the ubiquitous immigration warning; the Soyquick cereal ad; the BubbleRific poster with the sunny Valley Girl blowing a big yellow bubble; an appeal to orphans that read, 'Don't join the gangs. California has a home for you'; an ad for Shearson/American Express, 'Tomorrow is going to *work*! And we know how.'

A man was humming an old song: 'Jimmy Crack Corn'.

California is sun and the smell of watered lawns.

It is luxury trains and terror.

It is two-minute trials and prison farms.

And a beautiful prewar car, as exotic as a Maharajah's coach, hidden in a nondescript garage.

California is fresh food, and lots of it.

It is also a very nice place to leave, if you don't belong there.

The train was sitting in the Richmond station as the bus came to a stop out front.

We ran fast through the tiled lobby, past the ticket windows and directly to the train. A single Immigration Policeman lounged against the wall of the station.

The train was already in motion when we slung into the door a conductor was holding open for us.

'Come on, Fathers! You can make it.'

The *Zephyr* at last.

Soon it was picking up speed.

We went into the lavatory to change from the clerical clothes to our more ordinary jeans and shirts. We threw the incriminating clothes onto the roadbed somewhere between Richmond and Martinez.

Back in our seats, Jim began checking his discs to be sure none were damaged.

I leaned back, realising how deeply tired I was. Despite the handicap of our illegal entry, we had done fairly well in California.

In Martinez, three Immigration Police came through the train fast, but they didn't spot us. I suppose their eyes were going from throat to throat behind those mirrored sunglasses, looking for clerical collars.

I bought a soybean salad and some milk in the snack bar and sat watching the world go by. As we rounded Suisin Bay, I saw vast, empty docks that in the past would have been jammed with imported Japanese cars. Now there were perhaps a hundred of them standing in the afternoon sun, protected by chainlink fences.

Somebody began to play a tape of David Bowie's new album, *Dream Along*, and I did just that.

I didn't wake up until long after dark. There was a strong smell of salami. Jim was eating a sandwich that had been offered him by a magnificently uniformed British naval officer who now sat across the aisle from us, ready to give us what proved to be a truly extraordinary interview.

Jim glanced at me. 'We're in Nevada,' he said.

All I did was nod.

Interview: Captain Malcolm Hargreaves, Sub-Popper

I am on a five-day leave, on my way to see the Rocky Mountains. I'll shift in Ogden to the *Rio Grande Zephyr* for the scenery and go down to Denver. Then I'll fly back to base.

We have been in California for eight days. The Royal Navy has enjoyed learning about the famous California lifestyle. I'm from Yorkshire, and I believe I've seen more sunlight in a week here than we do in a whole Yorks' summer. And every time you turn around, there's another swimming pool. Not to mention an aspect my men have particularly enjoyed, which is meeting some of your wonderful girls. I confess to being unattached myself, so this hasn't been without interest for me, either.

Now I did tell you at the outset that I would not be discussing details of the range or speed of my ship, or exactly how our weapons operate. But of course we are what is popularly called a 'sub-popper', and that is not a completely inaccurate name. It does describe our mission very well. As you know, the war left a large number of unidentified submarines, armed with nuclear missiles, sailing about the oceans of the world. They are all what we call 'code blind', which is to say that there is presently nobody to send them the codes they need either to fire their missiles or to come home. So they continue on station, generally, until they get low on nuclear fuel or some essential supply, or break down in a critical part, whereupon they either return to base and are disarmed, or they sink.

If you are like three-quarters of the people we naval types encounter, you'll want to know something about the present naval situation. GHQ Pacific Office of Information gives us a prepared summary, which I can read into your machine.

'On Warday there were more than one thousand major combatant US and Soviet ships at sea, of which 380 were submarines, 100 of them American and 280 Soviet. Of these craft, as far as is known, only the *S. Shuvakov* actually fired weapons, and this ship was responsible for the destruction of the United States Seventh and Third Fleets in the Pacific. In this case, a single submarine of the *Typhoon* class destroyed the most massive assemblage of capital ships in human history and took, in a few moments, over twenty thousand human lives, utilising eleven SS-N-20 missiles, each deploying six warheads of four megatons each. The destruction of the other American surface fleets was carried out by land-based weapons, except the Sixth Fleet in the Mediterranean, which was an operation of unknown nature, possibly involving the firing of nuclear-armed SS-N-9 missiles by a *Nanuchka*-class corvette, or AS-43 fired by a TU22-M bomber. All American operational aircraft carriers on the high seas were destroyed within the first ten minutes of the war, including the four nuclear aircraft carriers and eight of the ten conventional carriers. Of the 190 other major combat vessels in the US surface navy, 141 were destroyed or damaged and later abandoned. With the destruction of the naval staff and all personnel records in Washington, the US Navy ceased to be an operational fighting force on Warday.

'The Soviet surface navy was also rendered nonfunctional on Warday. Both carriers were destroyed, the *Kiev* in Motovskij Gulf along with approximately one hundred other ships in the immediate area. The Soviet Baltic Fleet attempted to escape into the North Sea, but was substantially repelled by NATO forces, primarily UK and Danish antisubmarine forces, which were responsible for the confirmed destruction of eighty-two Soviet submarines of various classes, including numerous nuclear-powered types. The eight *Typhoon*-class submarines in the Baltic did not sortie. Three of these have subsequently been destroyed by the Royal Navy, one has ceased to be operational, and the other four remain functional, but the political situation in the Soviet area is too unstable to allow a determination of the present loyalties of the crews. These submarines are extremely dangerous, and will be sunk. The Pacific Fleet at Vladivostok was destroyed by American action. Some Soviet ships were found disabled for lack of fuel by French relief forces entering Vietnam in 1989. The bulk of these ships were at Cam Ranh Bay and were scuttled by their crews. The Soviet units stranded at Aden were interned by the Royal Navy. These included the helicopter carrier *Moskva*, with a complement of eighteen KA-25 helicopters; three GW-ASW cruisers fully armed and lacking only fuel; twelve GW destroyers in the same condition, all of the *Kildin* class; four GW corvettes of the *Tarantul* class and three of the *Nanuchka* class; and four *Matka*-class hydrofoils, which had been posted down from Black Sea ports during the Syrian affair in 1987. The fleet replenishment vessel *Berezina* was intercepted in the Indian Ocean at this time, and has been refitted as HMS *Triumph*.

'Remaining US naval forces are presently attached as the United States Special Detachment to the Royal Navy, commanded by Admiral the Rt. Hon. Vincent D. B. Hughes and Vice-Admiral (US) Charles Greene Phillips. These forces, primarily in the anti-submarine area, constitute a vital and important part of the free world's seagoing naval strength.'

Now that's the lot from the Office of Information. I'm supposed to give copies of that to any reporters who approach me, so here are two copies.

So, what can I say about myself? I am captain of the Type 12 antisubmarine frigate *Ulysses*, operating in cooperation with Fleet Air Arm antisubmarine forces and US Navy antisubmarine forces based in Hawaii, Midway Island, and San Diego. Our theatre of operations is the western Pacific. We are attached to STANAVFORPAC, the Standing Naval Force Pacific of the International Treaty Organisation countries. Our mission is to destroy unidentified submarines.

I am invariably asked, when I am on shore leave, whether we destroy American nuclear submarines. I can only repeat the aim of our mission. We do destroy all *unidentified* submarine craft.

That means that we may or may not know what countries those submarines are from. Perhaps some are American, although that would surprise me. Since they lost communication with their bases, most American submarines have returned to US waters and surfaced, or are in communication with us in some way. The mission of the Royal Navy with regard to submarines is not to destroy the remaining nuclear capacity of the United States and the USSR, or to impede them in the re-formation of government in their countries, but to remove the threat of the unknown – submarine crews, loyal perhaps to governments that no longer exist, under severe psychological pressure, suddenly firing their missiles in the mistaken belief that they are obligated to do so. There is also the possibility that both sides left 'long-trigger' ships with orders to hide for a period of years, then suddenly attack. These ships must be sunk before they open their orders.

I suppose the greatest engagement of my career was with a pack of one *Typhoon*-class submarine and three smaller vessels in the Aleutians about a year ago. These ships had been hiding under the Arctic ice for approximately forty-four months and were making a run for Vladivostok, evidently unaware that this port no longer exists. We suspected that they were there because of persistent reports from isolated communities in Alaska and Canada of raiding parties who spoke Russian to one another and who appeared out of nowhere to steal food. Sometimes these reports took as long as six months to reach us, because of unreliable communications, but we felt that they certainly indicated the presence of Soviet vessels under the ice cap. Indeed, there is no reason to believe that there are not still Soviet and American submarines on station there. Present long-range detection techniques do not offer us as reliable an indication of submarine activity beneath ice as we would like.

At any rate, we got a very good signal on these boats just as they were coming round the island of Umnak in the Fox Islands. Why they were there, and not hugging the coast of Siberia, we do not know.

As you might or might not know, a *Typhoon*-class submarine was the Soviet equivalent of a *Trident*, displacing twenty-five thousand tons and armed with twenty missiles of intercontinental range. We identified the presence of a *Typhoon*-class vessel by the emission signature of its reactor. Naturally, we were eager to destroy this ship, as it was one of four remaining

Typhoons and, next to the three *Tridents* still unaccounted for, is certainly the most dangerous vessel on the high seas. This one ship would, for example, be capable of reducing your California, in its entirety, to the present condition of Washington or San Antonio.

So we were very eager to get a kill while avoiding even the suspicion of detection ourselves. We found that we were out of range of the only Royal Navy carrier operating in the area, the old *Hermes* with its complement of Harriers. Thus we determined that the *Typhoon* would have to be located very precisely and then destroyed by *Ulysses*. The job was quite an exciting challenge, I can assure you.

It was one of those grey, cheerless days common in the North Pacific, when the wind blows with massive force and the sea birds fly before it. When I went on deck, bits of ice quickly formed in my beard. In addition to the winds, we had blowing fog. Earlier we had passed through a vast fleet of Japanese fishing vessels, including a huge automatic whaler. As fish meal is now the primary source of protein for that nation of ninety-seven millions, you can well imagine the size of this fleet. It was operating in INTO-foreclosed waters, meaning that fishing operations there are illegal except to signatories. In this case, the Gulf of Alaska. We had detached a frigate to check the papers of the Japanese fishermen; there have been many reports of Chinese fishing vessels operating illegally in American waters in recent years, and they are to be sunk if they are found. Only the Japanese, the British, the Danes, the Icelanders, and the Norse may fish former US-controlled waters.

We found ourselves approximately 420 nautical miles south-southwest of the target. The Soviet ships were deployed across an area of twenty square miles, with the *Typhoon* in the centre of its group of four support submarines. The pack was moving in a southerly direction at a speed of 20 knots. We were able to deploy a Nimrod aircraft from San Diego and maintain a continuous exact fix on the Soviet ships. Our objective was to destroy all five submarines simultaneously. We began closing at flank speed and prepared our weapons, which consisted of Harpoon missiles delivered via helicopter and directly from shipboard.

As the target was moving in our rough direction, closing time was fairly rapid. We were able to gain a positive identification of the support submarines about two hours after contact. These were E-1 class boats, attack submarines. Their purpose would be defence of the *Typhoon*, and they could be assumed to be carrying nuclear-tipped surface-skimming torpedoes. We had to assume that we were already in range of these vessels. Our Nimrod assistance began relaying satellite data to us at about this time, and we were able to project the exact position of each boat on our maps and supply our computers with all necessary coordinates. I then ordered our helicopter complement to the attack and stood back with the ships. It is known that Soviet aircraft-detection equipment has a much shorter range than the equipment that detects ship noise.

We released all five Harpoon-carrying helicopters, and waited the next two hours while they flew within range of the submarines. The moment they released their missiles, we activated our classified weapons aboard ship. Of this total firing, a classified number of missiles reached their targets, but all of the Soviet submarines were impacted. The E-1 class boats all sank. The *Typhoon*-class boat surfaced dead in the water.

Some hours later we boarded this boat. I recall vividly my ride across the sling between my ship and the sluggishly rolling submarine. She was an enormous vessel. By the time I went aboard, all the Soviet crew were off except the first officer, who had agreed to act as our guide. He spoke fluent English. His name was Benkovsky, and he informed us that his unit had been continuously at sea for nearly four years! They were only returning to base because their nuclear fuel was running low. As our missiles home on running reactors, the major damage to this boat, the *Teplov*, was to the engine room and rear crew compartments. The reactor was out of action but the enclosure was intact, so radiation levels aboard ship were normal. There was a powerful stench of burning electrical insulation in the boat, but the crew had contained the fire. We found American tinned foods, much from the prewar era, including Chef Boy-Ar-Dee Spaghetti Dinner and A&P Brand pork and beans with bacon, with prices in prewar dollars. The ships had been replenishing themselves by raiding grocery stores and larders in Arctic Canada and Alaska. Our reports from coastal towns had been correct.

We found this ship to be cramped and dangerously constructed, with much evidence of new welding and repairs of all kinds. Many of the electronic instruments were not operational, and never had been. It is not likely that this boat could have done much to defend itself, despite all the publicity its class received before the war. In addition, it was in poor condition and no longer capable of ultra-deep diving. Although it is a very silent-running vessel, the quiet was achieved at the expense of speed and power. By our standards, this boat was hardly seaworthy.

There was much evidence of low morale aboard, and crew members later indicated that there had been six executions for attempted mutiny or desertion.

One system on the ship that was built up to the highest standard was the missile fire-control system. After this boat had been towed to Hawaii and examined, it was determined that its complement of SLBMs was armed and on firing sequence when the boat was disabled. Another minute or so and the missiles would have been away. Evidently our presence had been detected, or, more likely, our incoming Harpoon missiles. The Soviet weapons were targeted against Seattle, Portland, and various communities along the California coast. They included three EMP weapons, which would have once again destroyed all the electronic devices in the United States and created every bit as much disruption as occurred before, not to mention ruining what communications systems your country has so painfully managed to reconstruct since the war. The ground-targeted missiles would have delivered a total of one hundred megatons to their targets, and killed outright nine million of the area population of twenty-two million. Residual radiation would have caused severe contamination throughout California.

After an encounter like that, we sub-poppers of the Royal Navy feel that we are doing a job vital to the security of the world.

Poll: The Grand Old Feud – Do We Still Believe in It?

First 'twas the Hatfields, and first 'twas the
McCoys. Or maybe 'twas the other way around.
– Traditional Tale

Looking back, it does not seem strange or even improbable that the United States and the USSR were rivals. Even without the ideological differences, geopolitics would seem to have made it inevitable.

But what does seem strange is the way the rivalry became so formalistic towards the end, almost a kind of ritual, which continued along its traditional lines despite the enormous changes in the two countries and the world around them.

It is not possible to assess blame; both sides were at fault, and both sides were trapped. Nobody knows what normal relations between the United States and the USSR would have meant because they never had normal relations, not at any time in their history. They either hated one another beyond reason or pretended to unrealistic friendship, such as during the Second World War or the 'Détente' period of the seventies.

With hindsight, we can see that they should have been neither mortal enemies nor fast friends. Some things about them suggested partnership, and others suggested competition, but nothing suggested the murderous war that occurred.

Do we think that the old rivalry will be rekindled in the future?

The polls say no. Perhaps the war has finally put the seal on the anguish of the old superpowers. Perhaps.

Do you believe that the Soviet Union will emerge once again as a world power?

	1993	1992
AGREE	27%	30%
DISAGREE	68	66
NO OPINION	5	4

Should the Soviet Union emerge again as a world power, do you believe that it will start another war?

AGREE	21%
DISAGREE	72
NO OPINION	7

Do you believe that an unfair portion of international war relief is being sent to the Soviet Union?

AGREE	61%
DISAGREE	29
NO OPINION	10

Do you believe that the United States should attempt to rearm itself militarily?

	1993	1992	1991
AGREE	49%	41%	39%
DISAGREE	44	53	54
NO OPINION	7	6	7

Some interesting differences appeared in response to the preceding question among age groups:

	AGREE	DISAGREE	NO OPINION
Ages 18–25	40%	53%	7%
25–35	46	51	3
35–45	45	49	6
45–55	49	46	5
55 and over	38	55	7

PART THREE

ACROSS AMERICA

I remember laundromats at night all lit up with
nobody in them.
I remember rainbow-coloured grease spots on the
pavement after a rain.
I remember the tobacco smell of my father's
breath.
I remember Jimmy Durante disappearing among
spotlights into giant black space.

– Joe Brainard,
'I Remember'

Jim: Prairie Notebook

When we crossed the border into Nevada, Whitley seemed almost too drained to react, but I felt like breaking out champagne. I contented myself with a quiet sip of water from our bag.

We are now on the western edge of the Great Plains. I wish I could have gone with Captain Hargreaves when he left the train at Ogden, but his world and mine are not the same.

I contented myself with this train's less scenic route. The going was slow and rough through the Rockies. We used old freight tracks for this part of the run. Now we are south of Denver, on our way to connect with the *Southwest Limited* in La Junta. Next year perhaps the *Zephyr* will resume its old route across Nebraska and Iowa, but not yet.

The great transcontinental migration passed through this land, and the legendary trains of the Union Pacific and the Western Pacific, their engines gleaming brass and black, their whistles stampeding the astonished buffalo.

That happened barely a hundred years ago. In the time since then, the Rockies have lost perhaps a tenth of an inch of their peaks from the ceaseless wind. Two thousand animal species have become extinct in this land, and the world that extinguished them has slipped through our fingers.

The grandsons of Buffalo Bill and Bat Masterson might well have been alive to see Warday.

We could still get dead drunk on Wild Bill Hickok's whisky. In a hundred years a well-sealed bottle will have lost no more than a shot to evaporation.

Long thoughts of the West. How impossibly fast it was discovered and settled. How quickly it matured and grew old.

My mind drifts away from ghost towns and empty ranches to the present, to my own work. I, who wrote books about atomic weapons, find myself writing one about a trip through atomised America. I've been shouted at by people who felt that writing about weapons glorified them.

Now is now, the rattling train and the night.

And the past is the past. I was sitting in a private dining room at the top of the Exxon Building in Houston when Warday occurred. My purpose was business; I was working on a book about oil exploration. My host had just lifted a cup of coffee to his lips when, from where I was sitting, his face suddenly seemed to glow with blinding, unearthly light. I closed my eyes. He pitched back, screaming.

We had just experienced the bursts going off over San Antonio, more than two hundred miles away.

It took fifteen or so minutes for the sound to reach us – a great, rolling roar that cracked most of the windows on the west side of the building.

My past had just ended. When I saw the cloud I knew at once what had happened.

I was well out of Houston before the fallout started. It was devastating when it came. The San Antonio bombs were at least as filthy with long-term radiation by-products as those that hit New York and Washington. Fission-fusion-fission bombs.

My only thought was to get on the road, away from any inhabited areas. My car radio wouldn't work, but every time I looked west I got all the news I needed. Over the course of the day, that cloud got bigger and darker and closer. And I drove on north, hoping against hope that I wouldn't see another such cloud over Dallas.

I stopped for gas and tried to call my wife in Austin.

There wasn't even a dial tone.

I couldn't reach my mother in San Antonio, either.

Reporting is a good job; you can put your heart into it. And the effort is worthwhile when you get something like the attached document. It is useful and important, and it took brave men to gather the information it contains. Even though I obtained it in Chicago, it belongs here, before we enter the great Midwestern plains.

The document concerns only the first few weeks. We have added two recent maps that show how the fallout developed at the end of one year, and which counties are still reporting live particles today.

Before the war we knew very little about secondary dissemination. It caused the famine by destroying so much stored wheat in the winter of '88–'89, at a time when farming conditions were chaotic. The loss of the grain supply led to local consumption of vegetables that would normally have been shipped to market, and to a massive meat shortage as feed supplies went to make the unforgettable oat bread that was around by the summer of '89.

It's too bad there are so many live particles still around the North Central States. I wish we could have seen the Dakotas. A trainman put it very vividly when I asked to be ticketed to Rapid City or Minot. He consulted his timetable, then looked up at me. 'Them places are gone,' he said.

Documents on the National Condition

He stood upon that fateful ground,
Cast his lethargic eye around,
And said beneath his breath:
Whatever happens,
We have got
The Maxim gun
And they do not.

– Hilaire Belloc,
'The Modern Traveller'

GENTLY, FROM ABOVE

Before the war, fallout was commonly thought of as a semi-permanent devastation that would at the very least doom us to death in a matter of days or weeks.

It didn't turn out that way. It was more subtle, and it was worse. Most of us have never experienced fallout directly, at least not in what we now think of as significant quantities. Like so many of the effects of Warday, by itself fallout was for the most part survivable. But when you combined it with the economic dislocations that started with the EMP burst, you had a prescription for disaster in the farm belt, a disaster from which we have by no means recovered.

The famine came about because of the negative synergy of fallout that contaminated stored grains and cropland in late '88 and '89, and the economic chaos that led to the breakdown of the system of farm subsidy and capitalisation.

A further synergistic effect occurred when the Cincinnati Flu broke out. It was a rough flu, but it would have been tenth-page news in 1985. Because we were already weak from malnutrition, and low-level radiation caused some immune-response suppression in many of us, the flu cut through the American population like a scythe.

So, for most of us, the drift from the sky has meant hunger and influenza, not the wasting of radiation sickness. How delighted I would have been before the war to find out that direct fallout wasn't a very serious threat. My own war fantasies often took the form of desperate escapes from the blowing dust.

Funny, that it was so much more benign than we thought, and so much more lethal, both at the same time.

SUMMARY REPORT ON EARLY DOMESTIC FALLOUT
JANUARY 5, 1989

EMERGENCY TASK FORCE ON DOMESTIC FALLOUT
U.S. DEPARTMENT OF ENERGY

INTRODUCTION

The Emergency Task Force on Domestic Fallout was created on December 15, 1988, as an interdepartmental unit to gather, assess, and monitor the radioactive fallout produced by the October 28, 1988, Soviet surprise attack against the United States. Data are presently being collected by field-based units within the Department, as well as from military and local government sources. This report is concerned only with the early fallout produced by the October attack, that is, the fallout produced and deposited within the first few days after the attack.

As a result of the Soviet attack, many monitoring facilities in the attack zones were either destroyed or disabled. Manned ground monitoring stations have been established on an emergency basis near bombed zones where human safety could be assured. Extensive remote/robot stations have been placed by helicopter or air-dropped into highly radioactive areas.

The purpose of this network has been to chart the extent and course of atmospheric fallout. A list of active major data collection stations appears in Attachment One.

For background purposes, each attack zone is briefly described in terms of target nature, weapon yield, etc. An abbreviated description of the causes and nature of radioactive fallout appears in Attachment Two.

This is a summary report only. Full details, as they are presently available, appear in other DOE documentation.

PARAMETERS

Radioactive fallout is an aftereffect of a nuclear detonation. Its nature, intensity, and range are results of weapon type (fission, fusion, or mixture), burst height (ground- or airburst), yield of weapon (usually calculated in megatons), and wind and other meteorological conditions. Brief coverage of these variables is presented in this report.

GENERALIZED OBSERVATIONS

For comparison purposes, the October 1988 Soviet strike may be considered two attacks: one against U.S. urban centers and another against underground missile installations. As a consequence, the Soviets employed different attack strategies, which in turn produced different fallout patterns. The attacks against urban centers utilized air and ground detonations, which resulted in both local fallout and broad distribution through the upper atmosphere. The attacks against missile silos produced intense ground-level radiation and severe long-range fallout. In both attacks, however, the multiplicity of warheads combined to produce aggravated fallout conditions.

The nature and extent of the attack and the prevailing winds produced in each case a unique fallout distribution. Some generalized, or averaged, comparisons can be drawn, however. In the case of the attacks on urban centers, it can be estimated that the following unit-time fallout conditions occurred similarly for all three attacks:

DOWNWIND DISTANCE FROM GROUND ZERO	DOSE RATE IN ROENTGENS/HOUR
50 MILES	1600 R/HR
100 MILES	360 R/HR
200 MILES	125 R/HR
300 MILES	55 R/HR
400 MILES	20 R/HR
500 MILES	6 R/HR

At the end of the first week, it is estimated that the dose rate for these distances was as follows:

50 MILES	3400 R/HR
100 MILES	2700 R/HR
200 MILES	405 R/HR
300 MILES	144 R/HR
400 MILES	42 R/HR
500 MILES	12 R/HR

In the case of the ground attack on missile silos, the following conditions are estimated:

DOWNWIND DISTANCE FROM GROUND ZERO	DOSE RATE IN ROENTGENS/HOUR
50 MILES	1400 R/HR
100 MILES	320 R/HR
200 MILES	75 R/HR
300 MILES	30 R/HR
400 MILES	8 R/HR
500 MILES	1.2 R/HR

Dosage rates for the end of the first week are estimated to have been as follows:

50 MILES	2200 R/HR
100 MILES	270 R/HR
200 MILES	68 R/HR
300 MILES	16 R/HR
400 MILES	3.2 R/HR
500 MILES	.8 R/HR

These are averaged estimates only, which have been scaled according to previously known fallout characteristics and limited current data. Complete analysis will not be available for some time, although local government and military authorities have been advised about fallout hazards and subsequent medical/health consequences.

REVIEW OF RADIOACTIVE FALLOUT CONDITIONS

A brief summary of fallout conditions and patterns is presented in the following target-by-target descriptions:

1. NEW YORK CITY–LONG ISLAND AREA
NATURE OF TARGET: Urban center.
TYPE/YIELD OF SOVIET WEAPON: Missile-delivered thermonuclear warhead in 9–10-megaton (MT) range.
NUMBER OF WARHEADS DELIVERED: Three land targets, with some evidence of several other weapons that detonated at sea.
BURST TYPE: Airburst and groundburst.

SPECIAL FEATURES: High concentration of fission elements suggests 'dirty weapon' type designed to increase fallout intensity of groundburst.

FALLOUT PATTERN: There was a frontal system active in the New York City area on this date, developing winds from a WNW direction at 10–12 knots. As a consequence, little upwind fallout occurred in upper New York–Connecticut area; most downwind fallout was seaward, with considerable centralized fallout in Staten Island, Brooklyn, Queens, and western Long Island areas.

2. WASHINGTON D.C. AREA

NATURE OF TARGET: Urban area.

TYPE/YIELD OF SOVIET WEAPON: Missile-delivered thermonuclear warhead in 9–10 MT range.

NUMBER OF WARHEADS DELIVERED: Six warheads with possible unknown number of other nondetonating weapons.

BURST TYPE: Airburst and groundburst.

SPECIAL FEATURES: Same as 1 above.

FALLOUT PATTERN: Prevailing winds created a fallout pattern that was generally easterly with some deflection SSE. Because of Washington's unique location, most fallout was into Maryland, and secondarily into Delaware and western New Jersey.

3. SAN ANTONIO, TEXAS AREA

NATURE OF TARGET: Urban area.

TYPE/YIELD OF SOVIET WEAPON: Missile-delivered thermonuclear warhead in 9–10 MT range.

NUMBER OF WARHEADS DELIVERED: Three.

BURST TYPE: Airburst and groundburst.

SPECIAL FEATURES: Same as 1 above.

FALLOUT PATTERN: A frontal system was developing winds of 10–15 knots in a SE direction. Fallout was into South and East Texas, including the Houston area.

4. GREAT FALLS, MONTANA AREA

NATURE OF TARGET: U.S. Minuteman missile fields.

TYPE/YIELD OF SOVIET WEAPON: Missile-delivered thermonuclear warhead in 1–2 MT range.

NUMBER OF WARHEADS DELIVERED: Unknown, but estimated at 25+.

BURST TYPE: Groundburst for maximum silo destruction. Some airburst detonations.

SPECIAL FEATURES: Intense surface radiation, with moderate to severe atmospheric fallout downwind.

FALLOUT PATTERN: Winds for late October were SE. Because of the attack nature, initial radioactivity was widespread over a large area. Radiation extended to Wyoming and South Dakota.

5. GRAND FORKS, NORTH DAKOTA AREA

NATURE OF TARGET: U.S. Minuteman missile fields.

TYPE/YIELD OF SOVIET WEAPON: Missile-delivered thermonuclear warhead in 1–2 MT range.

NUMBER OF WARHEADS DELIVERED: Unknown, but estimated at 25+.

BURST TYPE: Groundburst for maximum silo destruction. Some airburst detonations.

SPECIAL FEATURES: Same as 4 above.

FALLOUT PATTERN: Winds were SE, hence fallout pattern developed over Minnesota, with some low-level fallout in Wisconsin.

6. MINOT, NORTH DAKOTA AREA

NATURE OF TARGET: U.S. Minuteman missile fields.

TYPE/YIELD OF SOVIET WEAPON: Missile-delivered thermonuclear warhead in 1–2 MT range.

NUMBER OF WARHEADS DELIVERED: Unknown, but estimated at 45+.

BURST TYPE: Groundburst for maximum depth destruction. Some airburst detonations.

SPECIAL FEATURES: Same as 4 above.

FALLOUT PATTERN: Winds were SSE-S for attack date. Early fallout was concentrated in N. Dakota, with some fallout in S. Dakota and minor fallout in Iowa.

7. RAPID CITY, SOUTH DAKOTA AREA

NATURE OF TARGET: U.S. Minuteman missile fields.

TYPE/YIELD OF SOVIET WEAPON: Missile-delivered thermonuclear warhead in 1–2 MT range.

NUMBER OF WARHEADS DELIVERED: Unknown, but estimated at 35+.

BURST TYPE: Groundburst for maximum depth destruction. Some airburst detonations.

SPECIAL FEATURES: Same as 4 above.

FALLOUT PATTERN: Winds were SSE. Fallout line was largely into S. Dakota and Nebraska, with development into Iowa and Missouri.

8. CHEYENNE, WYOMING AREA

NATURE OF TARGET: U.S. Minuteman and MX missile fields.

TYPE/YIELD OF SOVIET WEAPON: Missile-delivered thermonuclear warhead in 1–2 MT range.

NUMBER OF WARHEADS DELIVERED: Unknown but estimated at 35+.

BURST TYPE: Groundburst for maximum depth destruction. Some airburst detonations.

SPECIAL FEATURES: Same as 4 above.

FALLOUT PATTERN: Winds were SSE. Primary fallout occurred in Wyoming, Kansas, Colorado, and Nebraska, with some development into southeastern Missouri.

ATTACHMENT ONE
LIST OF MAJOR FALLOUT DATA COLLECTION CENTERS
(Manned and Remote)

MONTANA

Billings	45D 48M North / 108D 32M West
Glasgow	48D 13M North / 106D 37M West
Great Falls	47D 29M North / 111D 22M West
Havre	48D 33M North / 109D 46M West
Helena	46D 36M North / 112D 00M West
Kalispell	48D 18M North / 114S 16M West
Miles City	46D 26M North / 105D 52M West
Missoula	46D 55M North / 114D 05M West

NEW YORK

Central Park/Manhattan	40D 47M North / 78D 58M West
Kennedy Airport	40D 39M North / 73D 47M West
La Guardia Airport	40D 46M North / 73D 54M West

NORTH DAKOTA

Bismarck	46D 46M North / 100D 45M West
Fargo	46D 54M North / 96D 46M West
Williston	48D 11M North / 103D 38M West

SOUTH DAKOTA

Aberdeen	45D 27M North / 98D 26M West
Huron	44D 23M North / 98D 13M West
Rapid City	44D 03M North / 104D 04M West
Sioux Falls	43D 34M North / 96D 44M West

TEXAS

Austin	30D 18M North / 97D 42M West
Corpus Christi	27D 46M North / 97D 30M West
Houston	29D 58M North / 95D 21M West
San Antonio	29D 32M North / 98D 28M West

WASHINGTON, D.C.

| Dulles Airport | 38D 57M North / 77D 27M West |
| National Airport | 38D 51M North / 77D 02M West |

WYOMING

Casper	42D 55M North / 106D 28M West
Cheyenne	41D 09M North / 104D 49M West
Lander	42D 49M North / 108D 44M West
Sheridan	44D 46M North / 106D 58M West

ATTACHMENT TWO
BRIEF DESCRIPTION OF RADIOACTIVE FALLOUT

Radioactive fallout is created by thermonuclear weapons as a result of residual radiation, that is, radiation that occurs or is induced in particulate matter approximately one minute after detonation. In thermonuclear weapons especially, large numbers of high-energy neutrons are produced, which interact with elements in the air and on the ground; these elements then become radioactive and in turn emit beta and gamma radiation.

Fallout may be considered of two kinds: early and delayed. Early fallout occurs within 24 hours and is the most severe. Fallout of this type produces contamination and presents a biologic hazard. Delayed fallout produces very fine particles of radiated material that are spread in the atmosphere. The hazard with delayed fallout is long term, especially because of elements with very long half-lives, such as cesium 137 and strontium 90.

Airbursts are more likely to produce delayed fallout because of the height of detonation. Surface bursts, conversely, produce fallout that is more localized but more intense.

Radioactive particles generally vary in size from 1 micron to several millimeters. The larger particles tend to fall within 24 hours and are the most radioactive. Between 50 and 70 percent of total radioactivity is produced as early fallout.

Weapons can be made to produce larger amounts of radioactive elements, hence the term 'dirty weapons.' This is done by using all-fission warheads or by enhancing thermonuclear weapons with additional fission steps. In addition, thermonuclear weapons can be wrapped in tungsten or cobalt casings.

Fallout is carried by winds and is affected by altitude, moisture content of air, etc. A 10 MT surface weapon, for example, can, on detonation, rise to a height of 80,000 feet, thus introducing radioactive particles into airstreams that circle the earth. More localized fallout is subject to geographical contour, nature of burst, and other factors that make statistical predictability unreliable.

FALLOUT PATTERNS

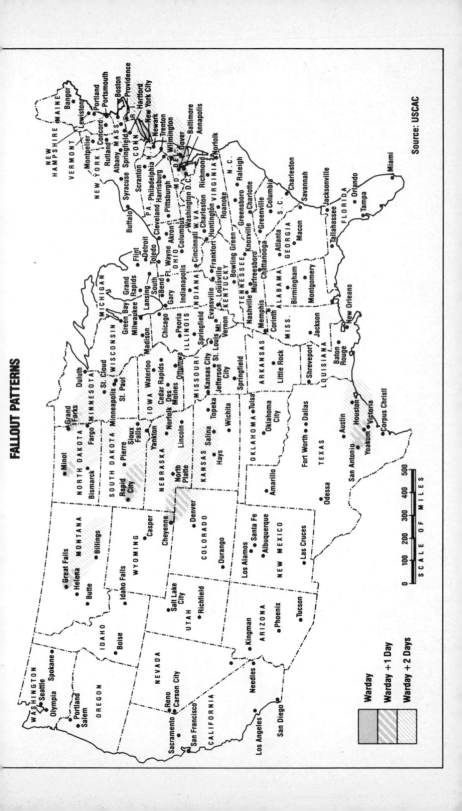

Source: USCAC

Warday

Warday + 1 Day

Warday + 2 Days

SCALE OF MILES
0   100   200   300   400   500

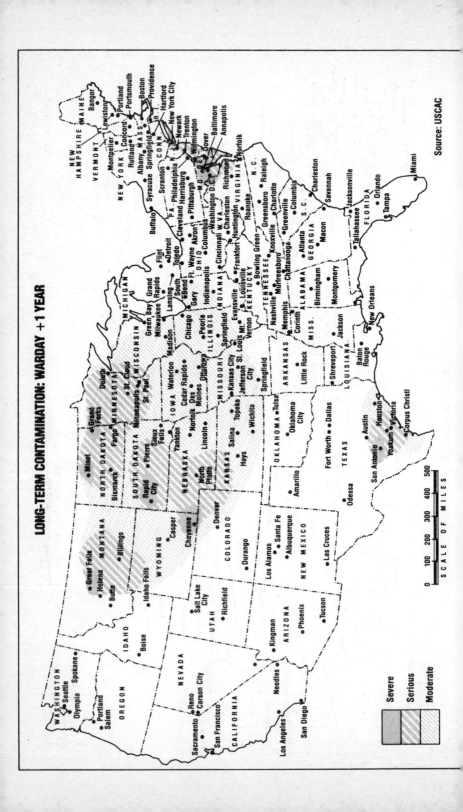

LONG-TERM CONTAMINATION: WARDAY + 1 YEAR

Source: USCAC

SCALE OF MILES

0   100   200   300   400   500

Severe

Serious

Moderate

LONG-TERM CONTAMINATION BY REPORTING COUNTIES: WARDAY + 4 YEARS

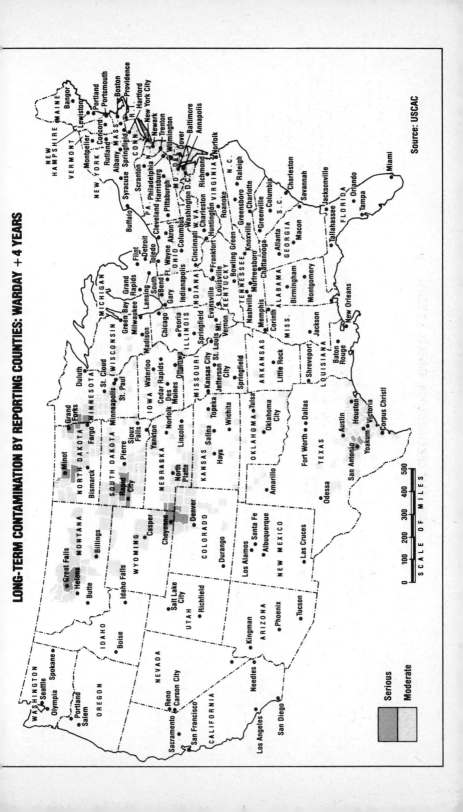

Serious

Moderate

SCALE OF MILES

0   100   200   300   400   500

Source: USCAC

The Rising of the Land

Just before a great storm is born in the plains, there often comes a time of perfect clarity. The sky becomes sharp, and the grasstops hang motionless.

Jim and I have been looking out the window of the train a long time. The air is a deep, clear blue all the way down to the northern horizon. But the horizon itself is the colour of baked clay. It is odd, something you look at very carefully. Something that makes you wonder.

We are between Topeka and Kansas City. The crop is sparse, and there are many empty fields.

All through '88 and '89, people left. One member of a family might get sick with some radiation-related illness or die of the flu and they would all leave, abandoning their acres to nature. But wheat and corn need tending. Left to themselves, these highly bred species do not go wild, they die. When the stalks rot or blow away, the raw dirt is exposed.

The wind has danced and eddied through the Midwest for years now, blowing the active particles about, depositing them as far south as Texas and as far east as Ohio.

It is not the kind of radiation that devastates bodies in hours – that was gone with the fireballs. It is the more insidious type that lodges in the ground or blows into the silos and the corncribs, and stays there.

'What's going on?' Jim asks.

At first I don't understand why. Then I realise the train has picked up speed. To reduce wear on equipment, Amtrak doesn't run much over fifty or sixty, but this train is doing seventy, maybe more.

Two rows ahead, a woman rises half out of her seat, shrinking away from the window.

I am shocked when I follow her eyes to the horizon. A vast black wall has risen there like some bloated mountain range, its topmost peaks streaming hazy fingers towards us across the sky.

People shout, their pale, frightened faces pressing the glass. The train sways, its horn sounding and sounding, and now I understand: we're running for shelter. If this dust storm stops us, we will be exposed to the full effect of whatever radiation it bears. A railroad car is little protection.

I feel bitter against myself. How dare I leave my wife and son to take risks like this! My own motives are inscrutable to me.

The light changes. Now the sun is being covered. The clear, still air around the train turns deep red. I can see the round orb of the sun behind a billowing cloud.

Then something incredible happens: in an instant it gets pitch dark. This is not the gloom of a storm or the darkness of night. It is the impossible, thick black of a cave.

The storm wails around the car as if the whole land had risen up and was screaming at us, screaming with a rage that went right down to the centre of the planet.

The conductor manages to get the lights on. The air is dirty tan, the dust already so thick we cannot see the front of the car.

We are so small in this rocking, shaking train, nothing but a few tattered bits of bone and flesh, eyes flashing in brown murk.

There is a squeal and a jerk, and the train stops.

'There's a shelter in the Shawnee Elementary School,' one of the trainmen shouts. 'Everybody out the second car. Hurry up, and take your stuff.' Shawnee is a suburb of Kansas City. I wish we had made it to the centre of town.

We form a human chain across the street, our way lit by tiny orange dots that must be streetlights. Somebody in full radiation gear is up ahead, waving a flashlight. I can hear the wind whipping his loose coverall. Then I see a black building. I am choking on dust, I can feel it getting deep into my lungs, smell the odour of dry earth, taste dirt.

As we enter the school, the wind whips through the open door, and the dust is soon thick in the hall.

'This way, keep moving, this way.' A policeman with another flashlight ushers us down some metal stairs and we find ourselves in the basement.

It's well lit, and the roar of the storm is more distant. Still, the building shudders, and I can hear windows shattering somewhere upstairs.

All around me, sitting in neat rows on the floor, are children. I'm stunned. I didn't expect a functional school. But why not? Kansas City still exists. There are people who didn't leave, and these must be their children.

'I'm your civil defence warden,' a young woman in jeans and cream-coloured shirt says. 'Welcome to Shawnee Shelter Number Twelve.' She looks at us, forty-odd scared people. 'I'm Joan Wilson. I teach third grade.'

Two more policemen come in. They have a geiger counter, which they proceed to sweep over our group. The ticking tells us that we have picked up a light dose.

I find that I take it like I might another blow in a place that has been hit a lot.

Other teachers have been bringing their classes down, and now the room is full. I realise from the blackboards and the desks that have been pushed aside that it is also Joan Wilson's classroom.

'Let's talk to her,' Jim says.

'Talk?'

'To the warden. Might be interesting.'

Also, it might take my mind off what has just happened to us. Being triaged can make you feel very naked at a time like this.

Joan Wilson isn't forthcoming, which is understandable, considering that she's got eighteen third-graders to worry about, not to mention the unexpected crowd from our train and the six or seven who have come in off the street.

She will not give us an interview. We have to content ourselves with a few quick questions.

'What are living conditions like here?'

She looks at me. She does not smile. 'It *was* getting better.'

'Do you have many dust storms?'

'This isn't a dust storm. It's the land, don't you understand that?'

'The land?'

Her voice is low and fierce. 'The plains themselves are blowing, right down to their core. There's never been a dust storm like this. But I'll tell you something, mister. I don't care how bad this storm is, or the next one or the one after that. I am staying here. I was born in Kansas City and I am not going to leave, and I'm not the only one. We made this place grow, and we'll make it grow again.'

She turns away. She doesn't want to keep talking. But there is one more question. In spite of her feelings, I must ask it. 'What about the children, Miss Wilson?'

She looks at me. The air between is brown now, as if a polluted fog had crept into the room. Wind screams outside. In the distance something clatters, maybe a tin roof blowing through the streets. 'The children?'

They do not look like the kids Andrew went to school with. They are as hard and tight as their Miss Wilson – quick, serious little people with sharp eyes. When I meet those eyes, they do not look away and they do not smile.

Soon one of the other teachers begins reading a book for the benefit of the whole student body, which counts perhaps eighty children. It is *Beauty and the Beast*. They listen in silence.

Kansas City – Children's Thoughts

Essays on spring from Miss Wilson's third grade, Shawnee Elementary School.

SPRING RAIN INSTRUCTIONS

If it rains get inside right away. And if you get wet you have to go to the office for geiger, then showers and get rid of your clothes. If you don't have any more you have to be in your underpants. You have to be careful, but spring rain is also nice.

I LOVE SPRING

The frogs croak and the mayflies fly. Mommy prays for the cabbages, which are just now coming out of the ground. They say spring is the time of hope. We read about lilacs.

SPRING RAIN DANGER

I got inside to keep it off me. I saw it go down on Barko. They won't let me have Barko. Spring rain danger. My daddy tried to keep it off our onions but he got all wet himself and there wasn't enough plastic from the allocation. Rain from the east is good, but if it comes from the west, just say your prayers, like it did Thursday.

RAINBOW

Lord Jesus sent a rainbow to say its OK, folks. Dad and Mom went on the cleanup. I was scared, I was home alone all night. Then Miss Wilson came and said come to the cleanup. They taught me how to get the particles with the Dustbuster, and I got a lot. They paint a red circle around them. Then you suck them up. Then you go to the next one, until your Dustbuster is out of juice. The Dustbusters are heavy because they have lead on them.

OUR FARM IN SPRING

Our mare is getting ready to foal. I am going to help deliver her with my dad. Mom and Dad said God gave us this foal, but I think War Cloud and Joanie did it when they jumped on each other last year. And we also have pigs.

WARM DAYS

To me spring is warm days. The sun is out and we don't have to worry about the coal. We are OK on money. I am often in the garden. We have a general permission because my mom is a garden freak. She makes salad all spring and summer. We sit outside on the back porch and shoot rabbits to eat with it. And I do not hurt when it is warm.

Documents on Limited War and the Limited Economy

> Red wine in the sunlight,
> May weather –
> While white fine fingers
> Break the thin biscuit . . .
> – Osip Mandelstam,
>   from *Stone*

LET THEM EAT WORDS

The official word from the Federal Complex in LA on the economy was one of cautious optimism.

In fact, there is no single American economy. It is possible to define the two big ones of East and West, but beyond those there are many, many more.

As we crossed the country from the prosperous valleys of the Pacific Coast to the dark Northeastern ports, we encountered dozens of economies. Life has focused down: people don't think in terms of long-range movement and trade any more, outside

California anyway. The concern is the farm on the hill, the plant down the street, the condition of one's own belly.

The following three documents illustrate how we have re-focused to microeconomies because of the suddenness with which the macroeconomy disintegrated and the deep conse-quences of the shortages that resulted.

The document on the effects of the electromagnetic pulse on Warday is in one way curious: it suggests that there has been steady recovery in such areas as communications and data processing, beginning shortly after Warday. But our lives tell us differently. Even today the overall amount of recovery seems smaller than indicated. It is probable that the document was prepared by people living and working in Los Angeles, who assumed that their local experience was being mirrored across the country, and wrote their projections accordingly.

The paper on shortages tells a central truth: the mineral resources upon which the fabrication of high-technology devices depends are no longer available in substantial quantities to the United States. In losing the electronic superstructure of our economy, we also lost the means to rebuild it, and we must now look to the outside for help.

There is also a report on the state of agriculture. If a bureaucrat could write a dirge, this is a dirge. It is about 450 words long.

With twenty-nine million dead in the famine, that is over 64,000 lives per word.

SUMMARY OF EFFECTS INDUCED BY ELECTROMAGNETIC PULSE
IN THE OCTOBER 1988 ATTACK BY THE SOVIET UNION,
AND THEIR IMPLICATIONS FOR RECOVERY

Defense Joint Systems Command
28 April 1991

1.0 OBJECTIVE

This report summarizes studies completed in the last seven months regarding multiple high-altitude nuclear detonations by the Soviet Union on 28 October 1988 over the United States of America. These detonations created powerful electromagnetic energy fields, known as electromagnetic pulse or EMP, which in turn produced widespread damage in both military and civilian enterprises. Data utilized in this report were supplied by the Department of Defense Joint Task Force on Nuclear Weapons Effects; Headquarters, Aerospace Defense Command; and the National Security Agency.

2.0 BACKGROUND OF THE SOVIET ATTACK

The nuclear attack in October 1988 by the Soviet Union against the continental United States was initialized by the detonation of six large weapons in the 8-10 MT range some 200–225 miles above the U.S. Comprehensive studies of the attack and its effects are limited because of critical wartime conditions, though it is believed, according to limited data from intelligence satellites, that as many as 12 large MT weapons were targeted by the Soviets as EMP devices. Only six such weapons actually detonated, however.

Nuclear weapons detonated at such high altitudes produce extraordinary electromagnetic fields, which in turn travel within the atmosphere and then strike the surface of the earth, where they can either severely damage or destroy sensitive electronic devices. A single weapon, detonated at a predetermined altitude, can affect an area of hundreds of thousands of square miles. The purpose of the Soviet attack, therefore, was to 'blanket' the United States with preemptive levels of electromagnetic energy designed to destroy or severely cripple communications, data storage and processing and electronic intelligence/detection capacities. Studies have shown that each detonating weapon apparently produced a peak field in excess of 100,000 volts per meter. Precise data are unavailable, though the energy fields thus produced far exceeded prewar military estimates of theoretical attacks. There were collateral effects on both surface installations and spaceborne intelligence satellites.

The six EMP weapons detonated in a pattern roughly forming two unequal triangles covering both halves of the continent. The effects were most pronounced in the U.S., but Canada, Mexico, and several Central American countries reported effects to one degree or another. There were substantial effects absorbed by both military and civilian populations.

A second attack wave followed, with strikes directed at three large urban centers and selected ICBM/SAC targets in the upper Central states. Recent data suggest that as much as 300 MT of total destructive yield were realized in this second and ultimately final movement. The Western, Southwestern, and Central states were unaffected directly, though it is not known at this time whether this limited attack pattern on the part of the Soviets was the result of retaliatory American counterattacks or equipment failures in Soviet weaponry, or whether it was simply one phase of a larger but uncompleted Soviet attack strategy.

3.0 EMP EFFECTS

3.1 General

EMP forces generate enormously high voltages, which destroy the atomic structures of earthbound or spaceborne objects containing electronic circuitry. This energy, which lasts only several billionths of a second, is sufficient to 'burn out' most circuits such as those utilized by microchips and similar devices. Consequently, six 9–10 MT Soviet weapons, detonated over 200 miles above the United States, produced a nearly simultaneous energy field that destroyed close to 70 percent of all microelectronics in use by both military and civilian organizations. Shielding, such as that employed in the late prewar years by both the military and industry, was largely ineffective in coping with blasts and subsequent EMP forces of such magnitude. The two areas most severely affected by the EMP effect, for both the military and civilian populations, were communications and electronic data storage/processing.

Brief summaries of the damage sustained by EMP are described in the following sections.

3.2 Military

3.2.1 Overview

Five broad areas within the military system sustained the most severe damage from EMP-generated effects:

AREA	PERCENTAGE OF DAMAGE SUSTAINED
Communications	75%
Data storage/processing	75
Guidance systems	65
Intelligence-gathering systems	60
Detection systems, including radar	70

3.2.2 Discussion

Overall assessment: Nearly catastrophic at 70-percent level.

The substantial dependence by the military establishment on microelectronics is demonstrated by the severe damage rates cited above. Prewar shielding procedures and methods proved to be largely ineffective. The failure to sufficiently employ 'hardened' microchips is only one explanation, however. Although experiments were conducted before the war to measure EMP effects, all experiments failed to consider the massive EMP forces created by large MT weapons geostrategically placed. As demonstrated above, most communications, guidance, and information storage/processing capabilities were destroyed. Continental radar systems were similarly affected and, because of orbital satellite conditions and in-flight aircraft locations, substantial intelligence-gathering capacities were destroyed. Communication facilities utilizing lasers, buried light fibers, and similar equipment survived relatively unharmed. Guidance systems in ICBMs in hardened silos also survived. Electronic equipment utilizing non-microelectronic components received little or no damage.

3.2.3 Recovery Projections

Recovery of microelectronic capacities is dependent upon three critical factors: (1) the ability to replace/convert damaged components and systems with stockpiled prewar components/systems; (2) the capacity to replace damaged systems with new systems utilizing imported microelectronic components; and

(3) the long-term capacity of the United States to rebuild its microelectronic industries.

Given these three factors, the following projections have been made:

AREA	PERCENTAGE OF RECOVERY IN CAPACITY TO DATE	PERCENTAGE OF CAPACITY NONRECOVERABLE
Communications	25%	45%
Data processing/ storage	20	65
Guidance systems	60	22
Intelligence-gathering systems	18	72
Detection systems	24	40

The 'Percentage of Capacity Nonrecoverable' statistics suggest estimated requirements for both imports and internal U.S. rebuilding efforts.

3.3 Civilian

3.3.1 Overview

This study has identified 12 major civilian business/industry/public enterprise areas most affected by EMP-generated effects:

TYPE OF ENTERPRISE	PERCENTAGE OF DAMAGE SUSTAINED
Computer/information systems	87%
Defense industry	57
Electronic/telecommunications	73
Financial industry	41
Government (all levels)	67
Heavy industry	31
Manufacturing	28
Petrochemical	38
Power/utilities	57
Service industry	39
Transportation	60

3.3.2 Discussion

Overall assessment: High-end damage at 5∅-percent level. The nation's civilian enterprises were affected almost as significantly as the military, perhaps because of inadequate shielding provisions. Although no precise figure can be calculated, it is believed that over 5∅ percent of the nation's civilian micro-electronic capacities were destroyed by EMP.

As with the military, the prewar civilian groups, including government, made extensive use of microelectronics, largely in computer applications for information storage and processing, and to a lesser extent in systems for manufacturing, airplane guidance, radio and television communications, and the like. Unfortunately, because of national defense and reconstruction needs, few prewar surplus components are available and current import allocations are limited. As a consequence, the rate of recovery is lower than that for the military.

3.3.3 Recovery Projections

Projections for civilian recovery are based on factors similar to those outlined in 3.2.3 above. They are as follows:

AREA	PERCENTAGE OF RECOVERY IN CAPACITY TO DATE	PERCENTAGE OF CAPACITY NONRECOVERABLE
Computer, information systems	24%	55%
Defense industry	27	57
Electronics/ telecommunications	37	72
Financial industry	21	60
Government (all levels)	32	45
Heavy industry	15	40
Manufacturing	15	57
Petrochemical	39	46
Power/utilities	42	37
Service industry	18	69
Transportation	26	59

4.0 SUMMARY

Prewar estimates of EMP effects have proven to be vastly understated and to some extent unforeseen. EMP effects are centered on microelectronic components, and all levels of both military and civilian populations were affected. Prewar efforts to shield sensitive systems were, to an unfortunate degree, ineffective. Only large-scale prewar efforts to stockpile critical components have permitted the constrained recovery which has occurred to date. There remains a severe shortage of these components and systems, which only accelerated Allied imports and long-term rebuilding can overcome.

DEPARTMENT OF DEFENSE REPORT D-8072

SUMMARY REPORT OF CRITICAL MINERALS NEEDS, 1991–1995
TASK FORCE ON CRITICAL MATERIALS
MARCH 31, 1991

There is at present a severe shortage of materials, especially minerals, necessary for reestablishing the defense capability of the United States. While many factors impact recovery, including the necessary commitment of resources by the government, no progress can be made in the production of many microelectronic components of aircraft and weapons systems without necessary supplies of certain critical minerals. Prewar stockpiles have been nearly exhausted and imports are at present minimal because of present conditions in the world trade system and breakdown of prewar alliances.

This task force has identified eleven minerals, or mineral groups, that are crucial to defense needs and are unavailable in any quantity in this country. Table One outlines these materials and the location of major reserves outside the United States. It should be pointed out that while reserves of these critical materials may exist, they may not be available to our industries. Recent political and economic postures put forth by the NATO countries, for example, suggest that internal restrictions may have been put on certain strategic materials. While it is not the purpose of this report to examine the rationale of these restrictions, they will no doubt further impede U.S. defense recovery.

TABLE ONE
PRINCIPAL SUPPLIERS OF CRITICAL DEFENSE MATERIALS

MINERAL	COUNTRIES WITH MAJOR RESERVES AND PERCENT OF WORLD TOTAL
BAUXITE	Guinea 28% Australia 20% Brazil 11% Jamaica 9% Cameroon 4%

MINERAL	COUNTRIES WITH MAJOR RESERVES AND PERCENT OF WORLD TOTAL
CHROMITE (Chromium Ore)	South Africa 68% Zimbabwe 30%
COBALT	Zaire 49% Zambia 15% USSR 9% Cuba 8% Philippines 8% New Caledonia 4% Australia 2%
COLUMBIUM	Brazil 79% USSR 17% Canada 3%
MANGANESE	USSR 45% South Africa 41% Australia 6% Gabon 3%
NICKEL	New Caledonia 25% Canada 15% USSR 14% Indonesia 13% Philippines 10% Australia 9%
PLATINUM GROUP	South Africa 81% USSR 17%
TANTALUM	Zaire 57% Nigeria 11% Thailand 7% USSR 7% Malaysia 5%
TIN	Indonesia 16% China 15% Malaysia 12% Thailand 12% USSR 10% Bolivia 9%

MINERAL	COUNTRIES WITH MAJOR RESERVES AND PERCENT OF WORLD TOTAL
TITANIUM ORES a. ILMENITE	India 23% Canada 22% Norway 18% South Africa 15% Australia 8% United States 8%
b. RUTILE	Brazil 74% Australia 7% India 6% South Africa 4% Italy 2%
TUNGSTEN	China 52% Canada 20% USSR 8% United States 5% North Korea 5% South Africa 3%

The minerals listed above, for all of which the U.S. is highly dependent on imports, are classified as vital to defense production and have limited convenient substitution possibilities in their major applications. The implications of worldwide reserves are as much political as economic. Only some of the nations identified are at present friendly with the United States. Other nations are themselves crippled as a result of the world economy and are experiencing difficulty in reestablishing prewar mining levels. Still others, including those under Allied spheres of influence, are perhaps being subjected to diplomatic pressures that make open exchange with the U.S. difficult.

It is recommended that this information be shared as soon as possible with the Executive Branch and with appropriate units within the Departments of State and Commerce.

UNITED STATES DEPARTMENT OF
AGRICULTURE NEWS

LOS ANGELES, CALIFORNIA 9Ø Ø48

Public Information Office
(213-555-6263)   FOR RELEASE 7/21/92

AMERICAN AGRICULTURAL PRODUCTION STILL DOWN IN 1991; WAR AND FALLOUT ZONES MOST AFFECTED

Agricultural productivity in America is still suffering from the effects of the 1988 war.

The first comprehensive study since 1987 of agricultural productivity in America has just been completed by the U.S. Department of Agriculture. The results reveal that even after three years, the United States still lags behind prewar productivity by nearly 5Ø percent. As a result, U.S. exports have dropped by more than 95 percent.

In 1987, for example, the nine major agricultural exports were wheat, oats, corn, barley, rice, soybeans, tobacco, edible vegetable oils, and cotton. In that year the United States accounted for more than 3Ø percent of the total world production in these nine products. In 1991, however, the U.S. accounted for only 14 percent of the total world production. Table One summarizes this trend.

The Department's recent study also confirms early surveys, which suggested that the 19 states most directly affected by the war remain considerably behind the rest of the nation in agricultural recovery. These states were either directly struck by the Soviets in 1988 or suffered from high levels of radioactive fallout. Total U.S. agricultural production is particularly affected because of the high prewar concentration of farms in these 19 states.

Although the study covers all phases of agriculture, wheat production is used as a standard to reveal the scope of diminished American productivity. Table Two uses wheat-production data for 1987 and 1991 as a benchmark for demonstrating the effects of the war in 19 critical states.

TABLE ONE
U.S. AND WORLD PRODUCTION OF KEY AGRICULTURAL PRODUCTS

	1987		1991	
COMMODITY	U.S. PERCENTAGE OF WORLD PRODUCTION	PERCENTAGE OF U.S. EXPORTS	U.S. PERCENTAGE OF WORLD PRODUCTION	PERCENTAGE OF U.S. EXPORTS
Wheat	18.1%	53.0%	7.9%	Negligible
Oats	18.3	5.1	6.7	Neg.
Corn	49.2	73.2	30.4	Neg.
Barley	7.3	11.9	4.2	Neg.
Rice	2.7	24.4	2.0	Neg.
Soybeans	65.0	87.0	42.3	10.1%
Tobacco	17.1	22.1	14.6	5.2
Veg. oils	28.3	14.0	16.7	.5
Cotton	20.2	37.6	9.4	Neg.

TABLE TWO
U.S. WHEAT PRODUCTION BY YEAR AND SELECTED STATES

		WHEAT PRODUCTION IN MILLIONS OF BUSHELS	
	STATE	1987	1991
	Maryland	6.1	less than 1
	Montana	181.3	32.2
	North Dakota	352.6	67.8
	New York	7.6	2.1
WAR	New Jersey	2.5	less than 1
ZONES	Pennsylvania	9.9	3.2
	South Dakota	93.2	8.7
	Texas	189.4	110.2
	Virginia	18.1	7.8
	Wyoming	9.2	2.5

| | STATE | WHEAT PRODUCTION IN MILLIONS OF BUSHELS | |
		1987	1991
	Indiana	68.3	43.2
	Iowa	5.1	3.1
	Kansas	331.1	170.3
FALLOUT	Michigan	46.7	30.2
ZONES	Minnesota	160.2	93.2
	Missouri	125.1	87.7
	Ohio	83.4	43.8
	Nebraska	115.5	23.2
	Wisconsin	7.2	3.7

In 1987, these 19 states accounted for 6Ø percent of all U.S. wheat production. Combined with the overall reduction in the number of farms since 1988, total American wheat production is approximately half of what it was before the war.

The full report, detailing all aspects of U.S. productivity, is available as A Comprehensive Study of American Agricultural Production, 1987–1991, AG92-S1-8. Copies are available for 25¢ from the Superintendent of Documents, U.S. Government Printing Office, Los Angeles, California 9ØØ47, or from the U.S. Department of Agriculture in major cities.

I Will

The rich farmland of northern Missouri was dusted brown, the towns were brown, the late-summer trees were hazed with dust. Each town we passed through granted us a secret glimpse down its streets. An occasional decontamination team could be seen in white coveralls, seeking slowly along the sidewalks, or a cleanup crew with a water truck spraying the pavement. We saw into backyards where people were cleaning clothing, furniture, and each other with hoses.

And everywhere, as passengers came and went, we heard tales of the storm. It was the biggest duster in history. Winds clocked at a hundred and ten miles an hour and more in town after town. Took roofs, cars, collapsed buildings, reduced a dozen trailer parks to pulverised aluminium.

Despite it all, we found a powerful spirit moving among the people that seemed at moments almost otherworldly, as surprising as sudden speech from a Trappist.

SYLVIE WEST, MARCELINE, MISSOURI: 'I'm goin' up the line to La Plata to see that my mother's okay. We been in Missouri a long time, us Wests. We aren't going anywhere. A lot of people from around here went south, down to Alabama and Georgia and Florida. There's trouble getting into Georgia. But this is good land, and we just decided we'd stick it out. The storm? I've seen dust before.'

Sylvie West was the colour of the land, yellow-grey. Her arms were as long and improbable as the legs of a mantis. She was missing her bottom teeth.

GEORGE KIMBALL, EDINA, MISSOURI: 'It wasn't all that hot. We got a real low dose in Edina. I'm looking at it this way – I just got myself a whole lot of good black dirt from Nebraska scot-free. Hell no, I'm not goin' anywhere. I stayed right in Edina through the war and the famine and the flu. That's the place for me. I'm a farmer, of course. I guess you could say I like the look of the town, and I like the people. The stayers, that is. The loafers and the new people all went south. But Missouri needs her people now, and I am not leaving.'

He carried a weathered Samsonite briefcase, which turned out to be full of warehouse receipts recertified that morning by the Knox County Radiation Board. He was on his way to Galesburg to present these receipts to the accepting agent for the Agriculture Department's Regional Strategic Grains Allocation Commission. His wedding ring was on his right hand, signifying his widowerhood.

ALFRED T. BENSEN, GALESBURG, ILLINOIS: 'I am in the practice of law in Galesburg, Illinois. I have been in my practice for twenty-eight years, and expect to continue until the day I die. I noticed some dust. But I was working through some title questions for a client and I did not have time to deal with it. This is a man who's been able to buy up over sixty thousand acres at auction in the past year. Abandoned farm properties. This man is twenty-eight. By the time he's fifty, you watch. Illinois will have done for him what it's done for millions in the past. It will have made him rich.'

He sat rigidly against his seat, his dark blue suit shiny from many ironings. He spoke as if he had memorised his lines, and been waiting for years to deliver them. Once I noticed him looking long and carefully at us, through brown, slow eyes.

GORDON LOCKHART, LASALLE, ILLINOIS: 'We got a little dust, but most of the blow was south of here. I am an International Harvester dealer. As of December of this year I will be able to sell you a tractor, a combine, just about any piece of equipment you want. What Harvester did was very smart. They just went out, over the past few years, and repossessed all the abandoned IH equipment they could lay their hands on. Meanwhile, they were getting the factories running again. Nobody was getting paid, but the company organised an employee barter co-op, so Harvester people didn't starve, either. We have company doctors and now a company hospital, so the triage doesn't mean a thing to us. IH people are a big, rock-solid family. We are going to make this land work for us again, maybe better than it did before. No question. Better.'

A moment later he was asleep, snoring, his head thrown back, the midmorning sun full in his face. One of the trainmen came and tried to get him to eat some soup, but after he was awakened he spent the rest of the trip staring out the window.

JOHN SAMPSON, JOLIET, ILLINOIS: 'We got the prison here, and a sure sign that things are picking up is that we got more inmates. Robbers, second-story men, mostly. No more drug dealers. That kind of petered out. Nobody wants to import drugs into a country where the money's worthless. We don't have many murderers, either. No car thieves. Joliet's kind of quiet. About half the bunks are filled. We got the electric chair back, and once in a while somebody gets the juice. Illinois abides by the US Supreme Court rulings, even though there isn't any Supreme Court any more. We still work under the old laws, just like before Warday. Why shouldn't we? This is part of America, and it is going to stay that way.'

The other passengers kept away from Mr Sampson. It might have been better for him to travel in ordinary clothing. His Joliet prison guard's uniform made his fellow passengers uneasy, and he had a lonely trip.

Twenty-five miles from the Loop, we began to pass through Chicago's suburban and then industrial outlands. The suburbs are mostly depopulated. People have moved into the city centres or rejoined the small-town economy rather than contend with the difficult transportation problems of suburban life.

Just as Chicago's skyline appeared ahead of us, we passed a tremendous sign, red letters on a white background:

CHICAGO, THE 'I WILL' TOWN
HAVE WE GOT A JOB FOR YOU!

I had again that sense of strangeness, as if I had come upon the spirit of the past alive and still moving in the land. It was a little frightening, but it could also fill me with the reckless energy of boosterism gone frantic.

We moved through a sea of factories with names like Ryerson Steel, Kroehler, Burlington Northern, and Nabisco. Some of these establishments were empty, but others were running – Nabisco, as it turned out, on what must have been an all-out schedule. A fifty-car freight was sided there, being loaded. People were swarming along the loading bays where trucks once came and went, hauling boxes on trolleys to the new rail siding. Another brand-new sign was in place here: NABISCO FEEDS AMERICA. I remembered them as a cookie manufacturer, but a passenger whose brother worked there explained that the company was now producing high-protein baked goods of all kinds: breads, biscuits, noodles, and other basic foodstuffs. I could not resist asking about Oreos. The answer: 'Available on a limited basis'.

By the time we reached Union Station, we had been thoroughly indoctrinated. Word had spread through the train that we were writing a book about the present condition of the country. 'We're sick of the "devastated Midwest" cliché,' Tom Walker of Chicago said. 'You guys make sure you see the real Chicago. Stay in the Loop. The Loop is Chicago.'

This is true, but not in the way he meant. From our own estimates, it appears that the city has lost perhaps half of its population in the past five years. Considering the destruction of agriculture, the famine, the flu, the lack of transportation, the economic chaos, and the massive depopulation, it is amazing that the city has retained such a strong governmental organisation. All that's left is the Loop. But the Loop is a good town.

Seeing the Loop, one would never know that Chicago had lost a single citizen. It has none of the subdued intensity of San Francisco or Los Angeles. The Loop is exploding with energy. The El works, and where it goes, the city works too. In the Loop there are buses and trolleys, seemingly by the thousands. At times it seemed hard to cross a street without stepping into one.

We are quite frankly at a loss to explain why this city, in the middle of what is arguably the most harmed area in the country, is so very much alive – or why the rural population we met on the train was so uniformly determined to reconstruct. We might have felt better about it if the energy of the place had seemed deeper and stronger. There is a frantic, gasping quality to it, as if the city were a runner who is beginning to know that, no matter how much he wants to succeed, he is going to have to drop back.

People who stay in places this badly hurt do so because they are in love with them. I suspect that the only people left here are the passionate.

A lot of prewar Chicago shops are closed. Jim stated this observation to a woman on Upper Michigan Avenue. She replied, 'Sure. And a lot of them are open, too.' It would be outrageous to fault Upper Michigan for being less grand than it was before the war. Gucci and Hermès are closed, as are Neiman-Marcus and Bonwit Teller. I. Magnin is selling suits for two paper dollars, and other no-nonsense apparel. They had a good selection of imported perfume, but all of it was priced in gold. This was generally true of imports throughout the store. The two exceptions were Canadian furs and British clothing. The British sell soft goods for paper dollars; they get their American gold through direct transfer for government services and such things as the sale of automobiles. Judging from the aggressive British presence in the store, the programme of tax incentives for accepting dollars, which Number 10 Downing Street announced last summer, is beginning to work. Jim and I both hope that Neiman's in Dallas (which is very much open) will have some British things by the time we get back.

The Gold Coast is densely populated, but it does not glitter as it once did. Many of the high-rises have a noticeable proportion of boarded windows. Glass is in short supply locally, as it is almost everywhere.

Lake Point Towers has had especially severe problems in this regard, and is no longer the uniform bronze colour it once was. In addition to boardings, there are many areas of differently tinted glass, some of it even clear.

The *Tribune*, which we were told by a number of people missed only six days after Warday, is much in evidence. The paper I bought for a penny was in one section of sixteen pages. Here are the front-page headlines for Wednesday, September 29, 1993:

DUST STORM STRIKES MIDWEST. WINDS TO 110 MPH. RADLEVEL MEASURES LOWER THAN EXPECTED.

TRACTION SCANDAL. NORTHSIDE TRACTION BOND FRAUD THREATENS TO STOP THE TROLLEYS.

BODY FOUND IN TRUNK OF CAR. FIRST WARD COUNTS ITS SIXTH FOR THE YEAR.

BOARD OF TRADE RIOT. DUST CAUSES BIDDING FRENZIES IN WHEAT, CORN. 'NO LIMIT' PRICES TRIPLE IN MINUTES.

MAYOR INAUGURATES FAR-REACHING ART RECLAMATION PROJECT AT ART INSTITUTE CEREMONIES.

The last story went on to explain that the Chicago Art Institute had joined with museums in Boston, Cleveland, and Pittsburgh to reclaim and restore paintings and other works of art abandoned in New York.

This project has been undertaken in response to the removal by many European museums of works by their national artists from New York galleries. A team from the Louvre even dismantled the Chagall murals from the Metropolitan Opera House in Lincoln Center and took them to Paris.

At the Art Institute, we stood looking at a painting from New York. It was Van Gogh's *Starry Night*, taken a week before by the Chicago reclamation team. It is greyed by soot, but beneath the haze there remains the extraordinary vision of the heart of the sky.

While at the Art Institute, we met a member of its board of directors, Chandler Gayle. He informed us that the reclamation project was essential not only to forestall further losses to Europe, but also to protect the paintings themselves, which were deteriorating rapidly.

Dr Gayle, it turns out, is director of the Nonspecific Sclerosing Disease Research Facility at the University of Chicago. We eagerly made an appointment to interview him about NSD later in the day.

By the time we were finished at the Art Institute, it was nearly eleven-thirty. Jim and I agreed that a visit to the Board of Trade was essential, especially in view of the headline in the *Tribune*.

We took a bus across Adams to La Salle and walked down to the weathered Art Deco structure.

Things have changed since the war. We asked a guard about this. 'Better than ever,' he snapped.

The first sign of change is the number of messengers running in and out of the building. This area is not nearly as heavily rewired as is, say, California, and the most reliable method of conveying information from rural communities about the state of farm output is by hand. These messengers would pull up in orange Americars and Consensuses with CBT markings on the doors and rush inside, bearing their field information in brief-cases similar to the one carried by the farmer on the train.

The whole length of La Salle was taken up with their cars, so much so that some of them had to scramble over the roofs to get to the building. A few had walkie-talkies, but most were without such sophisticated equipment. Inside the exchange were more runners, from the big trading houses and from individual traders on the floor. The Agriculture Department is also a major trader, using such warehoused grains as it has to attempt to stabilise prices.

As we entered the gallery and looked out over the Wheat Pit, a shout rang out: 'Aggie's out! The bull's buried Aggie!' A split second of stillness, and then there was a renewed frenzy of trading, and the clerks began racing back and forth, changing their prices on the big chalkboards that have replaced the electronic quotation devices of prewar days. November wheat went from thirty cents to thirty-two to thirty-three-and-a-half in minutes.

I noticed that some of the traders wore green hats with what looked to be a bite taken out of the rim. Later I found out that this had to do with the war. Traders so decorated had been present on the day after Warday. (The Board had already shut for the day when the nuclear exchange took place.) On that day, with no electric power and the Board's electronic devices out of commission, trading was active but extremely difficult. About noon, the Bond Pit closed for lack of information. Then a rumour swept the pits that there had been a nuclear exchange the afternoon before. Communications were so bad that Washington had been destroyed and New York burning for eighteen hours before Chicago learned about it.

The rumour precipitated a massive run-up in prices until one of the Board managers sounded the gong and entered the pit. The exchange was closed. At that moment the pit's oldest trader, Willie 'Eat My Hat' Dobbs, collapsed and died of a stroke.

The hats are in memory of him.

We stood in the gallery, watching the wild action. By twelve-thirty the price of wheat had gone to fifty-six-and-a-quarter cents. As we left, it reached sixty cents. The dust storm had

malnutrition and economic disruption. Of course, we knew that the population was debilitated. We Cincinnati doctors had organised into teams and groups to attempt to cope with the tremendous demand and the lack of communications. It was at a group meeting that I first heard of an unusual case of flu. We were very concerned. From the beginning, we saw a high potential for disaster.

The aetiology of the disease was suggestive of a produced, rather than a natural, factor. It occurred to us then that the Cincinnati Flu might have been released by enemy action or by an accident at a military facility in the area. It is also possible that there was a radiation-induced mutation of the common flu strain known as Influenza A. This is the sort of flu most often associated with pandemics. The serotype was unusual; usually each new serotype of this disease follows a pattern of extrapolation from the previous serotype. Only when a new serotype is radically different from the one previous can a pandemic occur, because only then is the entire population of the planet susceptible.

The Cincinnati Flu was a radically different serotype, at least four generations removed from Delhi-A, the previous serotype. We still have no way to explain this. The Spanish Flu of 1918 was probably a similar radical serotype. It could be that the presence of large, weakened populations encourages the proliferation of new influenza serotypes. We just don't know.

This influenza caused the most dramatic pneumonic infection we have observed. Infants and the elderly usually died within six hours. A strong, middle-aged adult might linger for three or four days. The mortality rate was about sixty per cent in Cincinnati, and about three out of ten people contracted the disease. What that meant in human terms was that, during the six weeks that the virus was active, we lost nearly eighty thousand people. To give you an idea of the magnitude of the problem, about five thousand people died in Cincinnati in 1987, the year before the war. All of a sudden we were dealing with close to two thousand new cadavers a day, and they carried a highly contagious disease. To make matters worse, seven out of ten hospital personnel and half of all mortuary and graveyard workers contracted the disease. Eight out of ten doctors contracted it. We actually had to abandon the hospitals. The real heroes of the flu were the people who went in there on their own to help out, and not only in

Cincinnati, but all over the country. All over the world, I suppose.

I have always been sorry that the flu had to start in Cincinnati. I love that town. It was my home and it was where my children were born. I would have stayed there happily for the rest of my life, if it hadn't been for the war.

But the flu's come and gone. We still have NSD with us. I'll turn to my work in this area unless you two have any more questions about the flu.

JIM: I was there during the worst of it. I remember the bodies in Eden Park.

DR GAYLE: We were desperate. That wasn't the only public park in the world where cadavers were stored. Look, this is tough for me. I'd really prefer to go on to NSD.

JIM: Sure. Thank you for sharing what you have with us. I know it's hard.

DR GAYLE: NSD is one of a cluster of postwar illnesses, previously unknown, which now affect the North American population. The combination of the radical negative alteration of the environment and the extraordinary and ceaseless stress of postwar life is believed to have caused the disappearance of these diseases, of which Nonspecific Sclerosing Disease is certainly the most serious. It is a central-nervous-system disorder and is apparently caused by unknown environmental factors. Current thinking is that contagion, if any, is limited to skin contact. NSD's early symptoms are dry, rigid skin occurring in patches, most often across the chest or abdomen. The development of massive cells leads to the 'lumpy' appearance that is the familiar presenting complaint. The progress of the disease is accompanied by generalised organic deterioration. As it spreads throughout the body, the dense, massive cell tissue causes various types of problems, ranging from interruption of ducted flows to actual destruction of organs due to compression or constriction. Death occurs sometimes as a result of a particular functional problem, such as the interruption of the heart or irreversible trachial constriction, but more often is caused by general collapse and exhaustion. The fatality rate is at present one hundred per cent.

At first the disease was approached by attempting surgical excision of the lesions. This was unsuccessful because of the broad-based nature of the disorder. A given patient at diagnosis will generally support two to three hundred lesions, most of them microscopic, spread throughout the body. Subsequently, chemotherapy and radiotherapy were tried, but the lesions were not responsive. Colour therapy, utilising so-called pink light, has tended to reduce speed of spread in early-diagnosed disease.

The permissible treatment group has recently been revised by the Centers for Disease Control to include only patients under thirty years of age, employed, and with dependent children. These patients will be treated with thrice-weekly exposures to pink light and hyperbaric oxygen therapy, which has proved effective in reducing itching in surface lesions. They will be allocated three hundred grains of aspirin per twenty-four hours. When they are declared in stage-three disease and unable to function, they will be offered the euthanasia option.

Euthanasia is mandatory for NSD-diagnosed children under twelve years of age. Responsible resource allocation prohibits treatment of children for this disease because there is no chance whatsoever of recovery. The extreme discomfort associated with the progress of the disease makes euthanasia the only humane alternative in childhood cases.

Patients over thirty are given the CDC publication *Blessed Relief*, which describes effective methods of euthanasia and explains how to stage the disease at home, so the patient can determine when further delay may lead to a *non compos mentis* situation developing, which would make it illegal to practice euthanasia and impossible for the patient to do it himself. There are many different types of health-care professionals capable of carrying out this type of care in a humane and dignified manner.

It is thus important that patients learn the symptoms of the third-stage preludium so that they can carry out their plans at the first sign.

The burning sensation commonly known as firepox is the most common initial sign of stage-three disease. This means that there has been invasion of the organs extensive enough to cause a build-up of uric acid in the blood. The firepox sensation occurs when acid-laden blood enters open second-stage lesions. Double vision, the seeing of flashes, hearing loud noises without known source, feeling of elation alternating with deep depression, sudden bursts of intense sexual desire, inappropriate laughter, 'Pell's sign', continuous vomiting, and the sloughing off of skin that had seemed healthy are signs that third-stage disease is fully developed. Euthanasia should be carried out without delay at this point.

The British Relief has determined that NSD is moving through the North American population at a nonexponential rate, suggesting that the illness is induced from something in the environmental background and is not spread person to person. British Relief statisticians have found that initial outbreaks of disease may occur anywhere on the continent, without regard to the background radiation level. For example, 3.34 per cent of the population of Greater Atlanta have NSD, even though GA enjoys a radlevel little higher than it was prewar. On the other hand, Houston, with its high radlevel, has only a 1.59 per cent incidence of the disease. Chicago, with a higher radlevel than Houston, has a 5.61 per cent incidence.

The possibility of an artificially induced vector – such as a delayed-activation biochemical weapon – cannot be discounted in the case of NSD any more than it can with the flu, but the spottiness of the outbreaks, and their tendency to cluster around specific small areas within the affected regions, suggests that some other factor is at work.

I guess that's all pretty technical, but it's the straight truth as I understand it. As yet, there is no central effort to determine the cause of Nonspecific Sclerosing Disease, because it affects a relatively small segment of the population and appears so intractable to even the most advanced attempts at analysis, much less cure.

As I said at the beginning, I am a medical doctor. I am also a recent convert to Catholicism. I converted a week after His Holiness declared that officially sanctioned voluntary euthanasia was not murder in North America and the Russian states. The chief thing I have to say is that I believe America is going to get through this. There will come a day when we doctors do not have to take life routinely, when we can help all people in need and not worry about the triage. I look forward to that day.

I have to stop now. I have a meeting with my Viral Particle Team now. Their job is to attempt to find a viral disease vector for NSD, but so far nothing has turned up.

Interview: Rita Mack,
Professional Rememberer

[THE ABSENT. We met Rita Mack on a streetcorner. If there is a truism about life in our times, it is that the poor die first. And in America that means, for the most part, the black.

In 1987 there were approximately thirty million black people in the United States.

I can remember walking the streets of Chicago a little earlier, in the autumn of 1983, and seeing black faces everywhere.

And now? The Loop is not empty of people, but blacks are rare.

There are stories of whole neighbourhoods starving, and there are long, blank streets.

We have no idea how many blacks remain alive in our country now. Their world was fragile because it was poor, and it obviously has not fared well. The loss of life among blacks must be much higher than among the rest of the population.

We saw very few black people on our journey. Certainly not in California, where Hispanics and Asians represent the major visible minorities. And on the road, the absence of black people was eerie at first, and finally terrifying.

By the time we reached Chicago we had come to feel an urgent need to seek out and interview someone who could effectively represent black experience.

Seeing Rita Mack, I experienced a kind of loneliness for the past. A black woman was partner in my raising. My earliest memory is of her face, peering down into my crib. There is thus some deep solace for me in the presence of black people. And their absence is fearful. These streets and buildings, this country, belonged to them just as certainly as it did to the wealthier elements of the society. When I saw Rita Mack hurrying towards me I wanted to embrace her, to greet her and hear her tell me that all was well, that black Chicago, once so powerful, had emigrated en masse to Atlanta or Birmingham or Mobile.

But she did not tell me that.]

I wouldn't say we were extinct. I wouldn't say that. But you look around this town and you see the worst emptiness in the black neighbourhoods. There was a whole world here that is gone now. I mean, a way of thinking and being alive that you would call the black way. There was a certain way of talking, a way of acting, a special kind of love. And violence, there was that too – kids running around with guns and knives and what-not. But the drugs were made in white factories – I refer here to the pills – and it was white capital in the form of Mafia money that brought in heroin from Asia. The black was the consumer. The black kid was the one they paid a dollar to let them mainline him out behind the school when he was fourteen years old. And why do they do this? They know that the black kid is strong, so the smack won't kill him before they get the profit, and the black kid is brave and smart, so he will be a good and cunning thief, and he is sad, wrapped up in that black skin of his, and he does not much like himself, so he will not be able to resist the smooth things the smack does to his body and mind.

But that's over, that's all gone. You had them dying in the millions, weakest first, step right up, and they just piled them up and they put up ropes around the worst neighbourhoods like the air itself had the infection, which I suppose it did. I looked at the way they treated the dead and I thought, 'They act like these are cardboard people, but they aren't, so show some respect, show some grief. They might be cardboard to you, but they had long histories in their minds, just like you do.'

I am referring to the flu now. These are my subjective impressions, you see. I consider myself a poet. I am not educated in the sense of having degrees, but in life, boy, am I educated. I have a PhD in starvation and an MD in Cinci Flu. I know how to sing. I am a rememberer of the old songs. I remember all the old blues, the songs of black people getting along somehow in the hot sun, the backs bent beneath the weight of work and the minds flashing with music, and also the songs of the urban street world, the songs that were like knives or like molten happiness. I want to say to you, we never had a chance. We were at the bottom of the list. The thirties saw a hell of a lot of black people starve. So did the forties and the fifties. We came out of the Depression only in the sixties. Then Martin Luther King said what was in our hearts. We *knew* how much we were worth, that we were sacred as all men of the earth are sacred, that we had in us the same spark of God any human being had, and we could lift up our hearts on high.

I was raised in Gulfport, Mississippi, and I remember the colour line very damn well. I'm fifty-six. They pulled down the colour lines in the sixties. I am stained by those memories, though, and I'll never really believe that anybody who lived under segregation is truly free. We cooperated, black and white, in mutual humiliation. They imposed it and we endured it. Separate water fountains in the bus stations, and separate lunch counters and sitting in the back of the bus and the top of the movie theatre. A thing like that stays with you. Sometimes I see lines where there aren't any lines. Sometimes I think it's still then. I could let it lie, but I owe this remembering to all black people who remain alive, and all human beings worth the title.

We moved to Chicago in '63, me and Henry. Let's see – '63 to '73, that's ten years. To '83 is another ten. Eighty-four, eighty-five . . . we lived together in this city for twenty-eight years. Lord, I was twenty-six when I came here with that man. Lord, I was a *girl!*

My Henry was a fine and loyal man and he made a good living. He was a baker. But big time, a factory baker. Sure, there was trouble. Some people didn't like a black man in that job. Naturally – it was a good job! But Henry, he knew what he was doing, how to bake ten dozen loaves of bread in those giant ovens and never burn a one. He also knew how to hold a good job and not let it go. As a kid he was on the migrant circuit, this and that, digging beets here and peanuts there, and picking cotton. He knew the difference between a good job and a bad job.

He got the flu, that man. He had lost forty pounds. We were living off roots and stuff. We would get some bread now and again from the city delivery. Bread and whatever else they had. Spinach one day. Collard greens another. Fried pork rind another. Then peas. You never knew. But thank the Lord for those trucks. There are good people in the world, black or white or you name it.

I spend my time working to preserve black culture. You have to hold on to things these days. The little details, they're important. I don't have any numbers to back me up, but I'll bet way more than half the black people are dead and gone. Right here in Chicago, you see all these empty black neighbourhoods. So many! Where are those people? They sure as hell didn't retire to the country!

We were the poorest, we starved first and worst. Because we starved the worst, we were the weakest, so the flu hit us the hardest. Look, I lost my husband. I lost my children. But a lot of whites had the same thing happen. The difference is, I also lost everybody I knew, and everybody at work, and all but a few of the people who lived around me. So now my life is full of new faces, and not a lot of them are black. And that is certainly not the white experience. Whites, you talk to them, and they lost a family member here, a friend there. I'm talking about loss on a different scale. The church I belonged to, for example – there are just thirty of us left, out of a congregation of a couple of hundred. Not to say they all died, but half of them did. The rest, they moved away, most of them looking for work or relatives or just a better colour of sky.

Whites look sort of surprised nowadays when they see this big coal-tar black woman, which is me, coming along. I see it time after time when I go down to the Loop. A Negro. A black. One of *them*. Before Warday they'd sort of close up on you. Look right through you. Like you didn't matter, or they wished you didn't matter. Now they just look and look. You can see that they are fascinated by your black face. I look at them, and in my heart I say, 'I am looking at you with two million eyes, for my face is a million black faces, and the look I am giving you is the reproach of a million souls.'

I hear the whole world singing in my memories. You'll never

guess it, but I sing for my supper now. You'll ask, 'How can this furious woman possibly be an entertainer?' But that's what I am. An entertainer. You ever hear of the Cotton Club on State? Well, I am the star attraction, practically. I sing for them. I am memory for them. Blacks and whites come. They mix together more easily now, probably because the whites no longer feel so threatened.

There I stand, on that little stage in that boozy and smoky hall, and I sing out all the sorrow that is in my soul. I sing until it hangs in the air around me and I am so sad I could die because that's the blues, but inside me where nobody can see there is God's glory, and that's the part of the blues they never talked about, but the part that's most important. The blues are true music of the human heart, the truest on earth, I think. How can we give up on the people who created this, and say they have no genius? Black genius doesn't have names attached to it. Black genius is not named Leonardo da Vinci or J. Robert Oppenheimer. Black genius flows in black blood, and has to do with pain.

I say we had a worse time than you did. Sure, why not? We were living from hand to mouth, most of us. Black meant poor. It also meant noble, and it meant good and full of joy that maybe had no business in there with the pain.

Am I angry? No, not any more. I am working and there is food on my table. I'm singing for my supper. Every night before I go to sleep, I remember Henry. I had a picture of him, but it got lost. My profession is to remember my people, and spread my memories among those who remain. I do it in songs. That is what they are for.

Anger

As we crossed Indiana on our way to Cleveland, the character of the passenger complement began to change. The train was still almost empty, but there was something familiar about the people. They pushed and shoved and muttered. They were noticeably more tattered than the passengers on the run from Kansas City to Chicago had been.

I recognised an accent, the harsh nasal twang of my old home-town. Refugees from New York have settled all through Ohio and Pennsylvania.

Jim went up and down the train and found that these people were almost exclusively former citizens of the Bronx, with a scattering of Manhattanites. Most of them were labourers, a few professionals. They were travelling for many different reasons: to visit or seek relatives; to look for work; to buy things such as clothing, car parts, or furniture, in Cleveland. None of them were making long-distance journeys. Although many expressed a desire to return to New York, those who had tried said that there was no way around the Army cordon.

Why the Army would cordon off what remained of New York was a puzzling question, one we were very eager to answer. It couldn't be radiation, not after five years. Of course, the radlevel will be higher by far than prewar, but we live with that in other places.

On the train there was a certain amount of talk about the World Series, which was being held this year at Fenway Park between the Red Sox and the Pittsburgh Pirates. We hadn't encountered much talk of sports on our trip. Dallas doesn't have a baseball team and we were running too hard in California to find out about sports.

Nobody on the train was going to the Series, but a lot of people were eager to see what the *Plain Dealer* had to say about it when they got to Cleveland.

We met one woman who was of special interest to me, as she was triaged and sick. She was going to Cleveland to visit a popular alternate practitioner, a witch named Terry Burford. I had been eager to interview an alternate practitioner, especially a witch. Since Warday our concept of witchcraft has, of course, changed radically, as they have begun to make themselves public as midwives, herbalists, and healers. How effective they are I do not know, but it seemed important to meet a modern practitioner, since so many of us may eventually depend on one for medical help.

Also on the train was one individual whose dress alone marked him as unusual and therefore of definite interest to us. We first saw this tall, elegant man heading from the sleeper to the diner. He was completely out of place on the train. Jim got out his recorder and we followed him into the dining car.

His name was Jack Harper. He was an exchange officer with the Royal Bank of Canada at Toronto. He told us: 'I am working on the development of the American Automobile Industry Refinance Plan with the Barclays Consortium, our bank, and the New Bank of North America. We're developing a private gold backing for a currency to be issued by the big three automakers themselves. We feel that the best way to deal with the problem of restarting the industry is to attract as many skilled workers back to the Detroit area as we can, rather than attempt to move the plants south. We are hoping that the prospect of being paid in a gold-backed currency will satisfy the concerns about nonpaid work that made them migrate in the first place, and we are guaranteeing a year's supply of Canadian beef to every registered member of the UAW who comes back. The combination of not getting paid and then getting hit by the famine has made these men extremely suspicious of their former employers.'

The waiter came up and Mr Harper ordered his lunch. The train had two meals available: soup and salad, or hamburger. Mr Harper ordered one of each, only to be told that there was a consumption restriction of one to a passenger.

'I hate the bloody States! Too bad there's no flight from Chicago to Detroit. It would have taken half an hour and I wouldn't be facing lunch in this diner.' He smiled tightly, but there was venom in his voice.

'Why do you hate us?'

'You mean you really can't think why? That's not surprising. I'll tell you, the US practically caused Canada to be destroyed. We were completely cocked up by Warday. The bank – you cannot imagine the anarchy. We lost not only our main computer but all our supporting computers as well. At the moment of the electro, we had about eight million in cash just evaporate, lost in the middle of electronic transfer. Within an hour the whole banking hall was filled with people shouting and waving paper records. We didn't know what we were doing or where we stood. It was madness, terrible madness. And it was caused by the United States and the damned missiles and the damned war. The phones were out, the lights were out, even the lockboxes were unavailable because the electronic locking mechanism was on the fritz.

'Canada had one hell of a time because of your little twenty-minute war, let me tell you. Then there was the Russian business in Alaska Territory, to add panic to the whole affair.'

'What Russian business, and what is Alaska Territory?'

'It used to be the state of Alaska until you ceded it to us last year.'

'We gave you Alaska?'

'The treaty was signed in LA and Ottawa in June of 1992. We interned the Soviet naval units that had docked in Anchorage, and it was decided in Ottawa that our national security depended upon our remaining in Alaska. We paid you thirty-five million gold dollars, so you needn't quibble.'

This did not seem like a very good price to us. 'What about Prudhoe Bay? What about the Alaska Pipeline?'

'It ends in Vancouver. Now, if I may, I'd like to attempt my lunch. What sort of grain do you suppose this false hamburger is made of?'

'Soy.'

'I'd say oatmeal, from the taste of the thing. The meat is indistinguishable from the bread. Oh, waiter!' The waiter came over. 'Bring me a half-bottle of Beaujolais, please.'

'We have Coca-Cola, sir.'

'Bottled?'

'Fountain, sir.'

'Sad it's not bottled. I really don't want to get the damned Uncle Sam Jump yet again.'

I recalled laughing to Mexican friends about the Aztec Two-Step. If they were as hurt and embarrassed as I felt, they concealed it well.

'What do Canadians think about the US now?' Jim asked.

'About the US as a country? Very little, because it isn't one. We deal with half a dozen separate governments down here. Illinois, Indiana, Michigan, and Ohio are one country we deal with a lot. It has four governors and on the whole is fairly disunited, but we deal with it. We also deal with the South, which has its de facto capital in Atlanta. There are other states, of course, but if you get Georgia on your side, they go along. We have a great amount of business with New England, of course. The Bostonians and the Vermonters are the two most vociferous lots. Then the states of Washington and Oregon are an independent entity. They have a joint legislature but two governors, so that can be complicated. California is the easiest. Governor Campbell is the beginning and end of power there.'

What sort of dealing do you do?'

'Canada in general, or just us bankers?'

'You personally.'

'I do financings, mostly. We offer Commonwealth pounds, Canadian dollars, British pounds, and gold, generally in return for substantial equity ownership, which we then sell on the American Trades Exchange in London.'

'The American Trades Exchange?'

'It makes a market for persons wishing to buy and sell instruments of ownership in American plants and equipment, trademarks, patents, and proprietary secrets. For example, one can buy a complete set of plans for the Boeing 747, including all supporting documentation, wiring diagrams, and subordinate electronic equipment schematics, and the right to use them, on that exchange. The 747 plans are going for eight million dollars gold or equivalent. I know this because a Canadian company has been attempting to buy them. We are financial guarantors in part of the deal. My involvement is in establishing acceptable currency equivalencies for the gold. Excuse me.' He called the waiter. 'Will you take this back and give me the soup, please? Amtrak really ought to get hold of some meat, if you want to have hamburgers on your menu.'

The waiter took back the partially eaten hamburger and returned with the soup.

'It's not hot. I want it scalding. Boiled, do you understand?' He turned to us. 'Sorry. Where were we?'

I had a question that was a little off the subject of banking, but after our experience in California, I was eager to know the answer. 'Is the Canadian border patrolled?'

He smiled. 'Very, very carefully. And it isn't because we don't like you, mind, or don't want you coming over, but rather for your own protection. There are Canadians, I'll tell you frankly, who are perfectly capable of violence against you Americans. So we think the passport/visa system is really best. They've pretty well cleared out the refugees that came into Saskatchewan and Manitoba from the Dakotas, so that particular disturbance is over. You've got to understand, it was *your* war and our country was just incidentally thrown into chaos in the process.' He waved his soup spoon. 'Let me ask you a question, and since I've been so frank with you, be frank with me. Before you encountered me, did you ever for even one moment think of what had happened to Canada? Of what we were going through because of you? Even that we were there? Did you?'

We had to admit the truth: we had not.

Jack Harper smiled his tight smile and went back to his soup.

Interview: Terry Burford, Midwife and Witch

I'm working towards delivering a baby a day. Right now I do about three or four a week. At the moment I've got fifty-eight patients in the midwifery and about two hundred in my general practice. I've got thirty psychiatric patients divided into four groups. Also, I have my own coven, Rosewood, and I'm elder of four covens that have hived off from Rosewood. I keep office hours from seven to seven, and I always visit my patients in the home. I can't really work on anybody unless I know them and what kind of energies there are in their home environment, and preferably at work also.

I'll take a fee of a dime for an office examination or fifteen cents for a home visit, plus ten cents to a dollar for the various preparations I might prescribe. Rosewood does healing rituals for free. I offer a complete midwifery service, with counselling and support throughout the pregnancy, for three dollars, which includes the delivery. If the child is defective or born dead, the fee is refundable. I lose about a third of the babies and one mother out of ten. My losses are almost always due to complications resulting from radiation exposure. I do euthanasias on profoundly crippled or retarded newborns for free. Also, I do abortion counselling and perform abortions.

I have been a witch since I was ten years old. My mom was a witch, and her mom before her, all the way back, but I went to Ohio State and NYU, where I got an MS in clinical psychology. I am a Jungian analyst, with a strong Wiccan override. Prewar, my kind of practice would have been on the periphery of society, but things have changed so much that people are flocking to us witches now, primarily for healing and midwifery. I am a good herbalist, and I really can accomplish a lot with my medicants. And herbs can give you the kind of dramatic cure that an antibiotic can achieve − if you can get an antibiotic.

My practice as a witch is also my faith. I follow the old pre-Christian religion. We worship the Earth as a Goddess, and Her male manifestation, the Horned God. Our emphasis on ecstatic union with the planet has accounted for the postwar growth of the Wiccan movement. As most Wiccans tend to be anti-hierarchical, we also feel comfortable with the Destructuralists − more than one witch is also a Destructuralist.

We work from our own homegrown rituals. Many covens follow various public traditions, such as the Adlerian method started by Margot Adler in '88, and the older Starhawk method. I am a 'fam-trad' witch in that my craft comes from an old tradition in my own family. To join one of my covens requires a two-year apprenticeship. Right now we have four trainees for Rosewood − all we can take at one time − and a waiting list of sixty.

Our lives are hard and our hours are long. Twenty-hour days are not unusual. Take the day before yesterday. Here's how it went:

3.55 a.m. My assistant, Kathy Geiger, wakes me up. Betty Cotton has come to term. Kathy has already gone to the Cottons' house and examined Betty. She is nearly fully dilated. I grab my instrument and herb cases and we are on our way. We've just bought a new Chrysler vanagon, so it's no longer necessary to go pedalling through the streets of Cleveland on a bike. For the past year, Cleveland has had a good fuel supply. Gas is twenty cents a gallon here, which is certainly higher than you'd like, but we manage.

I find Betty and her husbands managing her contractions very well. I use a modified Lamaze technique. These are very special people, in that they are totally radiation-free. Betty is one of the few people in the United States who had a bomb shelter, and she remained in it for a month after Warday, so even though Cleveland got a dusting from the Dakota strikes, she was not affected. Both of her husbands are from the deep South, Mike from Gulfport and Teddy from Savannah, so they are clean too. The chances of a mutant are very small. Betty also owns a geiger counter, which she uses to clean up hot spots in her immediate environment. This is her sixth child, so things are pretty well organised around here. The whole family is participating. The twins are boiling water, the middle kids minding the youngest, and the oldest daughter, Tabitha, is playing soothing music on her guitar. A good scene, and they get a boy of five pounds eleven ounces, healthy and strong. All I do is bathe him and get him breathing and give him to Betty and give her a cup of raspberry leaf and borage flower tea to promote lactation. Then I take off to grab some more sleep after making sure that we aren't going to have any haemorrhage, that nobody's got fever, and Betty's blood pressure is good. Betty Cotton – matriarch to a family of six kids and two husbands. I wish I had more as strong and happy as that bunch.

6.50 a.m. I wake up again and eat a bowl of boiled oats and drink some ground ivy and wild mint tea. My office is already full. First patient is a cancer case who's been triaged. He comes for counselling, staging of his disease, and visualisation therapy. VT works well for certain cancers, especially tumours of the cerebral cortex, but Joe T.'s bone cancer is proving resistant to our best efforts. He is in great pain. I have been prescribing wild lettuce juice rubbed in at pressure points – armpits especially – for its narcotic effect, but the pain is now breaking through even this drug, which is one of the strongest in my pharmacopoeia. I notice that he is coughing. His disease has spread to his lungs or he has acquired a secondary pneumonia. I tell Joe that he probably has at most a couple more months. He will suffer great agony. I recommend that he let me help him to sleep. His wife comes into the treatment room and the three of us agree. I know not to draw these things out. Joe could go to the hospital for euthanasia, but they would probably make him wait another week. Also, they do not do it with the same atmosphere of love and support. Kathy calls the Rosewooders who are available and we go together to the ritual space we have built at the back of the house. This is a large, pleasant room, full of sun from the skylights. There are flowers in vases. We take Joe to the big lounger and he lies back on it. I pour a tincture of henbane in his ear. His wife of twenty years sits beside him. They gaze at one another, talk a little. They cry. The henbane tincture is very powerful. When we see he is beginning to lose consciousness, we begin to sing. We sing 'Deep River', then one of our own songs, 'Joy in the Morning'. Sometime during the last song, Joe's eyes roll back and he coughs three times, quite violently. His wife calls him once, then again, louder. Then she bows her head.

7.45 a.m. I see a child with persistent diarrhoea. A manual examination of his abdomen indicates gas. The transverse colon is tender. A rectal feels clear. Still, there aren't any intestinal bugs going around and he has been eating his usual diet. He isn't triaged, so I call the hospital and order up a colon study, and refer it to my Project Partnership MD, Dr Stanford Gittleson. Sandy will see the boy at three o'clock this afternoon. The sonograms of the child's colon will be in his hands by then. I say a silent prayer, Goddess grant that all this child needs is a little sumac root and peppermint tea.

7.55 a.m. I see an elderly woman whose symptoms suggest NSD. I prescribe a depurative tea of burdock root and red clover blossom and a cataplasm of comfrey leaf, which we currently have available. One of the coveners takes her into the instruction room to teach her the use of the medicants and give her supplies. Because she is over sixty, I do not charge her. I will wait until the disease progresses a little more before I tell her what she has.

Over the next four hours I see thirty more patients. Then I stop for a lunch of soybean soup and a glass of milk. Afterwards I drink a cup of bee balm tea and read the *Plain Dealer*. There were two fires in Cleveland last night. Since insurance ended, the number of fires in this country has decreased dramatically.

2.00 p.m. I fill out my daily report for the Relief. Mainly, the English want to know about any contagious diseases. Except for a possible with the little boy I referred to Sandy, I don't have any. Unless NSD is contagious. If the English or the Research Group in Chicago know the answer to that question, they certainly aren't telling us.

I'd like a bath, but there's no time for that. I wash my hands instead, and then it's time to meet one of my psychotherapy groups. Since Warday the number of people in therapy has dropped by more than half. I think most of us work so hard we don't have time to be crazy. And nobody in this group is actually insane, not in the classic sense. There are ten members, five of them with touch neurosis, which is one of the more common current problems. There are many people who have developed a pathological terror of touching things because of the threat of hidden radiation. Two of my male patients suffer from impotence. Again, fear is a strong factor here. I have two women who have recently discovered they are gene-damaged, and one who is trying to cope with being triaged at the age of twenty-six, as a result of drinking strontium 90 in some milk she got last year in Dallas. Everybody is scared of milk because of the way cows concentrate strontium 90, but it has become a vitally important food. Milk, eggs, dairy products, soybeans, corn, and oats are our staples nowadays. Some chicken, but eggs are now too important to justify the slaughter of potential layers.

One of the things that sets people back nowadays is poor nutrition. I try to teach modern nutrition techniques, how to adjust to a reduced-protein diet. I get a lot of people coming in worrying about leukaemia or anaemia, who simply aren't eating right. Vitamin C and D deficiencies are most common, followed by proteins and amino acids. I can usually tell by looking at people or talking to them what their general deficiency problem is.

Most of the people in the afternoon group suffer from lack of good nutrition as much as anything else. People in therapy also tend to be the rigid personalities. This is an era of extreme change, and these are people who are afraid of change. Deep panic reactions are common. Most of them have very vivid memories of prewar times, and they are clinging to them. In better-adjusted people, prewar memories are always kind of hazy.

3.30 p.m. I go from the therapy group to the daily business meeting of the coven. One of our problems is record-keeping. We have applied to the Relief for a computer, but so far no response. They've been granting small computers to certain types of farms, so we decide to look into that programme. For a suburban community like Shaker Heights, we have a big farm, seven acres. Two are in herbs and the rest in corn, soybeans, and vegetables. We're even trying to grow watermelons in a semi-sheltered environment we've built, though they are officially an illegal crop here because of the likelihood of failure. As an experimental effort, they are tolerated. We also have a geiger counter, and run a radiation programme. I have the whole property checked every day.

4.00 p.m. I start on my housecalls, taking along Kirby Gentry, who assists me in this part of the practice and is going to take it over sometime soon. In the ideal world, I would devote myself to ritual, meditation, one-to-one counselling, and critical procedures such as deliveries and euthanasias. But this is hardly the ideal world, so we get in the vanagon and set out. First stop is the Barkers', where the little girl has chicken pox with a secondary staph infection. On the way in, I see that the Relief has quarantined the house. The little girl, Dotty, is really bad. I have prescribed applications of juice of sundew to the areas of most severe eruption, but I can see only slight improvement. This is one of the few herbs with a staph-effective antibiotic. The kid has acquired secondary pruritis from scratching. Her fever is 106. She is delirious and suffering agonies from itching. I think we might very well lose this child. I make sure her fingernails are trimmed back so that she won't break her skin so much. Then Kirby and I give her a bath in butterfat soap and water. She screams from the cold. We reapply a paste of myrrh, golden seal, and cayenne to the sites of infection and make sure she is comfortable. The mother tells us that the children's clinic won't accept her daughter because of the risk of contagion, but they have promised to send antibiotics if I approve. I sign the form.

Next stop is a house where both husband and wife have NSD. Their three children will soon be on what the English call the 'orphaned list'. We are getting to know these kids, because they will be in the fostering programme we do with the Diocese of Cleveland and the Council of Churches.

We do five more housecalls, and we find a situation where a diagnosis of tuberculosis is highly probable. Yesterday I gave scratch tests to Mr and Mrs Malone, and they are both positive. They also have hacking coughs and look generally debilitated. I have no choice but to isolate them and call the Relief. TB is a serious contagion, and we cannot risk letting it spread to the general population. The supply of curative drugs like Isoniazid is too limited to run that risk. The Malones will be hospitalised. Even though Hank Malone is triaged, he will get drug therapy, primarily because the disease is so contagious and long-term hospitalisation is too expensive. I encourage them as best I can, explaining that if a triaged person is going to get seriously ill, TB is his best choice, because all cases are treated.

Now it's six. I'm tired. I go home and sit down to dine with Kirby and four other witches. We eat, as usual, in silence, too exhausted to talk, too hungry to want to.

Rumours: The Garden of Eden

We had been travelling on trains almost continuously. To vary our experience, we took Trailways from Cleveland to Pittsburgh. It's a three-hour-and-ten-minute journey over the Ohio and Pennsylvania turnpikes, both of which are in rather poor condition. There is considerable shoulder erosion, and what the bus driver called 'settling', which makes the road look wrinkled and feel as if the bus is a boat on a choppy sea.

We asked a number of passengers if they had heard anything about a part of the country being a Garden of Eden.

They certainly had.

TOM MOON: 'Hawaii, where I took a vacation in 1977, is now a Garden of Eden. The islands were annexed by Japan in 1989. All non-Asians were forced to return to the States. The official language of Hawaii is now Japanese. There is no rationing and people are getting rich off Jap tourists. The Japanese consider American food the height of luxury, and have kept McDonald's and Burger King open. Cokes and Pepsis and milkshakes are readily available. You can go to a twenty-course luau for a dollar. There are theatres that play only old American movies, and the local television stations rerun old network tapes, complete with all commercials, which the Japanese love.'

FACT: Hawaii remains a part of the United States. There is, of course, a substantial Japanese presence, and the Royal Navy maintains its Western Pacific Fleet HQ there. The local fast-food establishments are closed – as they are everywhere – due more to a lack of cheap meat and soy protein from the mainland than to any local economic difficulty. The local Coca-Cola bottler has recently begun to get syrup again, and is expecting to restart production soon. As far as television stations are concerned, forget it. The functional parts were shipped to California years ago, which is one of the reasons LA and San Francisco have TV themselves. This is quite a sore point with Hawaiians, by the way. Rationing is worse than it is stateside because of the island's limited ability to grow grains and maintain its own herds. If you don't like breadfruit and pineapple, do not go to Hawaii.

JOAN R. HAMNER: 'There is a Garden of Eden on the Texas coast. The British have built a new port to supply Europeans in the States with luxuries we Americans can't get. This city has a huge entertainment complex where they show first-run European movies and plays. The Berlin Philharmonic and the Royal Shakespeare Company come. In this port there is a four-star French restaurant. Americans are not allowed, but only Europeans and Japanese. The city is all new.'

FACT: There is no such city in Texas, and we suspect that it doesn't exist at all. Walter Tevis placed a similar city somewhere on the Pacific Coast, but almost in the same breath discounted the story as a rumour.

CARL DIETRICH: 'Seattle is a Garden of Eden. The Japanese have taken over the state of Washington and are soon going to be turning out such things as high-pulse electromagnetic motors in the old Boeing facilities. They are planning to retrain former Boeing employees, to take advantage of the cheap labour. Soon the United States won't even need roads because of the off-road cars and stuff they will make. Also, the Japanese are now basing their fishing fleet there instead of in the home islands. As a matter of fact, things are so good in Washington that immigration is out and you will be turned back at the border.'

FACT: We are not aware of any major Japanese presence in the Pacific Northwest. This area has become a thriving agricultural and shepherding community. Vegetables, apples, and mutton from the state of Washington are beginning to be exported to other parts of the country, particularly California.

The Boeing facilities are not functioning at the present time,

although company spokesmen maintain that they will be producing the 800 series of aircraft there in the future. They will be
powered by conventional jets.

VERNA MCDUFF: 'Litchfield County, Connecticut, is a Garden of
Eden. Rich survival freaks escaped into Litchfield County right
after Warday and have formed a separate country, which has
been recognised by Great Britain and Japan. It is about the size of
Liechtenstein. It has its own gold currency and its own form of
government, which is based on family status. The Europeans
allow it to exist because these old families have such long-
standing ties with them. Many of them own parts of the world's
great companies, such as Phillips-IBM and Lever House. Litchfield has a fully functional telephone system and satellite TV
from Europe, and is full of luxury European cars such as Daimler-
Benz 4WDs and Leyland Stars. Unemployment in Litchfield is
zero, and there is no such thing as malnutrition or birth defects.
The living standard is even better than it was prewar.'

FACT: We learned in White Plains that Litchfield County has a
population of about a thousand, roughly twenty per cent of
whom are triaged because of Warday exposures. The county
hospital was closed in 1991 due to a lack of doctors, leaving only
alternate practitioners and religious organisations to serve the
population.

Interview: Amy Carver, Teacher

Well, I feel stranger than I thought I would, doing this. Although it's nice to talk about yourself. Ever since I got Joan Wilson's letter from Kansas City about you guys, thoughts have been running through my head about what I would say. I hope I can do the whole thing without talking about the World Series. But the Pirates won the first game, so we're all very, very excited.

Let's see. I'm supposed to identify myself? Yes? Oh, you're going to be totally silent. What is this, some kind of psychological thing? You're smiling. Is it? Are you really psychologists? Are you British? Joan said you were from Dallas.

Well, anyway, I am Amy Hill Carver. I teach junior high at the Baldwin New School in Baldwin, Pennsylvania. This school was reorganised in 1991, and serves as the central educational facility for all the surrounding suburbs.

I am thirty-seven years of age. Before Warday I was a freelance writer. I had done work for all the major women's magazines – *Cosmo*, *Good Housekeeping*, *Bazaar*, *The Journal*, all of them.

And then your next question is where was I on Warday. Well, I was on my way to Killington, Vermont, to ski. I was thirty-two years old, making good money, single, and there had been an early snowfall. So off I went for a long weekend. I heard nothing, saw nothing. The car radio went off. I thought, thank you, Mr

Ford. I continued on to Killington. When I got to the Holiday Inn, it turned out that all the radios and TVs were out in the whole place. There was an uproar. Nobody knew what had happened.

I skied anyway, all that afternoon. I remember it was powdery and not very settled, but it was still fun. I've never skied since, not after that day. So that's where I was on Warday. Skiing.

It wasn't until the next day that people started saying stuff – New York had been bombed, there had been a nuclear accident, a reactor explosion, that sort of thing. We saw a couple of helicopters. The out-of-town papers didn't get delivered. The second morning of my trip, I found the dining room of the hotel closed. No breakfast, and no explanations. That scared me. So I headed for home, which was New York.

I was in Hartford when I started seeing this immense black cloud to the south. It wasn't a mushroom cloud or anything. Just a huge black thing like a giant blob or something. By the time I was in Middletown, it was all the way across the southern sky.

It was the most terrifying thing I've ever seen. I stopped in Middletown and asked about it at the gas station. The man said there had been a bomb. He told me not to go any farther, because New York was burning.

I remember I just stood there staring at that old man. There was nothing to say. The radios and TVs were out. Many car ignitions were out. Even so, cars were streaming up from the south. And there was that cloud.

I stayed the night in Middletown – I was very lucky to get a motel room. Refugees were all over the place. When I got to the room, I found that there were six other people in it already. Two of them had these disgusting swellings, one all over his back and one on his face. I did not know then what flash burns look like if they're left untreated. I learned, though.

When the sun went down, we saw that the cloud was full of lightning. I decided then and there to stay inside the motel as long as I could. Other people did too. We were scared there was radiation.

We had a very hard time. Food ran out. My car got stolen. I lived at that motel for months. Nobody knew what to do. The manager kept a tab, but he couldn't get the bank to pay him on his credit-card chits. Then the bank closed. Food got really scarce. I used to get a slice of bread and make it into soup, seasoned with salt and pepper. No, wait a minute, that was months later. In the famine.

What saved me was staying in that motel as long as I did. I'm over thirty, single and childless. I didn't get much of a dose. I don't think I'm in a high-risk cancer situation. I have a little cluster of B cells on my nose, but they slough off as rapidly as they form, which is a good sign. Even if they do become cancerous, they will treat me because skin cancers are curable.

I was in that motel for six months. We became a family. The Brentwood Middletown Motel People. We had deaths and a marriage, and we foraged together during the food shortage.

One day a man came through, travelling from the West. He said Pittsburgh was good. There was food, and the people were okay. Outsiders were welcome there. So I thought, why not? Our motel family was down to ten or twelve people. We'd gone through the worst winter of our lives together, and we were ready to say goodbye. You don't necessarily want to stay with people you endured hell with. Every time you look at them, you see the past.

It took me two weeks to get to Pittsburgh. I hitched, took the bus, took the train.

You know, talking about Warday has a funny effect on me. I used to be very unemotional about it. But now I think about it in terms of humanity. And places. Not that motel. My beautiful prewar places. I had a loft in SoHo, can you believe it? A big white loft with the kitchen in the middle of the space. Light on three sides. I could see the World Trade Center and the Empire State Building. I remember the way the brick streets looked in the rain. I remember my friends. And my editors and co-workers. Cassie Stewart. I loved Cassie. She was full of laughter and fun. Sometimes I dream about those people. Cassie and Mindy and Janice and all the people at *Cosmopolitan*. That was really my best market. I did sort of self-help articles. 'Glamorise Yourself for that Special Him' – that sort of thing.

In those days I wanted to be a novelist. I dreamed of being a female William Kotzwinkle. Do you remember him? He was a novelist in those days. He did this novel called *Fata Morgana* that was practically unknown. But it was simply wonderful. I always wanted to write like him. And *Swimmer in the Secret Sea*, which *Redbook* published in '76. I was working on a novel called *Shadow-girl*. It was about a woman who thinks she is a shadow. About how she discovers she is real, and this basically destroys her. Before that, her life was a fairy tale of submission. Easy, but dangerously self-defeating. I had about three hundred pages done, and my agent really liked it. God knows where it is now. I must say, I do fantasise about going back to Manhattan and seeing what my old place is like. I bought my loft for a hundred and twenty thousand dollars. Forty thousand dollars down. My parents bought it. I hired a locator, a guy here in Baldwin, and he found out they'd died during the famine. I felt awful about it. For a while I had this nightmare where they are sitting in the kitchen in our house. It's a sunny morning and the birds are singing and the apple tree outside is blooming. Only the kitchen doesn't smell like bacon and eggs and coffee. And I look at them, and they are human skeletons.

I couldn't help them, I know that. The locator got the state of New Jersey to issue me a provisional deed to their house. It's a ruin, I guess. Nobody lives in Morristown, New Jersey, any more.

I have gotten to the point where I say, Amy, you just get through today. Or this morning. Or this minute. Whatever. I just want to survive the next ten minutes.

I love my job. Teaching is so very important. It's incredible to realise, but some of the very small children in the Baldwin Elementary School were born *after* Warday. They're going to grow up without reference to the old world. They'll never know what it was like.

So what are we teaching your children these days, you ask? Actually, most of the parents don't ask. They're too tired. The people of Pittsburgh work very, very hard. We're highly organised. This is a free-enterprise town, but we really do a lot of cooperating with one another. Our area is the most radiation-free in the whole Midwest. West of here, they got the dust from the missile fields.

Pittsburgh is an important place because it's healthy and strong. There is a lot of farming towards the Pennsylvania border and in eastern Ohio, just this side of the radiation areas. I heard there was this giant dust storm out there recently, but it didn't get as far as Canton, so we're okay. Pittsburgh sends its own agents to the farms in Ohio and Pennsylvania and West Virginia to buy up food. We have a unique system. The whole city is on a co-op food plan, the Greater Pittsburgh Sustenance Programme.

The programme figures out what we need and where to get it, and allocates the food by person. We all have these ration cards. You can get hung in the Allegheny County Jail for a class-one ration violation. That's if you steal food and sell it. That's the worst. To give you an idea of how well put together we are, the Relief has designated us a Prime Recovery Area, meaning that we get such things as computers for the school and demonstrable-need programmes like Sustenance. We also get extra shipments of medical supplies.

In junior high, we teach land management and radiation control, animal husbandry, principles of small-scale farming, FANTIX, reading skills, and business math. The kids endure it all, except FANTIX, which of course they love. And the new Phillips and Apple computers are great fun. We get feeds from the British via satellite, which is a great improvement because now the kids can communicate with students in England. They can have conversations, and it means a lot to them to know that somewhere across the sea, there is an unhurt world full of people who care about us.

I remember when we just assumed Europe had been hit. During the famine, for example. The world was ending, I thought then.

One evening a funny-looking jet flew over the school and we thought, oh God, the Russians. We lost the war and now the Russians have come.

All night there were planes landing at the airport, which is only a couple of miles away from us here in Baldwin. We hadn't seen a plane in six months. Boy, was this place in an uproar! I'll never forget, we were planning to surrender the town. I went out there with half the rest of the people and we saw all these planes on the runway with target insignia on the side. Most of us were on foot, a few in trucks and cars. We were coming up the road to the terminal when a man in a white uniform came out with a bullhorn and called out, 'We are a Royal Air Force Relief Support Unit. We are friends.'

The RAF! I just sat down in the road and cried. They came over and checked us for radiation. When they found we were clean, they sent up a cheer.

They were all in white uniforms. They'd come up from Atlanta. They gave us kippers. They had zillions of kippers that had been salted in Ireland and packed for export in plastic bags, so they were totally uncontaminated. We filled our pockets with kippers and went home.

One of the most vivid memories I have is of those kippers. They were so good. I'd never had one before in my life.

You know, another thing I'd like to tell the rest of the world about the people of Baldwin is this: we work hard, but we also have lots of fun. We have a rugby team and a baseball team and a Gilbert and Sullivan troupe and a little theatre and reading clubs and a thriving 4-H. Pittsburgh has the only satellite uplink in the Midwest, and we have been allocated short-wave receivers so we get the BBC North American service. As a teacher, the one special allocation I get is books and computer programs.

Which, by the way, reminds me of my Prince Andrew story, because it has to do with books. How long have I been talking? I'm getting hoarse! But this is really fun. I haven't actually sat down and talked like this before. Not ever, just talked and talked.

Now I have to tell you I was really impressed with Prince Andrew last June. We were so excited. I remember Martha Dorris – she's our Relief General Officer – got the RAF to give us shoe polish so we could get ourselves fit to see the Prince. Shoe polish! We hadn't polished a shoe for at least two years. But we shined 'em up for the Prince. The English were hilarious about the visit. Or, as they put it in their bulletins, The Visit. Polished shoes. Best clothes. He came to inspect a farm, the school, the Relief operation. He was here for two hours, which was considered a great honour. Most places he only stayed half an hour.

I must say that before he came I was not all that overawed. This is America, after all. We don't have a king. But I was totally won over by what happened at the school. We had all been out to watch the royal plane arrive, of course. The most beautiful white airplane. To see that huge Airbus and the royal entourage, you would not have known that there had ever been a war. Here is the world turned on its ear, and the royals are going on just as always, like saying it's all going to be all right. Civilisation isn't over.

The Visit was a totally self-contained production. First a band came marching down the stairs. Then they rolled out their own red carpet. Then a bunch of officers came along and saluted while some lords and generals came down. Then came the High Commissioner of the North American Relief. He had flown in from Toronto. He was dressed in a blue uniform, and did he ever look imposing! Then the Prince. He was in white. In my imagination I had visualised him as a very big man. But he was normal size. He moved quickly. They played 'God Save the King'. We sang 'America the Beautiful'. Then 'The Star-Spangled Banner'. Then he met the local Relief officials. Martha was very poised, but she was shaking like a leaf.

We teachers and the kids rushed back to the school. We had been selected for inspection, I think, mainly because we're so close to the airport. I thought it would be a very formal thing. But he spent half an hour sitting on a chair in the auditorium, asking questions. What is the most important thing you are learning here? Tell me about the curriculum. Is it useful? Is it interesting? He asked how well heated the school was. He asked after the health of the children. He went to the infirmary and read the records and inspected the medicine chest. He issued a Royal Warrant for tablet ampicillin, and we have never been without it since.

After he left, an equerry arrived with two suitcases of books. They were a gift from the Prince. He asked that we read one poem each day from *The Oxford Book of American Poetry*, and suggested that we form a Shakespeare society, which we have done.

Of course, I know there are people who resent the British, but without them I think the United States would really have had a very hard time. When it came time for them to repay their debt for our help and support through two world wars, they didn't hesitate. I will never forget that.

Interview: Charles Kohl, Student

I go to the Baldwin New School. My birthday is June eighth. I'm eleven. I like my school. There is always plenty of everything. We have all the sports stuff we want. I could have ten lockers if I wanted. We all stay just in the South Building. The senior high is on the top floor, we're on the second floor, and the elementary school is downstairs.

I go to school in the winter. From April to October, me and my family work to tear down houses on our land so we can increase acreage. We have some apple trees, and we grow corn and green beans and stuff. When we lived in New Jersey we had so many scrubdowns I got allergic to the soap Mom used to make. Mom and Dad tried to move to New Mexico, but this guy from the Relief said we were crazy, it was very bad there, because there was a revolution.

When I got TB, they gave me pills at the hospital. There are kids, like in Texas or somewhere like that, who probably die if they get sick. We pray in school that God will keep us.

Dad was a stockbroker before the war. He will not talk about those times, except he says he worked in an office. Dad is strong.

I used to think it was stock-breaking, like breaking horses, but Mom says it was a numbers job.

The United States is my favourite country. Of course, I love the King because of all the good things the Crown has done for us. When Prince Andrew came here, I saw him. England must be a great place, and my ambition is to go there. My dad says they still use his stock skills there, so he might be transferred to London someday. He put our names on the list. If we go before I am fourteen, I could get to be a British subject and have my own computer. They also have frozen food there. I would like to be a pilot. But the United States is the greatest country in the world, Dad says, although that is not right, Miss Carver says. She says we had a hard time but we will get back. One time there were aircraft carriers as big as our school.

We have big plants here. There are problems with furnaces and controls and fuel and all kinds of stuff, so they can hardly go, although I saw smoke last week coming out of the Bethlehem Number One.

Dad says life is to work from six to six, eat from six to seven, read from seven to nine, and sleep the rest of the time. Mom has NSD, but she thinks she will be better. I think when she puts mineral oil on her tummy it is better. Miss Carver says I should love her and pray for her.

Our school computers are tied into the international information network. I am working on a program to defeat the holds so we can find out more about the world. Miss Carver says okay, but store my programs on disks, not in the internal memory, and officially she doesn't know what I am doing. When a hold is imposed, it is always preceded by a synalog coding. It looks like it is coming in from the master program, but actually the master is just instructing your computer not to access the information. So I am revising our data-capture program to also capture the synalogs in the dump. That way I can find out their command sequences and probably get to where our program will automatically issue defeats anytime it sees a synalog being imposed.

Miss Carver wants to find out a lot of things she says are behind the holds. Miss Carver is from New York and she wants to know why people still can't go back. Also, she wants to know about Russia and China.

There is this guy in our high school named Buddy Toro who tries to scuzz me half the time when I am on the computer. He will chat into my work and scoop whatever I am doing. Then he'll alter my programs and superimpose something so my stuff comes out weird, like I'm supposed to have a geomorphic drawing but the earth looks like a pear, and I get a C. He only goes after me. Our dads have trouble together. They are both on the Baldwin Council, and they are on opposite sides. The Relief wants the city to keep food allocation, but Dad thinks it should go back to the state government, which we do not at the moment have. We have to get a new one, Dad says.

I have a girlfriend. She is Stacy Boyce and I like her because not only can she play rugby football, she is really neat. We are writing a saga together on our class computers. Fifth grade has a new Phillips that is really fast. It accesses ten kilobytes in the time it takes our Epson to do one. If they wanted to, they could pull up a thousand pages all at once and do instant correlations. Anyway, she is Morgan Le Fay in this saga and I am King Arthur, and we love each other even though we are brother and sister. Last night in the saga I kissed her, and she comes back, 'save'. That was so beautiful.

I gave her hard copy this morning, and she turned all red and said she would keep it for ever. Her dad and mine were brokers together when, as my mom says, America was still young.

But we are young now, Stacy and me.

A Wanderer

East of Pittsburgh there are mountains, then there are farms, then there are fields full of wild growth, and a tumbledown look to the towns. Not many people are aboard the *Empire State*, the train that runs from Pittsburgh to Albany via Scranton. We are carsick and uncomfortable. This was not a passenger line before the war, and the roadbed is brutal. I doubt that we're going much more than forty.

We reach Scranton after midnight. There is a cold, wet wind blowing out of the northwest. The air is fresh, with a tang of woodsmoke. We are leaving the train here, shifting to Trailways. To pare some hours off our journey, we'll take the bus across 84 to Poughkeepsie, then catch a midmorning train down to the end of the line in White Plains, the headquarters of the New York Military Area.

The terminal is empty, lit by a single light. There are no streetlights in this neighbourhood, and we are forced to rely on a map, reading street signs as best we can.

The Trailways station is more active. People camp here and there in the waiting room. Somebody is playing a dulcimer quite well, but I do not recognise the tune.

The restaurant is open, selling cheese sandwiches, cherry pie, and a local brand of yoghurt.

I eat a slice of the pie, which is far less sweet than what used to be sold in bus stations. We get coffee, which is generally made from toasted grain these days, and this is no exception. But it's hot.

There is one other passenger on the Poughkeepsie bus, a small woman of delicate beauty. Her eyes are large and dark, her lips full, her brown hair framing her soft face, which is as pale as a shadow.

She tells us she is on her way back to Boston. Her family lives in Scranton, but she is in school at Harvard. She is studying twentieth-century English literature. I am delighted. It was a discipline I thought might have been abandoned in the rush to prepare people for practical careers. 'I've applied to read at Oxford or Cambridge, but I doubt I'll make it. There are a thousand American applications a semester, just for my field. They take six in modern literature.'

'What's it like at Harvard?' Jim asks.

'Difficult, in the sense of physical survival. I'm a senior. I arrived there in the fall of '88, right? I was just starting my freshman year when the war happened. I stayed there because it was obviously mad to try to get back to Scranton. I couldn't even make a phone call home for months. I wrote, but the letters never got through. Harvard was in total chaos. People were leaving – students, professors, administrators. Trying to get home, wherever their homes were. Northeastern University, which is in the Fenway in Boston, officially closed. There were all kinds of problems there. The students rioted when they couldn't get food. I heard that there were shootings in the Fenway. In any case, one can now get a former student apartment there for next to nothing.

'Harvard was a bit better off than Northeastern. We thought of the war as an awful sort of irony, because there had actually been a joint US–Soviet physics conclave in session on campus when the war was fought, the first such conclave in years. The Russians tried to leave the next day. They set out for Logan Airport on foot, finally, even though it was obviously hopeless. Nobody ever saw them again.

'The famine caused riots in Boston, which grew so serious that the campus had to be sealed off. I found myself in the peculiar position of studying for my finals while doing guard duty in the Yard. I was lucky to fall only a semester behind. Despite everything, Harvard was still dutifully failing people at the usual alarming rate.

'Those times were very dramatic and dangerous. The worst problem was food. We ate odd things. The various kitchens kept coming up with jointly prepared meals. Pickles, corned beef, Wheaties, and Tang was the sort of thing we might get for dinner. Everybody was always babbling about how various unlikely things would make complete proteins when they were put together. To make a long story short, we all but starved.'

'What do you study?'

'Well, at this point my seminar in Joyce is probably my most interesting course. I went through a period of furiously deconstructing everyone from Barbara Pym to James Gould Cozzens. I think I agree with Cozzens about some things. You know what he said about Joyce? He said, "There's no point fooling around with the English language. You can't win." It's a hilarious thing to say, but I think there's something in it. Please don't think me a conservative, though. Actually, I suppose it's possible that's exactly what I am. I'm not really certain where I'm going, except that I feel most drawn to prose that is written with absolute clarity. Pym. Anthony Powell. Americans? Maybe Wharton, certainly Hemingway, although in his case the directness tends to bury what should have been subtle about the work.'

'Do you think it's appropriate for somebody to be studying a subject as impractical as English literature right now?'

'Impractical? It's not impractical at all. In fact, it's very necessary if we intend to keep the civilisation going. I can't make widgets, it's true enough. But not every single soul should. I'm a klutz anyway.'

We ride on, three people in a bus. If there weren't medical supplies aboard, we wouldn't be travelling at all. No bus company would release a bus with so few passengers unless there's another, better reason to move it than their needs. We are quiet for some time. I have just closed my eyes when the girl begins to talk again. This time her voice is low and rushed and full of tension.

'I have a lot of trouble with images that won't leave my mind. I have to make room for them. For example, I have an image of a kid who was executed in Cambridge. Can you believe it, he had broken into a house and killed everybody and eaten their food. Then he did it in another house. He was caught and put in the town jail. Two weeks later he escaped and did it again. This was the only way he could think of to cope. When he was caught a second time, the town made a decision to hold a public execution. We were deeply shocked, all of us at Harvard. This was in the summer of '89. We thought to mount some kind of protest, but there was no time. One morning there was an execution notice on various bulletin boards around town, and that afternoon they hanged him by pushing him out a window with a rope around his neck. He was left there for days. I am not sure that the threat of execution deterred anybody else from killing for food. Most people wouldn't do it anyway, not under any circumstances.

'I have an image of the police finding the house next door to mine with everybody in it dead during the first week of the flu.

'I have an image of my dog, Nancy, the night I let her go. People killed their pets during the famine, but I let Nancy go. She never came back. I hope she learned to live by hunting. She was a smart dog.

'When the kitchens began to fail, Harvard organised foraging teams. We ate rats, ducks from the park, geese when they appeared, all kinds of things. We ate the city-issue cheese and the carrots and potatoes the Army brought in. I've heard that lots of people starved during the famine, and I'm not a bit surprised.

'I've just had the satisfaction of going home and finding, once again, that my family is well. I go every few months, even though we can now talk on the phone. I really am compulsive about it.'

'Does your interest in family life mean you want to get married?' I asked.

'Am I wrong, or is there a whiff of fatuousness about that question? I'm twenty-two years old and ought, I suppose, to be eager to support a house-husband on my possible stipend of two quid a week, assuming Oxbridge accepts me. Is that a sufficiently fatuous answer?'

'What do you remember most about being in Cambridge on Warday?'

'That's easy. I remember the cloud. It blew out to sea before it hit us, thank God. All one day and night it could be seen from Boston Harbour, hanging over the Atlantic. God, it was big. It looked like a hurricane or something. People were leaving. The cops had bullhorns, telling you to go in the basement. It was awful. There was so much craziness. Kids went nuts in the

Fenway, kids from Northeastern running crazy, naked, kicking people, burning cars, looting apartments.

'My romantic streak makes me wish it was about 1985 and I was a high school girl again, in love in the way one could be before the war, but which seems so impossible now.

'I wonder what I will do with myself. In a sense, my degree is certainly an anachronism. If I don't make it into Oxbridge, I'll have to do my graduate work here, perhaps at Yale. At any rate, I've applied there and to the University of Chicago – and to Stanford, where I have no chance because you can't get a California Student Permit if you have a noncritical speciality. Oxbridge can lead to employment in England. If I have to stay here, I think I'll quit and join my father's company. They make windows. Dull, but it pays well.'

Again she falls silent. The bus roars and bounces. This is not a spectacular road. In places we can hear the hiss of grass scraping the sides of the bus.

'Anything else?' Jim asks.

'Years ago I had a mad love affair. We were going to marry and live together always, all the usual things. When I got back to Scranton I found he had died of the flu. I think we would have been happy together. For a little while, life would have been perfect. I missed that chance.'

She rests her head back against the seat.

'I'm so tired. These days I really need my sleep. When I go to bed I imagine a little warm cottage where I can cuddle up by the fire, sip wine, and be content.'

She says no more. Like most people who live at a very low nutrition level, sleep comes suddenly to her, this porcelain beauty. After a moment Jim touches her cheek, but she does not waken.

The bus pulls into Poughkeepsie in thin dawn light. When the driver wakes her up, she bustles quickly down the aisle and disappears without a word.

PART FOUR

NEW YORK

When pennants trail and street-festoons hang
    from the windows,
When Broadway is entirely given up to foot-
    passengers and foot-standers, when the mass
    is densest,
When the façades of the houses are alive with
    people, when eyes gaze riveted tens of
    thousands at a time . . .

– Walt Whitman,
'A Broadway Pageant'

The Approach to New York – Ghosts

Monday, October 4, 1993: The Northeast was more beautiful empty than it had been populated. Some of the drama of the old wildness had returned, in the thick foliage that scraped the windows of the train, and in the rioting fields that once were ordered. As we moved into the commuter belt, though, ruin took the place of wildness.

Images from the windows of the train: empty suburban stations whose parking lots once glittered with commuters' BMWs and Buicks; dark doorways and vines everywhere, spreading in the most unlikely places, along streets, up telephone poles, jamming the empty hulk of a bus.

Beneath all the brick and concrete, this land was always fertile. Green things, full of confidence and ambition, were reasserting themselves everywhere. The effect of all this was much more powerful than the kind of abandonment we are all familiar with, because this was so *total*, and the Northeast had been so vastly and intricately populated.

The thousands of fragile reminders of human presence intensified the emptiness.

The New York Standard Metropolitan Statistical Area con-

tained nine million people in 1987. The official population is now
seven thousand. According to General George Briggs, USA, the
Commandant of the New York Military Area, there are roughly
twenty thousand illegal inhabitants in the city. Officially, New
York is a Red Zone, under martial law with a twenty-four-hour
curfew, violators to be shot on sight. But General Briggs, a tall
man with narrow gunsights of eyes, said that his men hadn't
ever shot anybody. 'There's been sufficient death here,' he said.

Amtrak goes as far south as White Plains. From there it is
possible to take a bus east to Stamford, but there is no public
transportation into New York at all.

We arrived at the White Plains station on the *Twentieth Century*,
which we had left in Cleveland for our detour to Pittsburgh.

From the moment we got off the train, we were aware of two
things: this was US Army territory, and there was a massive
salvage operation going on.

First impressions: blank-eyed kids standing around smoking,
wearing uniforms that were threadbare before the war, carrying
M-16s the way exhausted majorettes might carry their batons, as
if all their magic had been transformed into weight.

It was cloudy, but there were signs of fair weather. During the
night it had rained, and the streets of White Plains were shining
in the shafts of light that were breaking through the clouds.
There was a smell something like creosote in the air. A convoy of
salvage trucks roared past on the Bronx River Parkway. There
were buses out in front of the station, and our thirty fellow
passengers all got into them. Soon quiet descended on the
station. A soldier, who had been playing Sunshine's 'Glee' on a
harmonica, stopped and began staring at us. He was wearing an
MP armband. He hitched up his web belt, unsnapped his holster
flap, and came over. He regarded us. His shoulder stripes said he
was a staff sergeant. His name tag identified him as Hewitt.

'Can we be of service, Sergeant?' Jim asked, when he did not
speak.

'Identification, please.'

'What kind?' I asked. My identification consists of a Texas
driver's licence and an ancient MasterCard, unless you count the
false California ID.

'Federal. British. Whatever you got.'

Jim showed him his *Herald News* press card. 'We'd like to
arrange an interview with General Briggs,' he said.

The young man looked at us. 'Okay,' he said, 'you'll find him over at the armoury. You know where it is?'

'You'll have to direct us.'

'We're goin' over there ourselves, now that the train's come in. You can come with us.' He turned to the knot of soldiers lounging nearby. 'Okay, guys, excitement's over. Time to get back to the Tyre Palace.'

The Tyre Palace?

We rumbled through the streets of White Plains in, of all things, a massive, roaring, turbine-driven armoured personnel carrier. 'What the hell is this?' I asked. 'We could've used a few of these in 'Nam.' It was like riding in a safe – massive steel doors, quartz window slits.

'This is the Atomic Army,' Sergeant Hewitt said. 'You could blow off a hydrogen bomb right on top of this thing, and you know what'd happen?'

'What?'

'We'd be vaporised.'

We rode on for a few minutes. Sergeant Hewitt pulled the lever that opened the door. Before us was a Gothic building of fairly massive proportions, designed to look like a castle, with towers and parapets and narrow windows set in red brick. Soldiers came and went. The convoy we had seen on the parkway was now parked across the street. Beneath the tarps I could see that the trucks were loaded with rusted steel beams and stacks of aluminium sheathing from buildings. One truck contained nothing but intact windows, each carefully taped and insulated against breakage. A soldier was walking along with a handheld computer, taking inventory.

This scene was my first experience of the work of the famous salvors, who are methodically dismantling Manhattan. Salvage is the latest business in which Great American Fortunes are being made, and the salvors, in their dashing khaki tunics and broad-brimmed hats, were romantic figures, lean men who stood around and gibed the neat officer with the computer.

A helicopter landed on a pad in the small park in front of the armoury, disgorging five men in white radiation suits, who began to examine the salvage with geiger counters amid a good bit of derisive laughter. A peacock, standing in the patch of grass in front of the building, gave throat and spread its tail.

'General's office is the second door to the right,' Hewitt said. 'It

says "Commanding General" on the door. At least that's what it
said the last time I looked at it.'

Even though I knew you couldn't see New York from the
streets of White Plains, I found myself looking south. The sky
revealed nothing.

The moment we entered the armoury, we found out why the
soldiers called it the Tyre Palace. The place reeked of rubber. The
central foyer was stacked with tyres. There were tyres in the
hallway. Farther back I could see a vast, dim room, also filled
with the tall, shadowy stacks.

Nobody ever explained to us what they were there for.

As we entered General Briggs's office, a bell tinkled above the
door. A master sergeant, lean and moist with nervous sweat,
laboured at a brand-new word processor, his fingers flying. I saw
Jim's eyes glaze with envy. I suppose mine did too. No writer
who has ever used one can forget the joys of the word processor.
I couldn't resist a look at the brand name. It was an Apple, a new
model called an Eve. The Eve had a nine-inch screen no thicker
than a pancake. I noticed that the sergeant typed normally, but
directed the word-processing programme by speaking into a
microphone around his neck. He said, 'File two-four-two,' and
the disc drives blinked.

How beautiful! Ever since I saw it, I haven't been able to get the
Eve out of my mind. What wondrous capabilities it must have. I
used an Apple II Plus from '79 to '84, and a Lisa after that, so I
have an affinity for Apple machines. Nowadays I am a pencil-
and-paper man.

We had no trouble getting in to see General Briggs, and he was
willing to give us a short interview. Most of our respondents
have agreed to an hour, but General Briggs gave us only ten
minutes, which, as it turned out, was a generous amount considering how busy he is.

Manhattan is almost free of radioactivity. It is still a Designated
Red Zone, though, because of the city's other problems. First,
there is no water supply. By Warday-plus-ten, the city's reservoir
system was drained dry because of thousands of uncontrolled
leaks in Brooklyn and Queens. The old water mains couldn't
stand the stress of losing pressure and drying out, and in
subsequent months many of them collapsed. It would take years
to repair the system.

It is contamination that prevents this work from being done.

Ironically, radiation is only a small part of the problem. The serious pollution is chemical. Hundreds of thousands of tons of hazardous chemicals were burned in the Brooklyn–Queens firestorm. Dioxins were produced, PCBs from insulation were released into the air, and deadly fumes mingled with the radioactive fallout.

Over the years, untended chemical-storage facilities deteriorated, especially along the Harlem River and on the New Jersey side of the Hudson. The whole of southern New Jersey is now uninhabitable, and Manhattan and the Bronx are severe hazard zones. People cannot remain in the Bronx for more than a few hours at a time, nor live in Manhattan north of Twenty-third Street.

Despite the dangers, we felt we had to go in. We asked for and obtained General Briggs's permission to enter the city. I suspect that he knew we would go in, even if he didn't give us the necessary papers. We were lucky to have gained his confidence. Had we not been under the guidance of Army and city personnel, we would not have lived through our trip to Manhattan.

Rumours from the Northeast

RUMOUR: The complete records of the United States government were preserved in a mountain in Colorado, and officials are just waiting for the right moment to put them to use in getting the country reorganised.

FACT: This is one of the most persistent stories we heard in this part of the country. In fact, there was and is a redoubt in the Rockies. It is the NORAD Aerospace Defence Command in Cheyenne Mountain, and it is back in operation despite battle damage. It is being run by a joint US–UK–Canadian command. But it contains only military equipment and electronics, most of it preserved by the mountain from EMP effects.

RUMOUR: There is a Council of State Governors that will soon meet to appoint an interim Congress, which will in turn appoint an interim President, whose primary responsibility will be the reorganisation of the federal government.

FACT: The federal government in Los Angeles gave no hint of any such plan, nor is there any functional national governors' organisation.

RUMOUR: Even though it was terribly damaged, the Soviet Union remained in one piece while the US did not. Thus the Russians won the war, but they need time to rebuild before they occupy America. Stories to the effect that the USSR has broken up are planted by Soviet intelligence to lull the Americans into complacency and create a false sense of security.

We think this rumour is false, and here's why: First, if Russia were still intact, Europe and Japan would be arming themselves as quickly as possible. There is little evidence of this. And the Russians apparently do nothing to resist the Royal Navy's attacks on isolated Soviet submarines, of which we have an excellent account elsewhere in this book.

Second, an intact Russia would already have invaded western Europe. The Russian armies in Poland and in some of the other Eastern Bloc countries disintegrated after the war because they had no orders from Moscow and no idea what had happened at home.

Third – the smallest but most telling fact – during the clothing shortage in '88–'89, the British brought in freighters loaded with uniforms. Everybody remembers them because we were all wearing them. They were dyed black, but they were Soviet summer uniforms, apparently liberated and sold to the UK as surplus by the Poles when the Soviet armies stationed in Poland collapsed.

Interview: General George Briggs, New York Military Area

What the US Army is engaged in here is the mission of protecting the property of American citizens and managing the most massive salvage operation in the history of the human race.

This salvage will continue until everything of value is physically removed from this area. And I mean everything. Let me read some statistics. In the past four years we have salvaged, among other things, 816,000 typewriters, 235,561 automobile parts, 199,021 kitchen appliances, over seven thousand tons of steel, four thousand tons of aluminium or other sheathing, more than three million metres of copper wire, eighty-eight thousand windows, 199,803 business suits and 204,381 articles of women's clothing from stores and factories, 9,100 toupees, 6,170 pieces of bridgework and artificial teeth, and one set of prosthetic rear legs suitable for a medium-sized dog, which were found at the Animal Medical Center. We have also saved 14,126,802 books, 2,181,709 phonograph records, and enough video and audio tape to stretch to the moon and back twice. Working in association with various art galleries and other types of museums, we are aiding in the salvage of such institutions as the Museum of Modern Art, the Metropolitan, the Museum of Natural History, the Guggenheim, the Whitney, the Frick, and many others. Among the items we have saved are the entire contents and panelling of the Fragonard Room at the Frick, which was transferred to the Isabella Stewart Gardner Museum in Boston. We have also saved the embalmed brain of a Mr A. J. Carnegie, which was found in a closet at New York University. The how and why of that one remains a mystery. If you wish, you can see the brain. It's in our collection here at the armoury, along with a number of other especially unusual exhibits.

The decision to salvage New York rather than attempt to repopulate it was made by the Joint Chiefs of the Continental Military Command, which consists of General Youngerman, USA, General Joe Point of the USAF, Admiral Whitaker, General Sir Malcolm Law of the British Continental Military Advisory Command, and General Topp of the Canadian Army.

Their decision was made as a result of the water and pollution problems I outlined to you earlier. The chemical spills have created an effective Dead Zone in eastern New Jersey every bit as lethal as any nuclear-impact area. Thus this region, in which most of New York City's primary petrochemical, food, and fuel supply points were located, has been evacuated. There is also the matter of the abandoned nuclear power plants, and the possibility that one or more of them could emit radioactive materials at some time in the future. Also, whenever the wind comes in from the east, Manhattan receives a dusting of thousands of particles of strontium 90 and cesium 137. Unfortunately, the bombs were so designed that the primary issuing particle was strontium 90 which has a half-life of nearly thirty years. Of the particles we collect, fifty-six per cent are this element, thirty-one per cent are carbon 14, and thirteen per cent are cesium 137.

Thus there are so many obstacles to the repopulation of the city that the Joint Chiefs were compelled to make the determination to undertake salvage instead of resettlement.

As you know, Manhattan is identified as a Red Zone, which means that unauthorised persons are liable to be shot for intruding. Nevertheless, the island supports a small population consisting of people who either refused to leave or have returned and are intent on protecting their former property. There is even an impromptu real-estate market. A few months ago, two individuals applied to the State Office of Title Reclamation in Albany for a grant to clear title to a property in the city, then the right to transfer that title between them. It turned out that both were active in this strange Manhattan real-estate market, and they lived in the city. Both were arrested.

Of course, what they were doing is meaningless. All property in Manhattan has been sequestered by the Army. The state government in Albany has no authority over military areas. Salvage proceeds go to the Special Refugee Account for use in areas where the most former New York City residents now live.

You requested that I add as much personal colour to this report as I can. I am married and have three children. My wife is Joyce Keltie Briggs. The kids are George Junior, Mark, and Nancy. We are members of the Baptist Church. My age is forty-three, and I have no living parents, sisters, or brothers. I was born on June 12, 1950, at Fort Sam Houston, Texas. I am an army brat, the son and grandson of army brats. I live with my family in Bronxville, in a home on Birchbrook Avenue, which has been designated as Residence, Commanding General, New York Military Area, by the Continental Army Command. This home was not owned or occupied at the time it was commandeered by the US Army.

I have held a commission since 1972, when I graduated from West Point. I was promoted to general officer on January 14, 1990, and assumed this command in February of the same year.

I see that I have a couple of minutes remaining before I have to inspect the Critical Minerals Salvage Holding Depot in the railyards, so I would like to make a statement to all Americans who read your book. My statement is this:

Since the war I have seen a tremendous change in our country. It has been terrible for us all, but nevertheless it has revealed toughness and gristle and fellow-feeling that we didn't even know we had. There was a time when I might have said, 'If a nuclear war will toughen us up, let it come.' Having lived through one, I would not say that now. I was a damned fool ever to have thought such a thing. By 1984 there was a substantial body of opinion in the military that a nuclear war was possible, and that we should therefore devote our attention to planning methods that would encourage the Soviets to engage in a limited rather than an all-out exchange, or reduce their ability to project their warheads into US territory. This was an error.

Not a day passes that I don't wish for the soft old America with all its faults. But everything has an end, and that world and way of life ended.

Those were good times. May God grant that we remember them always, but also give us the strength not to torment our children with tales of what has been denied them.

Documents from the Lost City

who created great suicidal dramas on the
apartment cliff-banks of the Hudson under
wartime blue floodlight of the moon & their
heads shall be crowned with laurel in oblivion . . .
                                    – Allen Ginsberg,
                                                Howl

THE MECHANICS OF ABANDONMENT

It is hard to believe silence in relation to so big a place as New York. You can hear a single truck coming for miles on the New York State Thruway. And that is usually a military truck. I cannot help wondering what it will be like here when even the soldiers are gone.

The documents I have gathered for this section are related to the management of the human withdrawal from New York. In an odd way I find their crisp tone reassuring. After the first panic, we did our leaving well. We were told that the city picked up tens of thousands of shoes in the days after Warday. But later there were staged withdrawals and organised retreats from Dead Zone to Red Zone to Orange Zone to elsewhere.

Beyond those early assessments, there really isn't much documentation about New York. I would have liked to include some sort of a list of paintings or books or valuables still in the city, or perhaps an evaluation of the present condition of buildings. Such documents did not present themselves.

I could have listed the orders of the day for the New York Military District, for every day since they have been here.

But those orders aren't important. The remaining valuables aren't even too important. There is no document that describes the emptiness of this city, no more than there is one to describe the immense complexity of the mind that caused it.

Nineveh, Babylon, and Rome each bustled a time in the sun. So also, New York. Nobody ever called it an eternal city, it was too immediate for that.

But we all thought it was one.

328

004 1500 ZULU April 93

TELEX TO 8th ARMY AREA COMMANDER
PHILADELPHIA HDQ. RECONPAC 34AQ
CLASS CONFIDENTIAL

You are hereby instructed that reconnaissance by RADPAC on 4/2/93 mandates following RADZONE assignments for New York area:

1.0 DEAD ZONE:

Original North/South strike centers from Bayville–Hempstead–Bellmore remain lethal and off limits to all personnel for foreseeable future. Radioactive levels remain at 300–500.

2.0 RED ZONE:

Eastern limit now set at Highway 27 with all entries to Dead Zone closed and monitored by electronic surveillance. Eastern boundary now set at Highway 110 with similar observation. Radioactivity levels vary. Damage not rectifiable. Looting reported by aerial reconnaissance. Shoot-to-kill order still in force.

3.0 ORANGE ZONE:

Radioactivity localized to standing structures and untreated ground surfaces. Highway 678 in Queens still usable with protected vehicles. No local traffic allowed. Eastern perimeter temporarily set at Highway 11.
The Brooklyn–Bronx–Manhattan areas remain under ORANGE ZONE designation. Radioactivity levels are negligible but damage is still largely uncorrected. Regular 'looting reported despite assignment of National Guard units. All major access points controlled as per continuing order.

4.0 BLUE ZONE:

New Jersey area to Hudson remains under control of 8th Army units. Radioactivity levels non-life-threatening.

New Assignments due 5 May 93.

ORDER END. STOP. RPX.54.30

REPORT FOR JT. DEFENSE TASK FORCE
NORADHQ. ACTING DESK FOR WAR ASSESSMENT
NOVEMBER 6, 1988

PRELIMINARY REPORT ON SOVIET TARGET NEW YORK AREA

1. RADCON SURVEY. Between 12/1/88 and 12/3/88, RADCON procedures were implemented to map the New York City Area in an effort to
assess the nature and extent of the USSR attack on this target. RADCON
implemented at Level Three employs aerial surveys and radiologic sampling. As of 12/3/88, Level Four earth-sampling and ground surveys were
impossible to implement.

2. SOVIET TARGETS. Aerial mapping reveals three strikes in a NE–SW
line, though preconflict data suggest that an additional 3–5 warheads were
directed at the same general area. Atmospheric sampling confirms total
radiologic levels to be consistent with a 6–7 warhead attack strategy. Data
indicate that the additional warheads detonated over water south of Long
Island. The three successful land targets were NORTHEAST, Glen Cove;
CENTRAL, a point one-half mile west of Elmont; and SOUTHWEST,
Oceanside.

3. SOVIET STRATEGY. The nature of the Soviet attack plan is not known
at this time, though it is probable that the intended target was the
Manhattan island area. Lack of precise target control may have occurred,
or the Soviets may have been unable to complete their full attack. Two
other urban targets were struck on 28 October in other parts of the
United States.

4. ATTACK STRENGTH. Radiologic surveys suggest that three thermonuclear warheads in the 9–10-megaton range detonated with high simul-
taneity. This prevented predetonation from first blast production of
extraneous radiation such as neutrons, gamma and X-rays, etc.

5. BLAST PARAMETERS. Two warheads detonated at an altitude designed to maximize ground effects. The airburst explosions occurred
between 8,000 and 8,250 feet and produced fireballs approximately 3.5

miles in diameter each. The third warhead was detonated at the surface.

Overall blast effects were constrained by the moderate variance in terrain, although the general flatness of the area encouraged destructive yield. Blast waves as measured in pounds per square inch, or PSI, varied by distance and terrain:

One Mile:	200+ PSI
Two Miles:	45+ PSI
Three Miles:	25+ PSI
Four Miles:	16+ PSI
Five Miles:	12+ PSI
Ten Miles:	4+ PSI
Fifteen Miles:	2.2+ PSI
Twenty Miles:	1.5+ PSI

It may be noted, for example, that reinforced concrete buildings can be destroyed by pressures of 14–16 PSI.

As a result of the high explosive yield, winds are calculated to have been over 2,000 mph at one mile from point of detonation; over 300 mph at five miles; over 125 mph at 10 miles; and over 50 mph at 20 miles. Physical damage from blast waves was amplified by the airborne dispersion of broken objects and particles.

Also, because of the close proximity of detonations – the warheads detonated between 1 and 3 miles of each other – the overall blast effects were intensified.

6. THERMAL EFFECTS. Over 25 percent of the total blast effects were produced as heat. Thermal effects on 28 October were lessened because the attack occurred during daylight with few clouds. Nearly 100 percent of the thermal energy produced was dissipated within 60 seconds.

Such radiation is produced in two waves, or pulses. Theoretically, at the high MT range, individuals have several seconds between the first pulse of thermal energy, which contains approximately 20 percent of the total energy emitted, and the second pulse. At 10 MT, the New York civilian population had 3.2 seconds to take protective action.

It is estimated that each weapon produced the following radiation calculated in calories per centimeter squared (cal/cm2):

One–three miles:	Over 1,000 cal/cm2
Three miles:	900 cal/cm2
Five miles:	300 cal/cm2
Ten miles:	66 cal/cm2
Twenty miles:	14 cal/cm2

Thermal radiation at these levels was sufficient to produce first-degree burns on all exposed individuals within 28–30 miles and second-degree burns on exposed individuals within 22–24 miles. It is estimated that as much as 20 percent of the population received thermal burns beyond normal statistical projections due to the number of weapons and their detonation points, which had the effect of broadening the radiation-exposure range.

Limited ground observations by trained personnel have been possible only in some localities. The data, however, confirm the dispersive effects of thermal radiation from three weapons. Numerous incidences of flash burns and 'ghost figures' of humans were noted.

7. RADIATION. Initial nuclear radiation was intense and, within a radius of 2 miles, virtually lethal to all life. Almost 100 percent of radiation produced occurred within 15 seconds. The following radiation doses have been calculated for the New York attacks:

DISTANCE FROM BLAST CENTER	INITIAL RADIATION DOSE
Up to 2.4 miles	100+ rems
Up to 2.1 miles	500+ rems
Up to 2.0 miles	1000+ rems

It is estimated that the fatality rate at 500 rems is 70 percent; at 1000 rems it is almost universally 100 percent. Generally, the effects of initial radiation upon the individual depend upon his/her proximity to the blast center and degree of physical exposure. In terms of overall protection for individuals not exposed to the blast(s) directly, it can be noted that a minimum of 18 inches of concrete or similar material is necessary in order to reduce 1000 rems of radiation to a tolerable level of 100.

8. PHYSICAL EFFECTS. A thorough physical survey of the New York area has not been possible as of this date. Aerial photographs, however,

reveal considerable damage to the Queens–Long Island areas, and severe-to-moderate damage to all adjacent areas. Given the variability of structures and terrain, the following damage table for the New York area has been constructed for each airburst:

TYPE OF STRUCTURE	DAMAGE LEVEL	DAMAGE RANGE IN MILES FROM BLAST CENTER
1. Wood houses and buildings	SEVERE	12 Miles (average)
	MODERATE	14 Miles
2. Masonry buildings	SEVERE	8.5 Miles
	MODERATE	10 Miles
3. Multistory wall-bearing buildings	SEVERE	5.9 Miles
	MODERATE	7.3 Miles
4. Reinforced concrete buildings	SEVERE	5.7 Miles
	MODERATE	7.0 Miles

Relating this schema to blast pressure (as discussed in Section 5 of this Report), the following table can be generated:

TYPE OF STRUCTURE	DAMAGE LEVEL	BLAST PRESSURE (PSI)
1. Wooden buildings	SEVERE	3–4 PSI
	MODERATE	2–3 PSI
2. Masonry buildings	SEVERE	5–6 PSI
	MODERATE	3–4 PSI
3. Multistory wall-bearing buildings	SEVERE	8–11 PSI
	MODERATE	6–7 PSI
4. Reinforced concrete buildings	SEVERE	11–15 PSI
	MODERATE	8–10 PSI

Within these parameters, therefore, total destruction of all structures occurred within 3–4 miles of each blast center; severe damage occurred within 10 miles; moderate damage at 14 miles; and minor damage, such as broken windows, at 20 miles. Groundburst damage was more concentrated.

This effectively places the geographical area bound by Highway 678 to the west and Highway 106 to the east as a Dead Zone, with total destruction at the 85–95-percent level. The remainder of Queens and the northern half of Brooklyn are estimated to have experienced severe damage at the 60–70-percent level, as has Long Island to Highway 110. Moderate damage, including downed power lines, broken windows, and roof damage, extends through Manhattan to New Jersey in the west, and to Riverhead and Southampton in the east.

Overall destruction in the above area is estimated to be 85 percent within five miles of Ground Zero; 65 percent within 10 miles; 30 percent within 15 miles; and 10 percent within 20 miles.

9. MORTALITY. Definite counts are as yet impossible to calculate. Preliminary estimates suggest that 2–3 million were killed instantly in the New York attack on 28 October; another 1–2 million died within 48 hours; and perhaps as many as 3–4 million will suffer premature deaths from trauma or radiation-induced diseases within the next 5–10 years. These estimates are based on 1980 Census counts and statistical probabilities for radiation illnesses.

10. PROJECTED STUDIES. Further studies of all aspects of the October 1988 Soviet attack are planned as soon as trained personnel are released by the appropriate military and Department of Defense units.

New York, New York

My first glimpse of it shocks me, not because it seems different but because it doesn't. I remember this skyline. From the back of an army truck bouncing down the Saw Mill River Parkway it gleams as it has always gleamed, tall and imperial and elegant. I can pick out the Empire State Building, the World Trade Center, the slanting roof of the Citicorp Center.

But then I notice an enormous difference. It is in my ability to see details. As it was when we arrived in White Plains yesterday, the air this morning is absolutely clear, more so than I have ever seen it in New York. I can make out the hollows of windows and see long black scars on the Gulf and Western Building. Then I realise that the Empire State Building has no antenna, and that makes me huddle into my jacket.

Jim stands beside me, his feet wide, his hands gripping the rail that runs along the back of the truck cab. He is silent, his careful eyes on the horizon.

We have been processed by the army bureaucracy in White Plains, and now carry mimeographed papers that, among other things, give us the right to be in Manhattan without risking arrest or being 'shot on sight'. I look at the kids in the truck with me – eighteen, seventeen, some even younger. They aren't very fierce, and I believe General Briggs's claim that nobody has ever actually been executed here. These kids are not soldiers in the prewar sense of the word. They are the uniformed custodians of a great, shattered treasure house.

I suspect that these soldiers might be obsolete, and they just might sense this also. Perhaps that is why they have chosen to protect empty places – the San Antonio and Washington perimeters, this ruined city.

Maybe the rivalry between the United States and the USSR went on so long because both sides knew that without it the central governments were as unneeded as they were unwanted.

So much of the ferment Jim and I have seen in our travels relates to this question of centrality. Perhaps there is a limit to the size of human states, beyond which they become too inflexible and inefficient to last very long.

We arrive at the rusting toll plaza that marks the entrance to the Henry Hudson Parkway. The truck stops. A spit-and-polish MP master sergeant walks to the back, his helmet gleaming in the morning light.

'Lay 'em out, you guys.' The men start handing over their Army ID cards. The master sergeant looks at each one, comparing it to the face of the man who handed it to him.

Jim and I give him our mimeographed sheets. He studies them both. 'We'll have to verify these. Come over to the command post, please.' I feel a surge of resentment, quell it quickly. His right hand rests ever so lightly on the butt of his .45. The CP is a tiny prefabricated building just off the road.

He hands the sheets to another spit-and-polish soldier, this one a second lieutenant. 'Have a seat, gentlemen,' the close-cropped boy says in a piping voice. 'I'll just make a quick phone call.' He picks up a brown telephone and speaks into it, reading off the serial numbers of our documents. After a moment more he puts the receiver down. 'Now if you'll just countersign on the first line,' he says. I sign. He spends a long time comparing my new signature with the old one. 'Your S is a bit off, but I suppose it's okay.'

He hands me my document, then checks Jim's. His J is the source of another mild complaint. Once these documents are countersigned twice, they're worthless – an assurance that they won't be reused. We are allowed one entrance to the city and one exit from it, and no more.

General Briggs put it this way: 'You will remain with your

designated guide. You will not contact anyone else you might
encounter there. For your own safety, you will not remain
overnight.'

We proceed. Soon we can see the George Washington Bridge
looming over the sparkling Hudson, and the red tile roofs of the
Cloisters. There isn't a boat on the river, and the bridge is empty.

The only sound is the roar of our truck. I wonder about the
Cloisters as we pass beneath the cliffs of Fort Tryon Park. I
believe that I might have first kissed Anne in the herb garden
there. Perhaps not, but that's where I fell in love with her. It
could easily have been the innocence of her enthusiasm for the
tapestries that did it. I wonder about them. Were they saved, or
do they lie now in heaps on the floor, providing nesting places
for rats and mice?

As soon as we pass the Cloisters, the bridge looms up on the
right. I see that there are long festoons of vines, some of them
scarlet with autumn, hanging from the cables and girders. The
truck begins to rattle and bump along as we pass the bridge and
enter the old West Side Highway. At this point Jim and I sit down
on the wooden bench at the front. We hunch forward, our hands
between our knees, bracing ourselves as best we can. The truck
growls and stumbles on. Soon the road is pitted, cracked, and we
pass over long stretches of grass. Up the side streets I can see
rusting cars, long loops of wire between the buildings, and rows
and rows of dark windows.

Our mission is to reach Columbus Circle, where we are to be
met by a guide who is, of all things, an employee of the City of
New York.

We turn off the highway at Seventy-ninth Street and take the
cleared route to our destination. I realise that the streets are
literally choked with abandoned vehicles of all kinds – cars,
trucks, buses, and an occasional piece of fire equipment standing
out from the jumble. Broadway has had a central path created
between the cars. There are vines everywhere, vines and shrubs
and things like stinkweed and dandelions growing in every
available crack. Some buildings are glutted with plants, others
are empty. I realise why: certain species of potted plants grew
and seeded, and expanded their dominion.

Then we pass a magnificent ruin. I recognise the Ansonia. Its
copper-sheathed roof has been salvaged. There has also been a
scarring fire. The Pioneer supermarket on the first floor is a

blackened hole laced by flame-red vines. As we pass there is a
fusillade of furious barking. It is low and aggressive and powerful. The soldiers nearest the rear of the truck finger their carbines.
'No good shots,' somebody says as we pull into Columbus
Circle. 'Shit.'

The Ansonia lingers in my mind. I can imagine Florenz Zieg-
feld coming down the steps to his enormous Packard, afloat in
champagne laughter.

There is an olive drab Chevy Consensus parked in front of the
New York Coliseum. But for the lack of glass in the entrance and
the grass spurting up through the sidewalk, the structure looks
almost unchanged. The marquee reads, 56TH NY AUT OC 18–3. I
remember the New York Auto Show.

A young woman gets out of the Consensus. We climb down
from our perch in the truck. Across the street, the vast glut of
Central Park roars with birds, a furious jungle just touched by
autumn. The sidewalks around it are completely gone to vegetation, as are the abandoned cars choking Fifty-ninth Street. There
are vines well up some of the elegant buildings that line Central
Park South.

'I'm Jenny Bell,' the woman says, shielding her eyes from the
bright morning sun. She wears a heavy tunic closed by a web
belt. There is what looks like a long-barrelled .357 Magnum slung
on her right hip. Her left hip bears a big, curved knife. She is
wearing leather trousers and heavy boots. She carries a canteen,
a backpack, a heavy-duty flashlight, and at least twenty feet
of rope and a selection of climbing equipment. She does not
smile, she offers no more words of explanation. She is simply
there.

We introduce ourselves and get a quick handshake. 'Let's go,'
she says. We leave our soldiers, who have instructions to pick us
up here at 5.00 p.m. The Consensus is cramped. I sit in front
because I can't manipulate my pad and pencil in the back seat.
Jim, with that fancy recorder of his, has to endure the confine-
ment of the hard bench in the back.

'I understand that you're a city employee,' I say to the young,
expressionless face. The beautiful face. How old was this girl on
Warday? Eighteen is my guess.

'That's right.'

'So there's still a city government?'

'That's right.'

Jim shifts in his seat. 'Is there any particular reason you won't talk, or are you just being a hardass?'

The girl drives in silence, bouncing us down Broadway. A spring has opened up in the middle of the street between Fifty-seventh and Fifty-sixth. We are forced nearly to the sidewalk to avoid the bed of the little creek it has made. I see crystal water dancing among the skeletons of electrical conduit and pipe. It is young water, wearing and active. The stream goes on for blocks, finally disappearing into the gutters at the corner of Forty-fifth. I remember from some book about New York in the early days that an oak tree grew where Broadway now intersects Forty-second Street. A snatch of song echoes in my head – 'those dancin' feet . . .' The melody continues until we reach our first stop.

When I start to get out, the girl reaches over and locks my door. 'Wait,' she says. She steps into the middle of Times Square. Her gun is out. She holds it in both hands. It is a heavy weapon, too heavy for her to aim accurately any other way.

There is a loud click, then the pistol cracks. The report echoes off empty buildings. Pigeons rise from eaves, and a flock of guinea fowl burst out of the ruined front of Tape City, leaving feathers around a crackling poster of Paul Newman in the '86 picture *Jury of One*.

Through the hubbub of the birds I can hear a dog screaming in agony, and more dogs barking. Many more dogs.

'Okay, come on out and take a look. You know Times Square?'

'I lived in this city for eighteen years,' I say.

'So I don't have to talk.'

The dogs are in front of Bond's Disco. They are dark, scruffy things. Two of them are worrying something long and angled like an arm. Our guide keeps her pistol in her hand.

'Many dog packs?'

'Yeah.'

'You love this city, don't you?'

'I was born a few hundred yards from here, at St Clare's. It's stripped. They stripped the hospitals first. I went to Dalton and then to Stuyvesant. I was in my senior year when it hit.'

'And you stayed on?'

'Most of my class did. We formed a volunteer action group. I've been working ever since. I haven't had a vacation in five years.'

'What's your group called?'

'At first we were Volunteers to Save the City. Now we're part of the city government. Officially we're called the Office of Salvage Management. I'm area manager for Chambers Street to the Battery. My job is to make sure that all salvage in my area is carried out by licenced salvors, and that the withdrawals are duly recorded and entered into the city's record books.'

A glance at her hands tells me that she doesn't wear a wedding ring. 'Are you married – if you don't mind me getting personal.'

'I haven't got time.' She gets back into the car. 'Come on. Next stop Sixth Avenue.'

'You don't call it Avenue of the Americas,' Jim says.

'What's the point?'

We move slowly down Forty-second. A narrow passage has been cleared between reefs of abandoned cars. Once again she takes out her pistol as she stops the car. There are no dogs about this time, so we get out. Through the distant overgrowth of Bryant Park I can see an immense and familiar shape. My heart almost breaks. There are vines pouring out of the windows of the Main Branch of the New York Public Library. I have the horrible thought that they must be somehow rooting in the books. Rot and mildew and moisture are changing them to a fertile soil.

'Is there any salvage for the library?'

'One-of-a-kind books only.'

It is a kind of lobotomy, the loss of a place like that.

Jim asks another question. 'Do you actually live in the city?'

For the first time, she smiles. 'I have a house on Eleventh Street. It once belonged to Nikos Triantaffilydis, the Greek shipping magnate.' Her smile widens. 'I commandeered it for special purposes. We have that authority.'

As she speaks I hear a faint but very familiar sound. 'Surely that's not the subway?'

'You better believe it.' She glances at her watch. 'That'll be the 9.00 a.m. Westsider. It runs on the old D line from 145th Street to Grand. A lot of salvors live up in Washington Heights and commute into the salvage areas.'

'I thought the subway was flooded on Warday.'

'Below Twenty-third. It drained away over the six months after Warday. There are two working lines, the Westsider and the Eastsider. Each runs a three-car train. There are three morning

and three afternoon runs, and one at noon. At nine-thirty the
Westsider will be back.'

Suddenly Jim curses and slaps furiously at his head. 'A bird! It
flew in my hair.'

'It's probably hunting for nesting materials. They don't see
enough people to worry about hands. It thought you were a nice
hairy dog.'

I smell a faint tang of diesel smoke rising from the subway
grating. I want to ask Jenny Bell if we can ride on that subway, if
we can go down to the Village, to my old neighbourhood. My
chest is tight. Until now I haven't realised just how much it
means to me. Jenny has opened up a little, but her steel shell is
just waiting to snap closed again. This matter will have to be
approached very carefully. 'You live on Eleventh Street. That
means that the Village is –'

'It's almost a countryside down there. Fires levelled most of
the West Village, and now everything's covered with green. I like
it. I like the look of it. And I like the sound of the wind in the
ruins.'

I think of 515 West Broadway, where Anne and I raised
Andrew, and had some very happy years. I knew everybody in
that building – there were only fourteen apartments – but I lost
track of them all. We left every single thing we owned at 515.

This is an entire city of haunted houses, rows and rows and
towers and towers, softly crumbling into obscurity.

'Can we go down to the Village on the subway?'

'We'd have to go over to Grand Central. The nine-thirty
Westsider is an uptown train. The Eastsider's downtown.
They're staggered like that.' She gets in the car and starts it. Soon
we are once again moving along the cleared path in the centre of
Forty-second Street. The silence in the car is split by a loud crash
and a lingering roar somewhere off to the left. 'Masonry falling,'
Jenny says. 'The Façade Law's unenforceable without any
owners. And we haven't got the manpower to identify all the
cracked walls. We just have to let it go.'

I wonder if there were civil servants like Jenny Bell in ancient
Rome – smart, tough people managing the death of their city.

The world has always had a great city, one place where all
races and occupations met – a rich, dangerous place where the
best men and women make themselves fabulous and the worst
come to unravel them. First the World City inhabited Ur. A

thousand years later it took its bells and moved to Babylon, then briefly to Athens, then to Alexandria, then to Rome. In Rome it lingered and made legends. Then the site was Constantinople, later Paris. It remained Paris for three hundred years, until, like all before it, the City of Light became too ripe, too perfect, and wars and fortune passed the jewel to London. Sometime between the first two world wars, the treasured office of man's great city came to New York.

I lived in its evening, when the sorrow was already painted on the walls. The World City has left America altogether. I don't know if the party has settled yet, in Tokyo or perhaps back in London.

A squirrel sits on some vine-covered stones that have long ago fallen from 500 Fifth Avenue. It is eating some sort of nut. The trees in Bryant Park, I realise, are swarming with wild creatures. There are so many birds that their sound is a roar. They rise in a cloud as the car passes, and the squirrels leap from limb to limb. A pack of dogs laze in the morning sun at the corner of Fifth and Forty-second. They pant at us, their eyes full of lusty interest.

We stop at the corner of Vanderbilt and Forty-second, across the street from Grand Central.

Here there is little foliage and the frozen, rusting traffic is solid the other side of Vanderbilt. I can see why the street hasn't been cleared further: there are at least thirty buses between here and Lexington. They stand silent, motionless, amid the Hondas and the Buicks and the yellow cabs and the vans. Details:

A cab from the Valpin Cab Company, its windows rolled up, doors neatly locked. The inside is thinly filmed with grey.

Signs on a bus: an ad for the musical *Willard* at the Uris. Another for Virginia Slims, a third for McDonald's.

A van from Wadley and Smythe, florists. When I was a gofer on *The Owl and the Pussycat*, I used to call in producer Ray Stark's orders. Flowers for Barbra Streisand, the film's star. Flowers for others of his friends. Spectacular flowers, exotic flowers, perfect flowers.

An Interdec Data Transfer truck with a notice painted on the door: 'Contains no valuables. Only bookkeeping records'. How funny, considering what happens when the bookkeeping records are erased.

I could continue this list for twenty pages. We pick our way across not to Grand Central but to the subway entrance in the old Bowery Savings Building.

'I'd like to see Grand Central,' Jim says.

'Structurally unsound. Our voices could be what makes the roof cave in. Sometime soon, it's gonna go.'

We follow her into the dank, swamp-stinking blackness of the subway station. Her flashlight provides the bare minimum illumination we need.

We descend into a maw, past encrusted turnstiles and across muck-slicked floors. The sound of dripping water echoes everywhere.

'You've gotta understand that the water table's been rising in Manhattan,' Jenny says. I wonder about the structural soundness of the steel girders that support these tunnels.

I am in a very strange state because of the difference between what is here and what I remember. These tunnels are weird and terrible, dissolving in the water. It's only a matter of time before they cave in.

To me there was something eternal about Manhattan. But it isn't even close to that now. It's flimsy.

I realise that I'd always imagined it was waiting for us to come home, that it was the same as before, except empty. I had forgotten that even this most human of places belongs, in the end, to nature.

My mind turns with half-remembered poetry. '*My name is Ozymandias . . . round the decay of that colossal wreck . . .*'

Jenny's flashlight hardly illuminates the long, echoing cavern. Soon, though, a flickering yellow glow starts up in the tunnel, and we hear a heartbreakingly familiar sound. Any New Yorker knows the noise of subway cars coming down the tracks.

As the light draws closer, the rattling of the cars is joined by the high bellow of a great engine. This subway is drawn by one of the old diesel work engines that the MTA used to haul disabled cars off dead tracks.

We are illuminated by its powerful headlamp. As the train enters the station it gives off loud blasts from its horn. 'Shave and a haircut, two bits.'

Brakes squeal and the thing stops. Diesel fumes are billowing around us. 'Hiya, Jenny,' the driver shouts from his cab. 'Where to?'

'Bleecker,' she shouts back.

The doors on the cars that this train hauls are permanently fixed open. Inside, the cars are lit by gas lanterns hung from the ceiling ventilators. 'Hey, Jenny,' shouts a huge man in a filthy radiation suit, 'who the hell . . . whatcha got here, *tourists*?'

'They're reporters. They want to do a story on the Big Apple.'

'The core or the damn seeds?' He laughs. 'You stick with me, you guys. You'll see a hell of a salvage. We're takin' out five tons of copper wire a day.' He extends a huge hand as the train lurches off. 'I'm Morgan Moore. I debuild buildings.' He roars with laughter. He is an incredibly wrinkled man, maybe fifty, his eyes glimmering like dark animal eyes in the light of the swaying lamp. 'You look so goddamn clean, you must be from Lousy Angeles. Am I right?'

'We're from the Dallas *Herald News*,' Jim says. He already has his recorder out. 'We'd like to interview you.'

'Whar's yer hats, cowpokes?' Morgan Moore cries amid general laughter. 'Y'all cain't be Texas boys without yer hats, can yuh?' There's no derision in Morgan Moore's voice, only humour. And his interpretation of a Texas accent is hilarious. We laugh too.

As we rattle along I observe that there are about ten people on the train, none of them minding their own business as in the old days, all interested in the phenomenon of the reporters.

'Seriously,' Morgan Moore says, 'you guys gotta put a story about what we're doing at the World Trade Center in your paper. It's worth front page.'

Another voice: 'We pulled over three miles of wire out of the South Tower just yesterday. You're talkin' eighty gold dollars' worth of copper in one day.'

'We'll be down to the structural steel in another three months,' Morgan Moore adds.

We stop at Fourteenth Street, and four people get on. One of them is a black man in a three-piece tweed suit and a homburg. He carries a neatly furled umbrella, and he doesn't say anything to anybody. He is totally unexpected, and there is no real way to explain him. The salvors do not make jokes about him. Jenny Bell might have smiled at him, and he might have nodded, but that is the only indication of familiarity.

He is a welcome indication that, despite everything, the old spirit of this town still flickers.

Soon the brakes squeal and we are at Bleecker Street.

' 'S dog country,' Morgan Moore says. The gentleman with the umbrella stands beneath the lantern, staring blankly. The other salvors murmur agreement with Morgan Moore.

Jim asks him if he will do an interview for us. He agrees at once – as long as Jim comes down to his World Trade Center site with him. There is a moment's hesitation. We are both supposed to stay with our guide. And we aren't even supposed to *talk* to local residents, much less record interviews with them.

'Have a big time,' Jenny says. 'We'll catch up with you at the TC by – let's see, it's ten now – say two o'clock. You wait for us there.'

Then she and I step on to the platform. The train grinds its gears and roars off down the tunnel.

'There's an awful lot of foliage in this area,' Jenny says as we near the stairs. 'And dogs, like Moore said. You stay close to me. And I mean close. No more than three feet away.'

'The dogs are that dangerous?'

'This is their city, Mr Strieber. They're the kings here. Our best defence is to stay the hell away from them. But since you want to see the Village –'

We emerge into the light and fresher air of Lafayette and Bleecker. There have been more aggressive fires around here. East towards the Bowery most of the buildings are caved in, their rubble spread into the street, covering the inevitable ruined vehicles. 'You go down towards the Holland Tunnel, the cars really get thick. And in the tunnel, all the way to where it's drowned down near the middle.'

My heart is beating faster. Many, many times I emerged from this same station on my way home. In a few minutes we'll be able to see 515 West Broadway.

Ahead is Broadway, the ruins of the Tower Records store on the ground floor of the Silk Building. I think to myself, the destruction of this city is so vast, so intricate, that it is not possible to grasp it, let alone tell about it.

New York was immensely wealthy, and so it was detailed. It is the ruin of this detail that impresses – the thousands of cars, the sheer weight of salvage, the numberless little things that together once defined the place: ballpoint pens, mag wheels, plastic raincoats, videotapes, canned goods, masonry and glass and asphalt, an endless list of objects destroyed.

It is a fine morning, though, and the light spreading down has the familiar sinister sharpness peculiar to New York skies. We begin moving along the centre of Bleecker, between Washington Square Village and Silver Towers. The trees are much taller than one would expect after five years, and the grass has extended on a bed of creepers right to the middle of the street. Bleecker seems like a country lane set amid exotic, crumbling colossi.

To the right, the Grand Union grocery where we used to shop is completely destroyed, burned to a few stacks of seared brick, and covered by vines and grasses.

Then I see 515. I am absurdly grateful. I could kiss this taciturn girl for bringing me here. The building does not look well. The slate façade has fallen off almost completely and lies shattered on the sidewalk. I can see broken windows with rotting curtains blowing out of them. Up close, the quiet of desolation is hard to bear. I took Andrew in and out of this building in a stroller. He learned to ride a bike on this sidewalk. Behind those walls my love for Anne matured and became permanent.

It is not until Jenny Bell puts an arm around my shoulder that I realise I've begun to cry.

'I want to go in.'

'These old buildings are dangerous.'

'Still –'

She sighs. 'You're crazy. But I suppose you know that. I'm crazy too. I work in New York, for God's sake.'

'The doors are busted. We could go right in.'

'A place like this never got cleaned. There might be particles.'

'I want to see my apartment. If you'll let me, I'd like to go. Alone, if you prefer.'

'You aren't going anywhere alone. What floor is it on?'

'Six.'

'Of course. Naturally. You wouldn't live on one or two, not you. A seven-storey building and you live on six. So come on.'

As we enter the building I see a couple of dogs asleep on the sidewalk about half a block away. Two dogs, not very big.

The lobby is badly deteriorated. The walls were carpeted, and the carpet now hangs to the floor. When I push some of it aside to open the door into the stairwell, at least two hundred roaches scuttle away. 'They like the glue,' Jenny says.

The place has a sweet, rancid odour, something like stagnant water. I suppose the basement must be permanently flooded. 'If the water table's risen, why couldn't people simply dig wells? We'd be able to repopulate Manhattan.'

'Toxins. The water's poisonous. Godawful. When dogs drink out of the basements, their lips get eaten away.'

'How do they live?'

'Rainwater, rats, and squirrels. And people.'

'You're not serious.'

'All the damn time. We find new kills every few days. Drifters figure that with so many buildings the city must be a squatter's paradise. Wrong. Those who don't get dogged die of waste poisoning from coming across Jersey. You can't walk from Newark to the Hudson and live. It just ain't possible.'

I think of the sins of the past. Then, it was so easy. Now I realise that I, like everybody else, was directly and personally responsible. The land was not despoiled by chemical companies, nor the war caused by countries. It was us, each one. We are all accountable for our era.

A sharp tang enters my mouth, something I wish I could spit out.

The stairs are dark in a way that the subway was not. This is absolute blackness, not the presence of dark but something more profound, the absence of light. I remember that these stairs were like this during the great blackout of '85. We set candles along the banisters then, and shared the hot night and songs, and survival stories. We were New Yorkers. We were getting through.

I am a little sick to be passing Joseph and Sally Boyce's bikes, the two beautiful Raleighs they got in June of '87. There is a bag beside them. Jenny's flashlight reveals a sweatshirt wadded up in it, so rotten that it turns to dust at a touch. I know that shirt; we gave it to Joseph for his birthday in '87. If it could have been opened out, it would have read WHIPPETS on the front and LAKE WOBEGON, MINN. on the back.

At the sixth floor I hesitate before the fire door. We peer through the glass. Jenny's flashlight reveals that the foyer on the other side is in perfect condition. It looks as if it has been preserved in a museum. The door creaks as Jenny opens it. Even the picture we and our next-door neighbours put on the wall of the foyer is still there. 'Deux', it's called. Photographs of two old men, one bright and smiling, the other in shadow. My neighbour was the bright one. The other represents me. There are just two apartments per floor in our building, and both doors seem securely locked. I put my hand on my old doorknob and rattle it. I wonder if we can even get in.

'Just a second,' Jenny says. She gives me the flashlight and produces a small hooked bar from a sling in her belt. 'We have to do this fifty times a day.' She inserts the tool into my supposedly burglar-proof lock and in an instant the door swings open.

Sunlight floods the living room. It was always a bright apartment. After a moment my eyes get used to the light. The first thing I see is the bulging, rotted ruin of our L-shaped couch, maroon with tan padding and foam jutting out. The ceiling above it slopes far down into the room.

But it's our apartment, very definitely. It hasn't been looted.

The rosewood dining table still has a note stuck in the crack in the centre. I take the brittle brown paper. *I am at the school*, says Anne's hasty scrawl. My first impulse is to take the note. But then I find myself putting it back, as if our whole past might collapse if this last, critical rivet were pulled out.

I want to see the rest of the apartment. But when I start for the back, where the bedrooms and my office are, Jenny stops me. 'Hold it.' She nods towards the floor. 'Spoor.'

'Spoor?'

'Animals have been in here.' She nods towards the fire escape. 'Window.' She touches a brown bit of the dung with her toe. 'Dry. Wish I knew what the hell dropped it.'

'Not a dog?'

She shakes her head. 'They don't come up this high. Big, though. Maybe a zoo animal. Some of them around. A few. All the way down here, s'funny. I wouldn't expect it.'

Jenny has her revolver out.

'You think it's still here?'

At first she doesn't answer. When she moves towards the back rooms, I follow. I make a mental note that we can go down the fire escape if we have to. Jenny takes a deep breath. 'Doesn't smell like animals,' she says softly. I notice that she cocks the pistol.

In places the floor has a disturbing springy quality to it. If I jumped, I don't doubt that I'd end up in the apartment below.

We reach Andrew's room. There is his Apple computer on his desk, his bed for ever unmade, his paintings on the walls, most of them rotted beyond recognition. His dresser has fallen apart. There is a dried cowboy boot in the middle of the floor. As this room faces west and north, winter blows in here, and his bookshelf is a bulging, sodden ruin.

The room echoes with so many past voices, him and his friends, a thousand bedtime stories.

It is in my office, where I wrote *The Hunger* and *Catmagic*, that I see my first clear sign of the last desperate days of this city. There is a can of Sterno on the floor, and three empty tins from the kitchen, their contents and even their paper labels long since eaten. I wonder who was here. Could it have been our neighbours? What might have happened to them? Elizabeth, the model, tall and gentle, her face at the edge of unforgettable beauty. Roberto, full of laughter, a native of Italy, wine importer, friend of evenings. Until this moment I have not remembered them, and I feel guilty for it.

'Come here,' Jenny says. She is looking into the bathroom opposite my office, where I used to soak in the tub to ease the lower-back pain of a sedentary life.

Bones, jumbled, gnawed, skulls pocked and pitted, teeth grinning, bits of clothing adhered to gnarls of ligament.

I cannot help myself. I scream.

Jenny neither scolds nor laughs nor sympathises. When I stop, she begins talking again. 'Stay-behinds. You see 'em all over the place.'

'How did they die?'

'Every way you can imagine.' She flashes her light into the bathroom. 'That vent. Probably brought in short-half-life dust, so they mighta gotten radsick. Or maybe they were scared to leave and they starved. That happened too. Or violence. Suicide. Take a coroner to tell you, and that I'm not.'

It is then that I see, standing in the door of our bedroom, the most enormous cat I have ever encountered. Its eyes meet mine and its ears go back. It crouches and hisses. 'Damn,' Jenny says. And then she pumps bullets into it until the head disappears into a red cloud of bone and blood. The creature slams across the room and then slumps to a tawny, blood-pumping heap on the floor.

'What the hell is that?' It looked like a cross between a blonde Persian and a Manx, but four times as big as either.

'Damned if I know. Big cat.'

'Giant cat.'

'I'm gettin' out of this hole, and so are you. You want to get killed, you can stay behind.' On the way out I see, lying on the floor of the living room, the china bud vase my mother gave

Anne for one of her birthdays. I snatch it up as if it were a gold dollar and put it in my pocket.

Jenny won't go near the fire escape, so we return down the stairs. The dark behind us seems so dangerous that it is all I can do not to run.

It will be a long time before I can think about that apartment again.

Interview: Morgan Moore, Salvor

I entered the salvage business in 1989. I've been a salvor for four years now. Mostly we work the New York Reclamation District, Southern Division. But I've also got permits for the District of Columbia and an iron permit for freelance railroad work in the Northeast Corridor. I have twelve guys and about six pieces of equipment, including a heavy-duty wire puller that strips copper wire out of conduits, a couple of rivet poppers, a wrecking ball, and one hell of a good set of torches.

My lifedose has put me on the triage, which means I'm untreatable, so I don't give too much of a damn about counts. I word hard, and when I can, I have all the fun that money can buy. Life's too short for anything else. I've got about eight per cent body coverage squamous, mostly face and neck. No pain. I'd like to wangle a trip to England. There's a doctor there who might be able to get me a number, but he wants a thousand in gold. A thousand! So I take black market radiums at a buck a pop. But I better not talk on that.

You want to know what we do? Simple. We work the salvage area for anything marketable. That's what we do. Our P-and-L puts us high, but that's mostly because of depreciation on the

Demon, which is our main cutting tool. It gets a lot of work. Mostly we're in for cutting out steel and copper from skyscrapers. We participated in the One Chase Manhattan Plaza demo for gold, though.

Now that was a hell of a demo. Salvors are still talking about it. We were new, a small company. In those days we didn't have the kind of equipment we've got now. I mean, I started up by just saying to myself, I want to make some of that goddamn salvage money. I was an assistant product manager for Triton Systems before the war. We marketed video games, can you believe it? That was a very big business. Multimillions. Even in new dollars we'd be grossing a hell of a lot. It was, like, I think thirty million in 1986. Big.

So I was out on my ass after the war. Triton's bank accounts had been erased by EMP. Then the stock market dissolved and all the Triton stock just ceased to exist. No different from everybody else. Except our inventory was destroyed. EMP burned every chip we owned, and ruined our fabrication equipment.

By '89 I was stealing food. Trouble was, so was everybody else. There was a point when I would have sold my sister for two minutes alone with a loaf of Wonder Bread. Here we were, living in a two-hundred-thousand-dollar house in Darien and there's the five-year Connecticut moratorium on mortgages declared, so we got no mortgage to worry about. You know what it was like. People were starving all around us. I remember, I went into a supermarket with a shotgun. Big deal. Everybody else had a gun too. Bread is eight dollars a loaf and I have, like, a dollar. I would have given away my house for that Wonder Bread, plus sold my sister.

When that hot dust drifted down into the wheat and corn belts, America learned what it was to goddamn not eat.

I figured we're all going to die anyway, so I'll just say the hell with rads and the hell with everything and go into salvage.

Now, of course, it's a different story. We got a waiting list to enter the Salvors' Association. We've been regulated by the Army. But back when I started, people were scared of salvage work. They still thought in terms of prewar life expectancies. People still thought they ought to feel young at forty.

Sally – that was my wife – she made my first rad suit. Sewed it herself out of an old swimming-pool cover. We used bonded lead epoxy in it that I made myself. I got the lead out of car batteries,

just like everybody else. Stole 'em. I don't mind admitting it. I
hurt people to get the lead for that suit, and I'm sorry. But most of
'em didn't last the winter anyway. I mean, we starved half to
death and then the flu came, just when we were weakest. Darien
probably lost half its people. Sally died in the spring of '89. Just so
weak, anything would have taken her. We had noodle soup that
winter, from the Connecticut Allocation when it got started up in
January. I remember, Christmas of '88 we were living on soup
made out of dandelion roots and salt and Fritos. We were just a
little hungry.

I went down into New York on the second salvor call in '89. I
remember they had this big pier on the Hudson, Jersey side. All
covered with plastic. About six government types. EPA, they
said. They got us to fill out forms and wear dose cards. They
checked our suits by putting a geiger counter in 'em, closing 'em
up, then sticking 'em out on the end of the pier. If you could hear
the counter, you stayed at home.

They gave a geiger to one of every twenty men. Those counters
were worth their weight back then, so half the men just took off. I
mean, what's the use of cutting steel and stuff all day that's
probably gonna be condemned hot anyway, when you can take a
geiger counter worth maybe five hundred in gold on the black
market and just walk away with it?

The government men stood on the pier in their orange Uncle
Sam rad suits and took potshots at the boats that were heading
downriver instead of across to Manhattan. They just did it
because they were pissed off. They didn't try to hurt anybody.

You think of New York as being, like, empty in those days.
Half burned out and empty and glowing like a goddamn hot
cow. It's empty now. But then it was still full of people. Manhattan, anyway. Part of the Bronx. There were taxis running.
Buses. The old stuff that hadn't been knocked out by EMP. There
were cops all over the place. People were starin' at our rad suits.
In those first couple of years, they'd condemn hot spots until
they could be cleaned up, and people would just move to another
building for a while.

That first night in New York I went to see *You're the Top* and
then we sat around at a place this guy knew, called the Monkey
Bar, where this female impersonator sang and played the piano.
A can of corned-beef hash was eighty dollars paper on the menu,
so we decide, we'll share one can between ten of us. We'd come

up a few bucks short, but they'd live with it, we figured. I remember that stuff to this day. God, it tasted good. One small mouthful, but it was the first meat I'd had in I don't know how long. The Monkey Bar, and that guy all dolled up singin' 'Memories of You', and eating Armour Star corned-beef hash off expensive hotel china. Holy God.

We slept in the basement of the B. Dalton bookstore on Fifth Avenue. The Plaza Hotel and the old Gotham had teamed up and made the world's fanciest dormitory in there. You couldn't sleep aboveground; you might get a dusting if the wind came from the east across the boroughs that did get hit. We were broke, but they let us in anyway. Salvors on their way downtown had credit. They figured we'd be back through, and God knows what we'd have with us.

Salvors were taking the treasures of the world out of that city. That was the year Salvage Team Victor, Inc., took out seventeen hundred pounds of gold, all assayed and ready to go, from the vault of the Republic National Bank. So when people saw that our paper said One Chase Manhattan Plaza on it, they just said, 'When you're on your way back, remember who gave you a free bed.'

I stayed in my rad suit the whole time. I was scared to death. Those people were all nuts in New York. There were people on the streets with the radiation trembles. People doing heaves right in the middle of everything. But they were staying put. There were actually only about a quarter of a million who stayed. But that's still a lot of people. They were the total New Yorkers, the ones who just couldn't imagine themselves anywhere else.

You still had the tail end of the long fires then, so the whole place was full of smoke all the time. Smelled sort of like a mattress fire, or burning hair, when the wind came across the East River. And you wondered, am I gonna inhale a particle or two? Maybe a little cesium is gonna get in my mask, or a little strontium 90.

Well, when we got to Forty-second Street, there was this barrier made of plywood, with skulls and crossbones stencilled on it. It went right down the middle of the street. You crossed it and there was nobody. They were living in the northern half of Manhattan and in the Bronx. The hits in Queens and Brooklyn had dusted lower Manhattan with the dirty stuff. I remember we went through the barrier. We tried to laugh it off. Nowadays the problem is more uptown, from the chemical spills to the north. But back then it was radiation. Every step we took, the geiger burped some more. By Thirty-fourth Street it was going continuously.

We were all set to walk to Wall Street when up comes the goddamnedest thing – a city bus all covered with black tarp. Comes right up the middle of Fifth Avenue, picking its way around the abandoned cars. They've been pulled here and there to make a path. It's slow going, but the bus is making it. The side streets were solid cars in those days, and so were all the avenues except Fifth and part of Sixth, and Broadway below Canal.

Anyway, it's an ancient jalopy of a bus and the sign says, 'Special'. So we get in. The driver's in one of those ancient city-issue rad suits, the olive drab ones from the civil defence stores that were put aside in the fifties. They weighed about a hundred pounds. He's slumped over the goddamn wheel. So what happens? We get on the bus and he says, 'Hey, don't you guys know you're supposed to pay a fare?' The guy is at the end of the world and he wants a fare. It's a buck seventy-five each. Nobody had thought about deflation yet. We don't have the money, but before we can give him the bad news this jerk says, real rude, 'You gotta have exact change. I'm not allowed to make change.'

We kind of displaced him by force and drove the damn bus ourselves. By the time we got to Broadway and Wall, where the cleared path stopped, we had a cop on our tail. Here comes this traffic cop, drags himself out of his car in his ridiculous heavy suit and writes us up a summons for 'unauthorised commandeering' of the goddamn bus! Not stealing. It was crazy. I never did anything about the ticket and I never heard about it again. The people who used those old rad suits in New York were all dead by the end of '89 anyway, so I guess the ticket got forgotten.

Now I'm starting to think about Warday. Three million people died in New York on that day, and the bombs damn well missed! Crap. Lemme tell you, we've been pullin' wire out of the World Trade Center for three months. Makin' a fortune!

You know, this was a grand place years ago. The Consumer Electronics Show was held at the new Convention Center in July of '86. We had a suite at the Waldorf. High times. Fat times.

'Never think about Warday'. That's my motto, and talking into your machine is making me violate it. I have a tough life. I don't wanta cry in my beer, but I've lost a hell of a lot. My wife. I had a boy –

Oh hell.

Listen, this has gotta be the end of this thing. I can't stand this. I work. I don't look back. I'll tell you about the salvage of One Chase Plaza some other damn time.

PART FIVE

RETURNING HOME

You cross with ease
at 80 the state line and the state you are entering
always treated you well.

– Richard Hugo,
'Goodbye, Iowa'

The Children's Train

Thirtieth Street Station in Philadelphia was an astonishing sight as we walked in, weary from the long bus ride that had brought us here from White Plains. We were planning to catch the *Southern Crescent* to Meridian, and from there take the bus to Dallas.

There must have been a thousand children in the station. We had just been to Independence Park and put our hands on the Liberty Bell, which you can do now, and stood before Independence Hall, seeking to renew our hope. There were hundreds of people there, including a doubled family, where a man had taken on his neighbour's children when the parents died. Such mixing is much more common in this part of the country than in Texas, where we tend to focus down on the unit rather than look to our neighbours. The spirit of the frontier, perhaps, still influences our habits.

There is at Independence Hall a daily schedule of recitations of the Declaration of Independence, the Bill of Rights, and the Gettysburg Address. This is a programme developed by the Philadelphia school system, and the speakers are children.

We listened with the rest of the crowd to the hasty voice of a girl reciting the Bill of Rights. Her eyes darted as she spoke. She was as frail as a bird, and her tone was high and thin, but something in her delivery came from deep within her, and set the breathless, mumbled words to ringing.

I had been thinking long thoughts of children as we walked through Philadelphia's quiet streets.

Now, here in the station, I was surrounded by children who had not gotten the chance to double up. Quiet children, sitting in rows on the floor. Here and there, one slept in another's lap. Older kids attended babies. The cries of babies echoed in the huge waiting room. A supervisor moved among the rows.

There was none of the hubbub of childhood among these kids. Their situation was serious, and they knew it.

They were all dressed identically, in white T-shirts and jeans, girls and boys alike. On the back of their shirts were stencilled their names, years of birth, blood types, TB susceptibilities, and Pennsylvania ID numbers. I began noting down a sampling of their names, but stopped when I saw the way Jim was leaning against the wall. We'd both dreaded getting sick on our journey. We were exhausted from too many nights in trains and too much third-rate food. Stepping between the rows of kids, I went to him.

'I'm sorry. I'm nauseated. I've got to lie down.'

'No – let's go outside. You'll be better.'

I did not say it, but I knew what had happened to him. The overpowering odour of unwashed people was stifling in that station. Out on the street he began to feel better.

'Jim –'

He stared off into the darkness. We both understood the stakes here. This scene was being repeated commonly all over the country. How many orphans are there? What are the support programmes like? What are we doing to protect the future?

We did not speak, not until long afterwards, when we were on the train. The children were jammed into eight passenger cars behind us. We were in the through-car. Ahead of us were three 'state cars' for people planning to leave the train in resident-only states, such as Georgia, the Carolinas, and Virginia.

'I want to find out about the kids,' Jim said.

'You mean why they're on the train?'

'Why they're on the train.'

Their presence worried him too. It must be an enormous undertaking to move so many children. Why was it being done?

We started moving back towards their cars. When we opened the door we saw dim lights and hard seats, and smelled their odour again. These were not the normal Amtrak cars, but old commuters with ceiling fans and dim bulbs, obviously put on at the last moment. They rattled and swayed. The night wind bellowed in the windows. The trainmen were giving out blankets and sheets, which the children made into beds on the seats and the floor. There was a gravity among them that was deeply unsettling, as if this bedmaking were the most important thing in the world, and these blankets were valuable beyond price.

Other passengers were coming back too, bringing food and water bags and whatever else they could spare. Soon the cooks appeared, bearing what later proved to be every scrap of Amtrak food in the train. But there were so many of them, and I know that the great majority must have gone hungry that night.

Jim found one of the adult supervisors at the rear of the car. She could have been thirty years old, or fifty, it was hard to tell. A little boy slept with his head in her lap, a girl of twelve with her head on her shoulder. She held a baby in her arms. Another baby lay in the girl's arms. 'We're writing a book,' Jim said. 'Can we talk to you?'

She smiled. 'I guess so, if you don't wake anybody up. I got some mighty tired kids on this train.'

'Are you the only supervisor?'

'Lord, no! I'd be *dead*! There are ten of us with this group, one for every hundred kids.'

'How did you get your job?'

'Well, I have my Master's in early-childhood education from Bank Street, and I have a degree in child psychology. But I didn't get the job on qualifications. I was with the State Department of Social Work before the war. Afterwards we found ourselves with tremendous numbers of orphans. It was natural that anybody in the Welfare Department who knew anything at all about kids, or just liked them, would end up doing what I'm doing.'

'Why are they on the train?'

She smiled again. 'These children are being transferred to an institution in Alabama. We've been informed by the Department of Agriculture that there's going to be another grain emergency by April, so we're evacuating them to a better-fed area. We do not want to go through another famine the way we went through the last one. My unit buried an awful lot of children. That will not happen again, not if there is any way on God's earth to prevent it.'

We returned to our own car. An hour passed. For a while I stared at my own reflection in the window. Haggard, thin, cadaverous even. I hadn't shaved since I was at Quinn's, in California. I was greasy and grungy and totally exhausted.

Jim read the *Philadelphia Inquirer* and then slept. I felt frightened, as if the delicate balance of the future were swaying and trembling with the movement of the train.

When I was twenty-two I went this way in a Volkswagen, on my way home from New York to San Antonio for a family reunion.

Years later I went in my Mercedes, through the Smokies and across the back of the South, through the piney woods of Arkansas and the hot plains of northeast Texas.

I went also in a bus, broke, hungry, to find work one year when it was too long between cheques from publishers.

My life has been punctuated by journeys between Texas and New York.

I can remember coming this way with my father, and seeing barefoot children with fishing poles in the Cumberland Valley and longing from my luxurious Pullman drawing room to be one of them.

To be a child.

I am tired of trains, tired of travel. Now that it's almost finished, I wonder what will become of this new book. These days it is not easy to gain publication, and the distribution of books is a difficult process.

I am very used to the rattle of trains, the smell of trains, the mood of travellers. In these past six weeks we have seen a fair sample of the country. And we have learned some things. America is changing, profoundly and probably irrevocably. In a few years there will be a kind of country here with as few references to us as we have to, say, the Kennedy years. Maybe fewer.

There is death in this, certainly, and the collapse of old ways. But there is also this other thing, which I heard again and again, in the voices along the road. I know it, and yet I cannot seem to put it down in words, except that it is America in us, the promise and the children. It is the common dream of gold – the golden valley, the golden door, the gold in the hills, the gold at the end of the rainbow.

The night deepens and the old diesel's horn sounds and sounds. This is another of those bumpy, slow routes around one of the dead areas, in this case Washington.

I close my eyes. Music comes into my mind, soft and slow, the music of the swaying car and the dark. I remember, so well, when I was a child.

Jim: My Final Image

When Whitley and I arrived in New York, I realised that, emotionally, I had reached the end of the journey. For me, New York exemplified the whole experience – both the folly of the war and the drama of our effort to recover.

Morgan Moore didn't talk much about his present project, but I must say that the dismantling of the World Trade Center is a work of tremendous energy and vision. Everything is being done on a gigantic scale. Massive devices pull wiring out on to huge wheels, drawing it like the meat from a crab claw. Dozens of scaffolds hang down from the towers, with men on them loosening sheathing while others work with cranes, taking the plates to the ground. Inside the buildings, window crews dismantle the good glass, floor crews take up usable wood and linoleum, decoration crews remove furniture. Behind all this, Morgan Moore sits in his command trailer, manipulating a sophisticated new Toshiba computer and talking to his people over an elaborate communications system.

I went as far as the thirtieth storey in the elevator that they have rigged along the side of the South Tower. From there I saw the whole of New York Harbour, from the Verrazano-Narrows Bridge between Staten Island and the black ruins of Brooklyn to the Statue of Liberty. I could see the arm and torch lying at the base of the great statue. Even if New York remains uninhabited, that statue ought to be restored – even moved, maybe to Philadelphia.

Moore has twelve workmen, all paid in gold on the basis of the market value of their salvage. Some of these men, skilled wire-pullers for example, can make the extraordinary salary of ten gold dollars a week.

But I could not love Morgan Moore's salvage operation. I could only think of the city before the war, with the sun on its towers and the throngs in its streets. It was a great work of art, New York, made up of millions of sophisticated, convoluted lives.

I find that I cannot really say much about it. It was Whitley's home, and fortunately writing about it has been his responsibility.

Instead, I am going to turn to other events that occurred towards the end of our journey.

We were unable to arrange a flyover of Washington. The Army refused without giving a reason. I think maybe the military is ashamed of losing the capital city.

Our money was nearly gone, which didn't matter much, since we couldn't leave the train once we crossed the Mason–Dixon line and entered the South, an area of the country almost as economically healthy as California. As long as one stays in the through-car there's no problem, so we watched Virginia and Tennessee pass by the window. We had neither the funds nor the emotional energy to do a repetition of California and become fugitives.

Watching the towns go by, the flash of a main street or a town square, big, leafy trees, kids waving from the backs of horses, I felt something I have never felt before, that under the circumstances was rather curious. I did not feel alienated at all, even though I could not walk freely down those streets, nor even set foot on this soil. I guess I understood. They can't afford too many immigrants. There have to be controls. I hope that what I felt never leaves me. It was a closeness to my fellow human beings, as if the very concept of the stranger were false. As if the borders, the restrictions, all were also false.

We belong to one another; in a sense we are married one to all. Before the catastrophe we had failed to notice this. But we all have as much of a stake in everybody else as we have in ourselves.

The thought of this great marriage brings me down to a much smaller one. Perhaps if Quinn Yarbro doesn't find Vivian, I will create some kind of a monument for her. A monument for one person still makes sense, I think, if she was your person.

In my mind I am trying to assemble the elements of my journey into some whole image: the people, their voices and faces and stories; the landscapes; the documents; my perceptions and what I feel about all of it.

The vision that remains of the journey is complex. It is a great mass of haunting images, of suffering and work, of people who keep on even when they ought to be unable.

I was affected by smiles. Before the war there were never such smiles. They can shatter you, the smiles of the Americans.

I listen to the rattle of the train. Beside me, Whitley rests from working on his own notebook. His head lolls on to the seat.

I realise that a radio is playing.

A radio?

Well, there are a lot more of them around these days than there were even a couple of months ago.

The music is soft, repetitive, peaceful. Typical popular music. I know the album: Brian Eno's *Persistence of Vision*.

I close my eyes. For a while, I'll sleep also. May my dreams be peaceful.

Georgia Patrol

The kids ran into trouble at the patrol station three miles across the Georgia border.

People in through-cars aren't supposed to get out in restricted-immigration states, but a restless murmur went among us when we saw them being herded off the train and into holding pens.

The Georgia Patrol wears green. They look like park rangers, not at all terrifying like the California Immigration Police. But they herded a thousand children into a fenced enclosure suitable for perhaps three hundred. They crowded them there in the blazing sun, the ten supervisors among them. A tall black man stood just inside the gate, clutching a sheaf of papers. We could see his mouth moving as he obviously tried to reason with the patrol officers.

'This is outrageous,' a woman said.

A man went to the door of the car. 'What's going on?'

He was ignored.

Jim got up. He took out his *Herald News* identification and strode out on to the platform. Most of the other passengers followed him, myself included.

'I'm a reporter,' Jim said, flashing his papers. 'Can I see the commanding officer, please?' The patrolman to whom he spoke shook his head, but in disgust, not refusal.

'Just what we need,' he said. 'Do you travel with 'em or what?'

'I think the press has a right to know what's going on here. These kids are bound for Alabama. Why are you taking them off the train?'

Another patrolman came over. His underarms were wet. He was haggard, his face covered with sweat. 'I'm Captain Howell,' he said. 'These children are not bound for Alabama. They're going back to Pennsylvania.'

'The hell they are, Bob Howell,' a man's voice boomed out. We all turned to see a stocky gentleman in a cream-coloured suit coming down off the Georgia car.

'Lord, if it isn't T.K. What the hell are you doin' all the way up here in Toccoa?'

'I just come from a meetin' of the Southeast Funeral Directors in Greensboro. Look here, Bob, I want to know what's goin' on. You can't just herd them kids into that hot corral. You'll have some dead babies on your hands, man.'

'They can't go any farther. We got a bulletin from Alabama about them. They haven't got room for them down there.'

'We've got papers,' the leader called from the enclosure. 'We've got all the authorisation we need.'

'What he has is a permit from Pennsylvania. The Northeastern states send these kids down here without so much as a by-your-leave. They figure we won't turn away a bunch of helpless orphans. You know how many of these kids have come down this one rail line in the past six months? Eighteen thousand and change. We can't handle 'em, T.K. We've got to send 'em back.'

The children, I noticed, were scarcely aware of the drama on the platform. They were going about making their new place as endurable as they could, tying blankets to the fencing to create sun shades. The babies and the little ones were kept in the shaded areas, watched over by the supervisors and the older kids.

The woman we had talked to on the train came to the edge of the enclosure. 'We're going to need water and milk,' she called. 'We can't stay in this sun without water and milk.'

A woman on the platform began to cry. She wept bitterly, her fists clenched, her body bent as if the least weight would break her in the middle.

'Do you have supplies for them, Captain Howell?' Jim asked.

'There's plenty of water. And we can give them a few gallons of milk for the babies.'

'They sure must be hungry, Bob,' his friend T.K. said.

'We don't have a budget to provide food for detainees.'

'I hate to hear you talk like that, Bob. It makes you sound like a nasty little peacock, and I don't think you're really that way at all.'

'Look here, T.K., I've got a job to do – a job you wouldn't do when you were asked.'

'I'm in a critical profession, Bob, as you well know. I'll tell you something, if you can't find a way to provide for these kids, you shouldn't be in this job yourself. Now you find them more than water and milk. They need food. They've gotten little enough on the train.'

'I can't go all out for every bunch of orphans –'

'The hell you can't! And don't you dare say "orphan" like it was a dirty word. Kids like these are the future and honour of this country. There's no shame in being an orphan, Bob. Look at 'em. They oughta get medals, the way they behave. Now you take care of 'em or I swear I'll see you outa that pretty uniform inside a week!'

The people on the platform broke out into applause. The captain promised to provide the children with food, and let them wait for the northbound *Crescent* under the trees beyond the platform.

As our train pulled out, I found myself full of a mixture of anger and a curious sort of hope. I saw something in those kids that is strong. And I saw strength also in the way the passengers jumped in on their side.

The train picked up speed past Toccoa, and we moved on towards Atlanta through the warm October morning.

'T.K.' turned out to be a funeral director from Savannah. His opinion was that one of the other Southern states would probably agree to take the children. 'There's a lot more to it than you might think. And old Bob Howell's a good man. That uniform's gone to his head a little bit, but he'll do his duty.'

We never found out what happened to the children.

On the road, one gets used to lost people. You see roadies all the time, walking the bus routes, following the railroad tracks, or just hiking across the countryside.

But you also encounter another type on the road, those whom

it seems nothing can stop, who keep on no matter what happens to them, those who will not give up.

It isn't that they aren't afraid. They all have their nightmares. But when they wake up, they find a way to go on.

No doubt the children do the same.

Interview: T. K. Allerton, Funeral Director

What happened in Savannah, the way the war hit us, was that the radio and the TV went off. I remember I was in the showroom with some clients, and all of a sudden, no Muzak. I thought, hell, the bastard's on the fritz, and went on with my consultation.

After I'd sold the funeral I went back into the office and found Frances Tolliver trying to get the Apple to boot the database management program. She said the computer had made this funny popping noise and that was it. So I told her to call Computerland and we then discovered that the phones were out. I turned on the radio in my office and couldn't get a sound out of it.

That was the first sign of the war in Savannah. We never got a scratch, and we've never suffered any fallout. We were damn confused for about a week. But we knew, we all just knew, that all hell had broken loose. A lot of people couldn't start their cars. My broker's line to New York was dead, and it stayed dead. There was no TV. Even the civil defence sirens weren't working. And out at the airport – you couldn't get anything beyond an ultralight into the air.

Of course, cars can be hot-wired, and soon people were on the road again. People went up to Charleston and down the coast towards Florida, hunting for news.

Meanwhile, things began to happen to my business. At first I just kept going, no real problems. No computer, but that was only an inconvenience for us. The phone was a pain in the neck, but we got used to that, too.

But coffins are shipped by rail, and no trains were coming in. Plus there was the bank rush. I participated in it when the Southern & National stopped taking cheques. I tried to get at my money. The banks just handed out all the cash in Savannah and closed their doors. They were electronic basket cases from the EMP. I had about eighty thousand in the S&N, and I ended up with two thousand. Better than some did. Some people didn't get a dime. And there was no more FDIC insurance, although we didn't know that at the time.

First off, I got a lot of heart attack and accident situations, where people who were on the edge died. I think about half the people with pacemakers, which was about eight hundred in Savannah, died on the spot when the EMP blew out their units. The rest of them either kept up without the pacemaker or they somehow were shielded, like sitting in a car, that plus the body itself shielded the pacemaker enough, apparently. Accidents, there were a lot of those. There were fires. People couldn't get the fire department on the phone. In those days right after the war, we were still living as if nothing much had happened. There was no panic. There was no idea how much things were going to change.

People were strong and confident in those days. They're good now, and we've learned something about just how tough we can be if we've got to be, here in America, but in those days we were basically happy people. There was none of this talk like there is now that the human race is sort of fundamentally defective. And of course movements like the Extinctionists and the Destructuralists didn't exist.

You were proud of your government in those days. America was the land of the free, from sea to shining sea. Not like it is now, a jumbled-up whatnot. Do we even have a President? I don't think the Europeans and the Japs even *want* us to become self-governing again. Don't quote me on that. Or you probably can't say it anyway – look at you, smiling at me! You can't say that, can you?

A couple of days after the war, I had all of a sudden sixty deceased in the fridge. Sixty! We stacked them in there like logs. Later I found out how lucky Savannah was we didn't lose our electric power. God knows what they did with the cadavers where they had no refrigeration.

All of mine were either accidents or, like I said, pacemaker. I never worked so hard in my life as I did that couple of weeks after the war. I was in real trouble. No coffins, low on formaldehyde. I had to go to the county and get body bags. Can you imagine that? Here I was, selling the most beautiful funerals in Savannah, and all of a sudden I'm doin' body bags.

Had to. They would've stunk. I was just draining away the blood and putting in a weak solution of formaldehyde. I'd display 'em in a real fine casket, and then take 'em to the cemetery in it. When everybody went home, we'd bag 'em and bury 'em. Had to be that way.

I got a carpenter to start making me boxes. He'd use pine, and sand 'em down. Shellac 'em if he could. So for a while I was turning out a fairly good funeral again. The boxes were just boxes, but the smell of uncured pine is a good smell. I've got it in my brain, that smell.

It was about six weeks after the war that we got a visit from the National Guard in Atlanta. They called a meeting of all the VFW and the American Legion and the Sons of the Confederacy and the Rotary Club and the Lions and all those clubs, down at the Hilton. General Trowbridge was the speaker. He announced that an organisation called the Georgia Patrol had been formed by the Governor, and this group was supposed to keep refugees out of the state. I thought that was awfully harsh. I don't have anything against people who need help. But then he started talking about radiation poisoning and looters, and things like people with rabies, and fleas carrying unknown diseases, and all of that. Then he tells about the problem with medical supplies, how the plants have been damaged or are irradiated. Most of them were in the Northeast, and those that weren't are hardly shipping to Georgia, even if they are operating, and I see that we really are in a hell of a mess.

So then he says there is going to be a voluntary sign-up, that they need five thousand able-bodied men from Savannah for the Georgia Patrol. They are going to be covering the border complete. The patrol would consist of a hundred thousand people, and they were just to keep the foreigners outside of the state altogether, except if they were known to have business here.

I realised as he talked that he and the Governor and all of 'em in Atlanta were nuts, to think a state in virtual economic chaos could field an army that size and supply it with food and weapons and all – it was damn foolishness.

They must have thought we'd lost the war, and they didn't want to say it, but they were preparing a last-ditch defence of Georgia in case the Russians showed up.

But hell, if it was a last-ditch defence, I was damn well going to do my part. So on that assumption I joined up. As soon as I put down my job, funeral director, I got an earful about how I could carry a card as an auxiliary, but I couldn't go on patrol because mine was an essential service, and under the Emergency Services Act passed that week by the legislature, I had to stay in my present business and I had to follow new regulations being worked out now.

I left that meeting mad and all confused. What regulations? And what about the Georgia Assocation of Funeral Directors? Were they involved, had they been consulted?

I buried fifty people that week, and found myself selling cremations real hard because fuel for the digging tools was getting scarce.

In those days the mail was still working, but it was slow, slow, slow. Not like it is now. You mail a letter in the morning collection here in Savannah, and it will be anywhere in Georgia in the afternoon. One thing that goes real good is the mail. Mail's as good as the phone is bad. I mean, I still can't get used to phone-call rationing. Hell, I was going to call my coffin company up in Illinois to special-order a real good casket, and here I find myself on a waiting list, the operator says ten days! That was Monday. How the mighty have fallen! I remember the days when you hardly even thought about the phone.

Well, no damn more.

So, getting back, let's see, they started in dropping like flies. Then we got gas-pressure trouble. The furnace won't take 'em in my crematorium. I call the other guys and they all got the same problem. What the hell, we're in trouble. We get together, and everybody's in the same boat as me, doing maybe four times his usual business, no coffins, no preservatives, not even any damn cosmetics! And trouble with the digging tools and nobody to fix the damn things because you used to take 'em up to Atlanta for that and now it's a long drive and they might not be able to help you, and on and on like that. We're paying people fifty cents an hour to predig graves. We figure we can get some stoop labour if we just make some posters and put 'em up.

We each put up a poster, a meeting down on Cotton Exchange, fifty labourer jobs at half a dollar an hour. Can you imagine? The minimum wage was two-fifty, then. But there was no federal government now, was there? And we did not have that much money. It was a wild time, then. People would buy and sell stuff for peanuts.

I remember, during the famine, I would have to go out and barter funerals for food. Now isn't that a hell of a note? But I was watching my own kids die. And Jennine did die, that's my wife. That was the flu as much as the hunger. And Ed's not right, we don't know why. He's gone what they call catatonic, and the GP is saying it's against the law for him to have hospital care. I guess it won't be long before we put that boy to sleep. The hospital'll do it for free since he's on the triage due to mental incompetence. Or I could take him to a private practitioner. That death clinic over on Eleventh, the one called Sunshine House, is real nice. They have a live country-and-western group that does your favourite song, and you just go to sleep. 'She'll Be Comin' Round the Mountain' would be for Ed. He used to love that song back before the war. Jennine'd sing it to him at bedtime, and he'd laugh his little head off. Then I'd give him to Weedon's. I couldn't do the funeral myself. I remember that boy used to bring me my lunch for a quarter when he was on holidays. Oh Lord. He was a fine kid. Full of imagination and fun. Getting good at Little League.

I've gotten real close to the Good Lord. I pray all the time. My whole heart and mind is a prayer. I'm burying more than people now, I'm burying a way of life. Praise the Lord. I am burying a world that was so fair.

Whitley: Dallas, October 10, 1993, 2.15 a.m.

I am home again, sitting at the kitchen table with my notebook and a fresh pencil. It is two o'clock in the morning. I arrived home at nine, but so far I haven't been able to sleep. Jim came back with me but he didn't stay long. He has nothing like this, and must find it hard to be with another man's family. The worst losses are those without end, where there is only the question. His own wife is such a loss.

I have seen my wife and son to bed, and now I am alone.

Being on the road so long has made me sharply aware of ordinary household things: the refrigerator's humming, the kitchen clock's ticking. Through the window above the sink I can see the moon hanging low in the sky. The night is rich and warm and fills me with expectancy. There is a faint smell of flowers on the air.

I have in my mind's eye a picture of Anne on the front porch when I came home. At nine the shadows were already dense. I could see the white of her head against the red brick wall of the house. She did not cry out, but came quickly across the lawn, through the tall grass. Then she was standing before me, and I opened my arms and took her in them. She uttered a long sound, soft, and then laid her head against my chest. When she raised her eyes to look at me, I kissed her.

I gave her the little vase from our apartment. She held it a long time, examining it in silence. When we went into the house she put it in a drawer, and I understand that.

That was hours ago. I look at the drawer beneath the kitchen counter, wondering if before Warday any object could ever have been charged with such a combination of remembrance.and threat that it could neither be displayed nor discarded.

A mockingbird sings, leaves rustle. I respect how fine a moment the world can yet make. We have been in shattered years, but there is peace in our consciousness now. I saw it in the eyes of the ones we interviewed, heard it in their voices, felt it in the gentle shuffle of travelling America. We are not like we were before. Now our habit is more often to accept and heal rather than to reject and punish. Would things have been different if our postwar consciousness had, by some miracle, arisen before the war?

My son came up to us when we were still standing together in the front yard, and put a surprisingly big hand on my cheek. 'Dad,' he said, 'we're in good shape.'

'Good, Andrew,' I said, and I was glad to feel his name on my tongue. 'Andrew. Anne.'

They fed me an enormous supper of fried chicken, green beans, biscuits, and, for dessert, egg custard. Afterwards I took out my notebooks and read to them for a time of our experiences on the road. Anne and Andrew told me the chronicle of their life here at home.

The bus service into town is improved.

Andrew has started his sophomore year in high school.

The price of bread went up twice last week, so Anne is back to making her own.

I have eight orders for gardens, and I think I'd like to get back to that.

It was nearly midnight when we went to bed. I do not think I have ever felt anything as good as lying down beside my wife in the dark and feeling the softness and warmth of her.

I expected to fall into deep black sleep after our intimacy, but I did not. The voices of the road came back to me, all the words at once, softly, persistently possessing me.

I got up, stood looking long at the shadow of my wife in our bed, filled with an emotion so rich that it hurt. I went past my son's room, listened to his heavy sleep, and then came down here to try to write this last little bit.

I suppose the world is passing through a thundering moment of history. I do not feel it that way, though. Words like *history* have lost their weight. They seem as indefinite as memories, and as unimportant. Anything real means more to me than history. My own house, my kitchen, my chair. Sitting here, I feel something I can only describe as a kind of austere ecstasy, as if I had found my way in a black desert.

The 'US' and the 'USSR' I grew up with are gone, and that is strange. It is, I suppose, also history. If we could have our old America back, I suspect that most of us would gladly take the old Soviet Union, too. We could live so well together, in the calm of present maturity.

In retrospect the war seems odd and exotic, as if it was fought not by us, but by innocents disguised as ourselves, who, in their fury, forgot how fragile we were. It is eerie to remember the bitter hatred I felt against the Russians when they shot down that Korean airliner in '83, or after the Kabul firebombing in '85. Those brutal acts seemed the work of pride, but time and experience has revealed that they were the fearful doings of the trapped. I wish we could reach back through time and heal our relationship. And how would we have done it? The Soviets were punished without surcease for the whole sixty years of their existence. It would have been a remarkable adventure to give up our punitive habits and try to view them as one does a friend who has fallen from the grace of accepted ways.

But what that past world might or might not have done matters little now. It has disappeared so utterly that even granting it consideration seems an indulgence.

I think much more of healing my own body. I touch my hands to my face, running my fingers over the wrinkles that complicate my cheeks. These are the hands and this is the face of a Warday casualty. I wonder what is going wrong in the depths of my body, in among the pulsing organs and the blood. Are there cells that should not be there, obdurate and growing in the softness of me?

I want to die right here in this house, attended by my wife and son. Even if I must feel pain, I will not choose euthanasia. I want my pain. Perhaps that is a silly and outmoded notion, but I do not recall giving myself life, and feel uneasy about taking it from myself.

I look down at the table, listen to my pencil scratching along the pad. Lord, heal me. Heal my world. Heal the past. If we could accept one another so completely that we were free of all judgment, of all anger, of all denial, would heaven not shine through us then?

Would it shine even through the engineers of Warday, the soldiers and the fliers, the generals and the bureaucrats who worked the machine? The greater justice is not to punish evil, but to give the evildoer the courage to experience his own conscience.

If we are all participants in the glory of mankind – the songs of children, the joy in the bedrooms of the world, the great cathedrals and paintings – then are we not also each responsible in some way for the failures? Or at least, if we accept them into our hearts as our own, can we not heal ourselves?

I wonder. I hope I can come to terms with the feelings that this journey has evoked in me. We bear weighted memories; we all hold the dead in our hearts. Our humanity demands that we do this. Their memory is the conscience we so urgently require if we are not, in the future, to drift back to the old recourse to war. The Europeans, especially, need to remember this. Otherwise another century will see them again battling for senseless dominion.

To decide that a given war can be endured and survived is to let oneself come that much nearer to fighting it. War's greatest tragedy is not the destruction; it is the lives that are prevented from unfolding. And size counts: the greater the war, the more profound the wrong.

The mere existence of nuclear weapons was the most revealing symptom of what was out of balance about the past. Two societies, in varying degrees acceptable or unacceptable to one another, were so interested in their differences that they came to hate their common ground. That obsession was as a cancer in the mind and heart of the old world, which spread cruelty and blindness through the whole enormous body, and finally killed it.

When I awake in sweat and dread, sensing that things are starting to grow in my body that shouldn't be there, imagining my flesh tricked into destroying itself, I get my heart to stop its thrashing by remembering that at least the war is over. I must still live with my personal consequences, but I am coming to terms with that.

Now I am going upstairs. I'll finish these last few lines in bed.

As I slip into our room, I see that Anne is sleeping heavily, her right arm stretched across my side of the bed. I lay it on her breast and get into bed beside her. There is a sense of completion now. At last I am going to sleep.

I lie down, drawing the sheet up around my chin. I sit with my pad on my knees. Music comes to me, an unknown melody, and an image of my son rises in my mind. I want to allow myself to have hope for him and his generation.

If only we have gained wisdom from the fire. If only we can accept how alike we all are, one and another.